# Controversies in Political Economy

# Controversies in Political Economy

## Canada, Great Britain, the United States

Harold D. Clarke, Euel W. Elliott,
William Mishler,
Marianne C. Stewart,
Paul F. Whiteley, and Gary Zuk

Westview Press
BOULDER • SAN FRANCISCO • OXFORD

This Westview softcover edition is printed on acid-free paper and bound in library quality, coated covers that carry the highest rating of the National Association of State Textbook Administrators, in consultation with the Association of American Publishers and the Book Manufacturer's Institute.

All rights reserved. No part of this publication may be reproduced or transmitted in any form or by any means, electronic or mechanical, including photocopy, recording, or any information storage and retrieval system, without permission in writing from the publisher.

Copyright © 1992 by Westview Press, Inc.

Published in 1992 in the United States of America by Westview Press, Inc., 5500 Central Avenue, Boulder, Colorado 80301-2847, and in the United Kingdom by Westview Press, 36 Lonsdale Road, Summertown, Oxford OX2 7EW

Library of Congress Cataloging-in-Publication Data
Controversies in political economy : Canada, Great Britain, the United States / Harold D. Clarke . . . [et al.].
   p. cm.
Includes bibliographical references and index.
ISBN 0-8133-7770-6
1. Business cycles—Political aspects—United States.  2. Business cycles—Political aspects—Great Britain.  3. Business cycles—Political aspects—Canada.  4. United States—Politics and government—1981–1989.  5. Great Britain—Politics and government—1979–  .  6. Canada—Politics and government—1980-  .
I. Clarke, Harold D.
HB3743C68  1992
338.9—dc20
                                              92-7996
                                                 CIP

Printed and bound in the United States of America

The paper used in this publication meets the requirements of the American National Standard for Permanence of Paper for Printed Library Materials Z39.48-1984.

10   9   8   7   6   5   4   3   2   1

# Contents

*List of Tables* ix
*List of Figures* xiii
*Preface* xv
*Acknowledgments* xvii

**1 Introduction: Contemporary Political Economy** 1

   The Controversies: An Overview, *3*
   Economic Influences on Political Support, *5*
   Responsibility Attributions and Political Choice, *11*
   Political Control of the Economy? *17*
   Methodological Issues, *19*
   Three Contexts of Controversy, *22*
   The Controversies Considered, *25*
   Notes, *29*

**2 The Economics and Politics of Presidential Approval: The Reagan Years** 31

   Measures and Methods, *33*
   Reagan's Presidential Approval Ratings, *35*
   Trends in Inflation and Unemployment, *36*
   The Subjective Economy, *38*
   Political (and Economic) Interventions, *39*
   Models of Presidential Approval, *39*
   Models of Economic Evaluations, *45*
   Conclusion: A "Teflon" President? *47*
   Notes, *49*

**3 Through a Glass Darkly: Economic Evaluations and Governing Party Support in Mrs. Thatcher's Britain** 51

   Theoretical Considerations, *53*
   Modeling the Subjective Economy, *56*
   From the Objective to the Subjective Economy, *60*

Do Subjective Economic Evaluations Matter? *66*
Conclusion: Through a Glass Darkly, *70*
Notes, *72*

**4 The Dynamics of Third-Party Support: The British Liberals and the Alliance, 1979–1987**     75

Theoretical Perspectives on Party Support, *77*
Measures, *81*
Economic Conditions and Economic Evaluations, *82*
A Model of Alliance Support, *84*
The Economics and Politics of Alliance Support, *89*
Conclusion: The British Party System—Bent, Not Broken, *93*
Notes, *96*

**5 Regional Political-Economic Contexts and Party Support in Canada, 1985–1988**     99

The Canadian Political Context, *100*
The Economics and Politics of Party Support, *103*
Measures and Methods, *110*
The Determinants of Party Support, *112*
Region, Economy, Politics, *117*
Conclusion: The Politics (and Economics?) of Party Support, *118*
Notes, *120*

**6 Campaign Context, Economic Evaluations, and Electoral Choice: The 1988 American Presidential Election**     123

Contemporary Approaches to Economic Evaluations, *124*
The Model of Economic Evaluations, *125*
The Distribution and Structure of Economic Evaluations, *127*
Recent Controversies over Economic Voting, *130*
A Contextual Model of Presidential Voting, *131*
Economic Evaluations and Presidential Voting in 1988, *134*
Conclusion, *137*
Notes, *139*

**7 "It's Their Fault!" The Economics and Politics of Governing Party Support in Canada Since 1988**     141

Changing Economic Evaluations, *143*
Economic Issues, *149*

Modeling Attitudes Toward Free Trade and the GST, *152*
Progressive Conservative Support, *156*
Conclusion: From Disaster to Dismissal? *159*
Notes, *161*

## 8 Macroeconomic Theories and Political Interests: The Political Business Cycle — 165

The Macroeconomic Foundations, *166*
Reaction Functions: Theoretical Perspectives, *171*
Looking for the Political Business Cycle, *175*
Manipulating the Economy for Political Profit:
   Britain, 1983–1987, *180*
Conclusion: The Future of the Political Business Cycle, *186*
Notes, *188*

## 9 International Developments and Presidential Factors: Political Business Cycles in the United States — 189

The Controversies over Political Business Cycles, *189*
Two Models of the Macroeconomy, *191*
Measures and Methods, *195*
Presidents, International Developments,
   and the Economy, *197*
Conclusion, *201*
Notes, *204*

*Appendix A: Box-Jenkins-Tiao Time Series Analysis* — 205
*References* — 209
*Index* — 231

# Tables

2.1 Effects of Retrospective Sociotropic Economic Evaluations and Political Interventions on President Reagan's Approval Rating, 1981–1988    41

2.2 Effects of Subjective Economic Evaluation Index and Political Interventions on President Reagan's Approval Rating, 1981–1988    42

2.3 Effects of Subjective Economic Evaluation Index, Inflation and Unemployment on President Reagan's Approval Rating, 1981–1988    44

2.4 Effects of Inflation, Unemployment and Economic and Political Interventions on Subjective Economic Evaluations, 1981–1988    46

3.1 Crosscorrelations of Retail Prices, Unemployment, Real Income Growth and Interest Rates with Public Perceptions and Expectations of Prices, Household Finances and General Economic Conditions    58

3.2 Effects of Economic and Political Variables on Public Perceptions of Prices, Household Finances and General Economic Situation    63

3.3 Effects of Economic and Political Variables on Public Expectations of Prices, Household Finances and General Economy    65

3.4 Bivariate Models of the Effects of Subjective Economic Evaluations on Conservative Share of Major Party Support, 1979–1987    67

3.5 Multivariate Models of the Effects of Objective Economic Conditions, Political Events and General Economic Expectations on Conservative Share of Major Party Support, 1979–1987    69

4.1 Effects of Retrospective Sociotropic Economic Evaluations, Prospective Egocentric Economic Evaluations and Political Interventions on Liberal/Alliance Support, 1979–1987    89

| | | |
|---|---|---|
| 4.2 | Effects of Subjective Economic Evaluations Index and Political Interventions on Liberal/Alliance Support, 1979–1987 | 91 |
| 4.3 | Effects of Inflation, Unemployment, Subjective Economic Evaluations Index and Political Interventions on Liberal/Alliance Support, 1979–1987 | 92 |
| 5.1 | Pooled Cross-Sectional Time Series Analysis of Progressive Conservative, Liberal and NDP Support, February 1985–November 1988 | 113 |
| 5.2 | Pooled Cross-Sectional Time Series Analysis of Third-Party Squeeze Effect on NDP Support, February 1985–November 1988 | 116 |
| 6.1 | Responses to Economic Evaluation Questions, 1988 | 128 |
| 6.2 | Confirmatory Factor Analysis of Economic Performance Evaluations, Entire Sample, 1988 | 129 |
| 6.3 | Covariance Structure Analysis of Presidential Vote, Entire Sample, 1988 | 136 |
| 7.1 | Evaluations of the National Economy and Government Impact, 1983–1990 | 143 |
| 7.2 | Evaluations of Personal Economic Condition and Government Impact, 1983–1990 | 146 |
| 7.3 | Government Impact on Personal Financial Condition and National Economy by Economic Evaluations, 1990 | 147 |
| 7.4 | Confirmatory Factor Analysis of Economic Performance Evaluations, 1990 | 148 |
| 7.5 | Attitudes Toward Free Trade Agreement, 1988 and 1990 | 151 |
| 7.6 | Attitudes Toward the Goods & Services Tax (GST), 1990 | 152 |
| 7.7 | Probit Analyses of Attitudes Toward Free Trade and the GST, 1988 Post-Election–1990 National Panel Survey | 154 |
| 7.8 | Multiple Regression Analysis of Support for Federal Progressive Conservative Government, 1988 Post-Election–1990 National Panel Survey | 157 |
| 8.1 | Factors Affecting Growth of the Money Supply (M1), 1983–1987 | 183 |

| | | |
|---|---|---|
| 8.2 | Factors Affecting Inflation and Unemployment, 1983–1987 | 185 |
| 9.1 | Effects of Presidential Factors and International Developments on Inflation, 1947–1985 | 198 |
| 9.2 | Effects of Presidential Factors and International Developments on Unemployment, 1947–1985 | 200 |

# Figures

| | | |
|---|---|---|
| 1.1 | A Model of Political-Economic Relationships | 4 |
| 2.1 | Presidential Approval, Eisenhower to Reagan | 35 |
| 2.2 | Reagan's Presidential Approval Rating, January 1981–September 1988 | 36 |
| 2.3 | Inflation and Unemployment, January 1981–September 1988 | 37 |
| 2.4 | Retrospective Economic Evaluation Indices, January 1981–September 1988 | 38 |
| 2.5 | Impact of Iran-Contra Scandal on President Reagan's Approval Rating | 43 |
| 4.1 | Liberal-Alliance and Conservative Support, June 1979–June 1987 | 76 |
| 4.2 | Inflation and Unemployment, June 1979–June 1987 | 83 |
| 4.3 | Retrospective Economic Evaluation Indices, June 1979–June 1987 | 84 |
| 4.4 | Prospective Economic Evaluation Indices, June 1979–June 1987 | 85 |
| 4.5 | Liberal-Alliance Support and Economic Evaluations, June 1979–June 1987 | 90 |
| 4.6 | Impact of By-Election Victories on Alliance Support | 93 |
| 5.1 | Federal Party Support in Canada, February 1985–November 1988 | 102 |
| 5.2 | Federal Party Support in the Prairies, February 1985–November 1988 | 103 |
| 5.3 | Federal Party Support in Quebec, February 1985–November 1988 | 104 |
| 5.4 | Regional Trends in Unemployment, February 1985–November 1988 | 105 |
| 5.5 | Variance Explained in Federal Party Support by Region, Economic Conditions, and Political Events | 118 |
| 6.1 | Measurement Model of Economic Evaluations, 1988 | 127 |

| | | |
|---|---|---|
| 6.2 | Structural Model of Presidential Vote, 1988 | 135 |
| 7.1 | Evaluations of Federal Government's Handling of the Economy, 1983–1990 | 144 |
| 7.2 | Probability of Favoring Free Trade and GST by National and Personal Economic Evaluations | 155 |
| 7.3 | Variance Explained in Support for Federal Progressive Conservative Government | 158 |
| 8.1 | The Political Business Cycle and the Phillips Curve | 172 |

# Preface

Political economy long has been a disputed field of inquiry. The strong resurgence of interest in political-economic relationships during the past two decades has perpetuated this intellectual tradition by stimulating important new debates and reinvigorating old ones. In this book we address a number of these controversies in a series of studies of the political economy of political support in three Anglo-American polities—Canada, Great Britain, and the United States.

Our investigations focus on two topics central to recent research on the interaction of economics and politics in contemporary Western democracies. The first of these concerns the proposition that a healthy economy is a *sine qua non* for the continued electoral success of governing political parties and their leaders. Although this hypothesis has acquired the status of conventional wisdom among politicians and political scientists alike, efforts to determine, as George Stigler (1973:160) once put it, if "this fact in fact is a fact" have produced discordant results and fueled a variety of theoretical and methodological disputes. The second related topic concerns what have come to be known as "political business cycles" (PBCs). The idea that governments can manipulate the economy for political advantage has intrigued political practitioners and academic analysts at least since Napoleonic times, and disputes over the theory and practice of PBCs have been prominent themes in the new political economy.

In addressing these topics we have adopted an explicitly comparative perspective. This perspective is consonant with our general argument that political-economic interactions are conditioned by political contexts in which they occur. These contexts can vary between political systems and within them over time. Recognition of the significance of the settings within which political-economic interactions occur prompts us to address a range of theoretical issues concerning which variables properly belong in political economy models and how the effects of these variables should be specified.

In developing and testing these models we also have been sensitive to the criticism that many previous studies of political-economic relationships have involved "high-tech analyses of low-grade data" (Miller, 1989:143). Lacking adequate data, such studies have not been able to confront crucial issues that have fueled ongoing debates among political economists. Many of these issues involve the psychological underpinnings of political economy. Examples include relationships between objective economic conditions and subjective economic evaluations, the conditions under which people attribute responsibility to government for prevailing economic conditions, and the relative importance of retrospective and prospective judgments about national and personal economic circumstances in the skein of forces influencing political support. The American, British, and Canadian survey data we use enable us to address these issues.

Nearly a half-century ago the prominent political economist Joseph Schumpeter (1962:73) argued: "Bourgeois society has been cast in a purely economic mold: its foundations, beams, and beacons are all made of economic material." Since the rebirth of interest in political economy in the early 1970s, Schumpeter's argument has resonated strongly in the many studies that place a heavy accent on the economics of political-economic relationships. Although the resulting simplifications extend the seductive promise of theoretical parsimony, we argue that reality-oriented models of such relationships must be based on recognition of the importance of the *politics* of political economy. Such models will be more complex than many existing ones, but, by providing a more accurate portrait of political-economic interactions, they will help to resolve long-standing controversies and suggest new areas of inquiry.

*Harold D. Clarke*
*Euel W. Elliott*
*William Mishler*
*Marianne C. Stewart*
*Paul F. Whiteley*
*Gary Zuk*
*Denton, Texas*

# Acknowledgments

This book is the product of collaborative research conducted by the authors over the past several years. We wish to acknowledge the assistance of those people and organizations that have facilitated our efforts. We owe a special debt of gratitude to Allan Kornberg, whose intellectual contribution to our enterprise extends far beyond his coauthorship of Chapter 7. Many thanks also are due Roy Fitzgerald, the coauthor of Chapter 3.

Additionally, we are pleased to acknowledge the generous financial assistance of the National Science Foundation and the encouragement provided by the Foundation's political science program director, Dr. Frank Scioli. Two grants from the Foundation enabled Clarke and his co-principal investigator, Allan Kornberg, to gather much of the data on the political economy of political support in Canada presented in Chapter 7. Other Canadian data were gathered using grants from the Institutional Research Grant Programme of the Public Affairs Division, the Canadian Embassy, Washington, D.C. We thank Dr. Norman London, the Embassy's academic liaison officer, for his continuing interest in the project. A special note of thanks goes to Mary Auvinen, senior project director, Canadian Facts Limited, for her invaluable assistance with the design and execution of the Canadian surveys conducted by Clarke and Kornberg. Mary also provided us with the data on party support in Canada employed in Chapter 5.

Other individuals and institutions helped as well. Our data analyses were performed using the computing facilities at the Universities of Arizona, North Texas (UNT), and South Carolina and at SUNY-Buffalo. We greatly appreciate the use of these facilities as well as the assistance provided by Dave Molta and his helpful colleagues at the UNT computing center. We also appreciate UNT's financial support via its membership in the Inter-university Consortium for Political and Social Research. This gave us access to the 1988 U.S. National Election Study data analyzed in Chapter 6. Of course, the analyses and interpretations of these and other data presented in the book are the responsibility of the authors.

We also wish to acknowledge the many efforts of Jo-Ann Lutz at North Texas, who helped us to prepare our manuscript for publication by performing the word-processing and table-preparation chores carefully and cheerfully. Last, but certainly not least, we wish to thank Amy Eisenberg, our editor at Westview, for her patience, encouragement, and helpful advice.

*H.D.C.*
*E.W.E.*
*W.M.*
*M.C.S.*
*P.F.W.*
*G.Z.*

# 1

## Introduction: Contemporary Political Economy

*The Government's responsibility for the economy is a fundamental assumption of the contemporary dialogue between the parties and the electorate in Britain as well as America.*
—Butler and Stokes (1976:245)

Political economy is both old and new. Although studies of the interplay of economics and politics have a lengthy intellectual lineage and were a thriving enterprise during much of the 19th century (Heilbroner, 1972), afterwards economists and political scientists tended to go their separate ways. Now this has changed. During the past two decades both groups have become increasingly fascinated by relationships between economics and politics. The renewed interest in such relationships is especially evident in political science where the volume of work at the interface of economics and politics has expanded exponentially.[1] The study of political economy is now a major subfield in the discipline.

There are a number of reasons for the intellectual vitality of the new political economy, but two are particularly important. First, there has been a general growth in the popularity of what might be termed the economic approach to political science. As Keech, Bates and Lange (1989:1) observe, contemporary political economy is characterized by an emphasis on the utility of economic concepts and "choice-theoretic" reasoning for understanding a broad range of political phenomena. The influence of the rational choice approach is evident in many fields of inquiry (Monroe, 1991; Ostrom, 1991; Riker, 1982), but its impact has been especially pronounced in research on voting behavior, which previously had been dominated by the social-psychological approach developed at the University of Michigan in the 1950s (e.g., Campbell et al., 1954, 1960, 1966). Building on seminal works by Downs (1957) and Key (1968), studies (e.g., Alt, 1979; Kiewiet, 1983; Kinder and Kiewiet, 1979, 1981) have focused on the influence of economic issues and evaluations of national and personal economic conditions on electoral choice, and some analysts (e.g., Fiorina, 1981) explicitly reinterpreted the major concepts of the "Michigan model" in rational choice terms. In so doing, they provided intriguing explanations for the enhanced volatility in party support in many Western countries during the 1970s and 1980s.

A second, related, reason for the heightened interest in political economy involves changes in the relationship between government and economy in Western democracies since the end of World War II, and the patterns of economic decline and political change that have occurred in these countries in the past two decades. Increased government involvement in managing national economies, as exemplified by the Keynesian revolution in macroeconomic management (Stewart, 1986), was accompanied by greatly heightened public expectations about what government could do to improve economic performance and personal well-being. These expectations did not develop *ab nihilo*. Rather, political parties of all ideological hues, believing that Keynesian demand-management techniques enabled them to ensure continuing prosperity and overcome the "boom and bust" cycles that had plagued capitalist economies earlier in the century, felt free to promise that they could deliver a never-ending supply of economic and social well-being. Electorates became convinced that they could and should demand strong economic performance and the many popular social programs fueled by an expanding economy.

When the remarkably strong economic growth in Western countries during the 1950s and 1960s gave way to a protracted period of spiralling inflation, high unemployment and sluggish growth in the 1970s, these new and unpleasant economic realities were accompanied by a rising tide of public discontent, diminished support for governing parties, and enhanced political instability. Radical critics reacted by interpreting the growing disaffection as the harbinger of the long prophesied legitimacy crisis of advanced capitalism (e.g., O'Connor, 1973, 1986; Offe, 1972, 1984). Mainstream political scientists and conservative commentators also joined the chorus, and offered theories about the causes and consequences of government "overload" and "bankruptcy" in the era of the welfare state (e.g., Brittan, 1978, 1983; King, 1975; Niskanen, 1971; Olson, 1982; Rose and Peters, 1979).

At the same time, the deepening economic malaise and the seeming inability of Keynesian techniques to alleviate the situation prompted renewed interest among economists in monetarist and neo-classical economic theories. As the decade wore on and the stagflation continued, popularized and, in some cases, unorthodox, variants of these theories were propagated by neo-conservative intellectuals and politicians who combined their new economic wisdom with an explicit rejection of the central tenants of the post-war consensus on government role's as economic manager and social provider. In a number of Western countries these politicians and the parties they led came to power, promising to restore prosperity by implementing varying mixes of monetarist, neoclassical and supply-side economic policies, and curbing the perceived excesses of the welfare state (Clarke, Stewart and Zuk, 1989; Cooper, Kornberg and Mishler, 1988).

This combination of shifting intellectual currents and real-world economic and political developments has strongly oriented research on political economy toward studies of interactions among objective economic conditions such as unemployment, inflation and economic growth, subjective perceptions of economic performance, and support for political parties and their leaders. Despite the dramatic growth in scholarly as well as more popular analyses of these relationships, and a strongly held conviction that they are important, much remains to be learned. As Miller (1989) recently has noted, studies of political-economic interactions are characterized by a welter of conflicting theories, sharp disagreements about the significance of various explanatory variables, and unresolved arguments about how to measure and analyze the economic and political phenomena of interest. In this chapter we discuss these controversies in contemporary political economy.

## The Controversies: An Overview

Figure 1.1 provides a convenient starting point for analyzing debates in the study of political-economic interactions. Starting in the bottom right-hand corner of the diagram, public assessments of national economic conditions and personal economic circumstances influence support for governing and opposition political parties and their leaders. At election times one can examine relationships between economic performance and political support using voting data, and models of such relationships are known as *vote functions*. In the interims between elections, when feelings about parties and party leaders are measured using data from public opinion polls, such models are known as *popularity functions*. The effects of variables in vote function models can be estimated using aggregate-level data on economic conditions and parties' vote or seat shares in national elections (e.g., Fair, 1978; Jacobson, 1991) or, alternatively, by using individual-level survey data on voting behavior or voting intentions and evaluations of national and personal economic performance (e.g., Fiorina, 1981; Lewis-Beck, 1988a:ch. 4). Popularity function models, in contrast, are invariably analyzed using aggregate time series data (e.g., Hibbs, 1987a:ch. 5; Norpoth, 1987a).

Since governing parties and their leaders are well aware of the potential impact of the performance of the economy on their popularity ratings,

FIGURE 1.1  A Model of Political-Economic Relationships

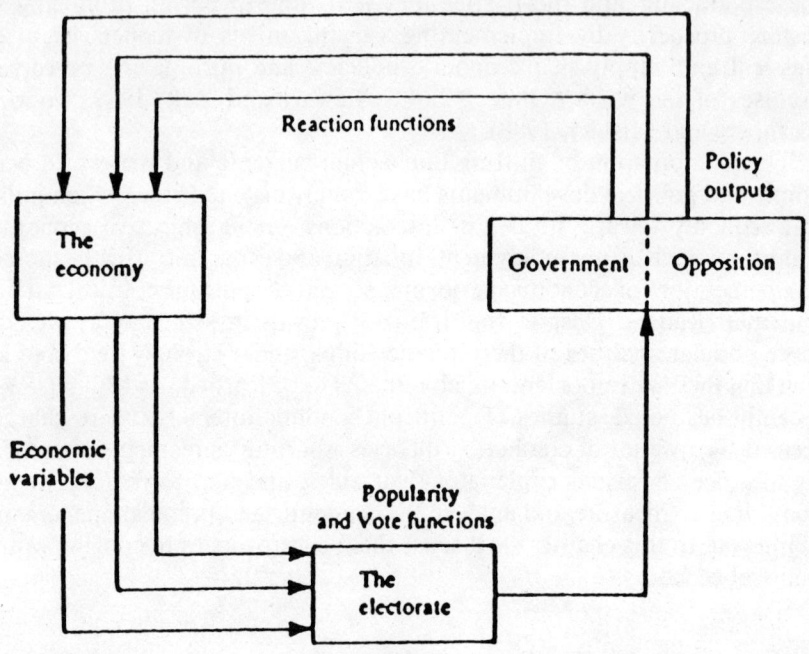

they can react by attempting to manipulate the economy for political advantage. Analyses of the efforts of incumbents to respond to changes in their support involve the construction of models known as *reaction functions* (Figure 1.1, top). What is being explained in these models are variations in the policies governments use to influence the macroeconomy. Two principal policy instruments that governments employ are: (a) *monetary policy,* which concerns the quantity of money in circulation, and interest rates (Elliott and Whiteley, 1989); and (b) *fiscal policy,* which concerns government taxation and expenditure (e.g., Alt and Chrystal, 1983:ch. 3; Lowery, 1985).

The third segment in the process of political-economic interaction involves the impact of these policies, and models of these effects on macroeconomic outcomes such as rates of inflation, unemployment and income growth are known as *outcome functions* (Figure 1.1, left). Efforts to develop such models historically have been located squarely within the research program of the economist, and this means that the whole of the disputed field of macroeconomic theory is at issue.

The agenda of contemporary political economy is thus both large and diverse. Since the impact of economic variables on support for governing parties and their leaders has been a primary concern of political scientists, several chapters in this book examine linkages between economic outcomes and party and leader popularity. However, because the flow of causality between politics and economics is bidirectional, we also consider how political variables influence economic policy and economic outcomes. In the next section, we will delineate some of the key debates that characterize research in these fields.

## Economic Influences on Political Support

Although attempts to analyze the impact of economic conditions on political support have engendered many separate debates, they can be classified in terms of three overarching issue areas. First, there is the issue of how voters perceive economic outcomes, which raises the topic of relationships between *perceptions* of economic performance and actual economic conditions. At the core of this debate are questions about how voters process information about the economy, and which aspects of the economy are salient in particular contexts. Second, there is the issue of how voters *attribute responsibility* for economic performance, which encompasses questions such as whether they simply reward governing parties and their leaders for good or improving economic conditions and punish them for bad or worsening ones, and whether noneconomic events and conditions can override the effects of the economy. Third, there are *methodological* issues concerning how best to estimate the effects of economic variables in political support models, particularly models that try to capture the dynamics of such effects. These methodological issues are complex and highly technical, but typically they involve debates about the merits of aggregate-versus individual-level data, and the utility of various statistical procedures.

**Public Perceptions of the Economy:** One of the most important controversies in this area relates to the question of whether people think primarily in terms of personal self-interest or national economic conditions when making electoral choices. Following the language adopted by Kinder and Kiewiet (1979, 1981), the former typically are termed *egocentric* evaluations, and the latter, *sociotropic* evaluations.

The presence of sociotropic variables in political support models presents problems if one wishes to assume voters are rational and self-interested. Such a "narrow rationality" assumption long has been axiomatic in economic theory (Monroe, 1991), and it is central to economic models of electoral behavior as well (e.g., Downs, 1957). Even if one is willing to discard the argument that a rational self-interested person will not bother to vote at all because the probability of influencing the outcome is negligible (Barry, 1970), the notion of sociotropically motivated voters encounters a paradox of collective action of the type discussed by Olson

(1965) and others. Briefly, it is not rational for individuals to respond to national economic performance which is unrelated to their own pocketbooks, since by doing so they are providing a collective good, the benefits of which go to society as a whole rather than to themselves. An additional problem of sociotropic voting is that it contradicts the strongly individualistic strain in the political culture of a country such as the United States (Schlozman and Verba, 1979; Sniderman and Brody, 1977).

Collective action problems and cultural anomalies notwithstanding, most of the evidence gathered in the United States and elsewhere suggests that voters *are* motivated primarily by sociotropic rather than egocentric concerns (e.g., Kinder and Kiewiet, 1979, 1981). A number of analysts have sought to account for the whereabouts of the elusive "pocketbook voter," whose presence is crucial to traditional rational choice theories of political support. One prominent explanation is methodological. Kramer (1983) has argued that cross-sectional survey data tend to obfuscate the impact of personal economic circumstances on voting behavior by failing to distinguish between those conditions which can be attributed to government, and those which are beyond its control (see also Peffley, 1984). Thus, the relatively weak impact of personal economic conditions in vote models may be an artifact of an inability to measure the influence of government on voters' pocketbooks.

The argument, as stated, applies to objective measures of economic welfare such as household income, but not to voters' *perceptions* of their individual welfare. Empirically, however, it also is the case that when voters are asked to make retrospective evaluations of the financial situation of their households over the last year, the answers typically have only very weak correlations with voting behavior (e.g., Lewis-Beck, 1988a:56). Taking account of voters' *responsibility attributions,* i.e, whether they attribute responsibility to government for their economic circumstances, would seem to be an important missing piece to the puzzle (Peffley, 1984). However, recent analyses with data from four Western European countries show that even such "mediated" egocentric judgments have significant effects only in the British case (Lewis-Beck, 1988a:60, 61), and sociotropic concerns remain influential net of the possible impact of egocentric evaluations. Thus, the mystery that economic voting appears to be primarily sociotropic is not solved by considering responsibility attributions.

Other approaches have been tried as well. Some analysts have attempted to salvage egocentric voting by constructing more complex models in which evaluations of personal economic circumstances have indirect effects via their impact on other variables (e.g., Lewis-Beck, 1988a:ch. 6). Others have employed complex research designs which "pool" several cross-sectional surveys conducted over time (e.g., Markus, 1988). The results of these analyses are mixed and, even when egocentric effects can be detected, sociotropic ones remain significant.

The persistence of sociotropic voting in a wide range of sophisticated analyses points up the need for an explicit theory of how voters acquire and use information when making political support decisions. One possibility is that in a world of conflicting and imperfect information, people may rely upon information about the state of the national economy as a basis for making judgments about their personal well-being. Mebane (1988), for instance, has argued that while voters are motivated by concerns for their own and their families well-being, evaluations of economic performance are gleaned from "collective oriented" interpretations of information about the economy derived from various sources. Moreover, Weatherford (1983a, 1983b) has pointed out that electorates are not homogeneous with regard to the information they possess, and such differences may prompt them to rely upon different decision rules—persons with relatively limited information may tend to rely upon personal experience, while more knowledgeable individuals may utilize information about collective economic well-being.

One weakness of the focus on egocentric versus sociotropic thinking is that the distinction between the two types of evaluations typically is imposed *a priori* without investigating how people actually think about economic performance. Do they distinguish between national and personal economic well-being and, if they do, does one type of economic evaluation affect another? Some analysts recently have started to investigate the cognitive structures underlying economic thinking (Elliott and Zuk, 1989; Kinder, Adams and Gronke, 1989), and some have explored the causal linkages among different types of economic evaluations (Clarke and Kornberg, 1989; Lewis-Beck, 1988a:ch. 6).

The development of a more sophisticated understanding of information processing may go a long way to clarifying how voters think about the economy in different political contexts. Such an understanding also may throw light on how *noneconomic events* and conditions affect relationships between the economy and political support. For example, one strategy for information processing in the face of uncertainty might be to use noneconomic events, such as a government's handling of an international crisis or war as a surrogate measure of its competence to achieve economic policy goals. Some analysts contend that this is exactly what happened in the case of British involvement in the Falklands war. The argument is that the "resolution" Prime Minister Thatcher demonstrated in quickly recapturing the Falklands after the Argentine invasion in April 1982 helped to convince the electorate that she and her government had "the right stuff" to quell the country's economic difficulties as well (Clarke, Mishler and Whiteley, 1990; Norpoth, 1987a, 1987b). As a result, public evaluations of national and personal economic prospects improved markedly in the wake of favorable news about the war, and these sanguine economic judgments, in turn, prompted substantial increases in government popularity. Thus, in addition to directly influencing government support, a salient noneconomic event can operate indirectly by modifying public judgments about a government's ability to manage the economy.

*Time Horizons:* The example of how the British public reacted to the Falklands war suggests that voters' thinking about the future course of national and personal economic well-being can have an important impact on government popularity. The relative importance of past (*retrospective*) versus future (*prospective*) economic evaluations is a second important debate in studies of the political economy of political support. If the retrospective-prospective distinction is interpreted narrowly as one between past performance and future promises, then it is rational for individuals to rely on the former rather than the latter when making judgments about the economy. Downs (1957:40) explains why when he discusses electoral choice in a two-party system:

> [The voter] must either compare (1) two hypothetical future utility incomes or (2) one actual present utility income and a hypothetical present one. Without question, the latter comparison allows him to make more direct use of concrete facts than the former. Not only is one of its terms a real entity, but the other can be calculated in full view of the situation from which it springs. If he compares future utility incomes, he enjoys neither of these advantages. Therefore we believe it is more rational for him to ground his voting decision on current events than purely on future ones.

Ferejohn (1986) argues that retrospective voting can be best understood from the standpoint of principal-agent relationships (see also Beck, 1991). Since the agent (government) has a huge advantage in the amount and quality of information available to it, voters (principals) seeking to economize on information processing rely on the *performance* of the incumbent. Moreover, if they discount the promises made by governing and opposition parties in an election campaign on the assumption that all parties will say whatever will further their office goals, the only trustworthy information available is past performance.

However, the distinction between retrospective and prospective evaluations is not necessarily one between performance and promises. During an election campaign, the rational voter will make a judgment about what will happen in the future, since it is the future performance of a party or candidate which is really at issue. The past is "over and done with" and cannot be changed. Promises made by competing parties and their leaders are only one component of a prospective evaluation. The rational voter will consider how best to use existing information in order to make a judgment about what the future will hold if one rather than another party is elected. In this sense there is no such thing as a rational prospective evaluation which is independent of retrospective considerations.

This latter point explains why models of expectations in macroeconomics are based on evaluations of past performance. Three models have been particularly influential: extrapolative, adaptive, and rational expectations. Extrapolative expectations models assume that voters forecast the future as a simple linear trend of present and past conditions. Adaptive expectations models assume that voters continuously update their expectations about the future using information about actual economic performance and giving the greatest weight to current performance. Finally, rational expectations models, which have become increasingly popular among economists in the past decade, assume that people have accurate models of how the economy works which they use to forecast the future. As a result, they do not make systematic forecasting errors (Begg, 1982). All three models constitute different ways of using retrospective information to predict the future.

Political psychologists recently have developed an alternative perspective on how people forecast the future in the context of electoral choice (e.g., Conover, Feldman and Knight, 1986, 1987). This perspective challenges the rationality assumption by relying on the insights of cognitive psychology to explain how individuals process information. Voters do not simply use data on past economic performance to forecast the future. Although the process of information usage basically conforms to an adaptive model, predictions are strongly affected by noneconomic considerations. "In effect, economic forecasts reflect more a combination of hopes and politicized guesses about the future than they do an awareness of current economic conditions and an understanding of how the economy functions" (Conover, Feldman and Knight, 1987:579).

A closely related debate concerns the *cognitive* and *affective* content of economic evaluations. In the rational choice literature decision-making is seen as being very much an exercise in objectively evaluating the costs and benefits of different courses of action. But Conover and Feldman (1986) argue that this image of the "coldly calculating" voter is mistaken, and that economic evaluations have important affective components. Voters' responses to the economy and their personal economic situation generate emotional, politically consequential, reactions. Individuals can become angry and upset about rising unemployment even when it does not affect them personally, and this can override considerations of self-interest. However, there are affective components (e.g., anger, anxiety, disgust) to egocentric evaluations as well, and some of these strongly influence judgments about the government's economic performance.

However retrospective and prospective evaluations are formed, it can be argued that their effects are dependent on the context within which political choices are made. Some authors (e.g., Clarke and Kornberg, 1989; Powell, 1989) have hypothesized that electoral systems characterized by fragmented authority or the absence of clear distinctions between parties encourage voting decisions based on retrospective economic evaluations, while decisions based on prospective economic evaluations are more likely to take place in systems where parties differ clearly in their policy programs and more general ideological stances. There may be more general incumbent-challenger differences as well. Miller and Wattenberg (1985), for example, argue that incumbent parties and candidates tend to be evaluated in terms of retrospective economic judgments, whereas prospective judgments are more important for assessing challengers.

*Modeling Economic Effects:* Virtually all studies of party popularity in interelection periods are aggregate time series analyses which rely exclusively on objective measures of national economic conditions such as rates of inflation, unemployment and growth in real disposable income. Such measures of economic performance have been exploited because they readily available but, by themselves, they tell us nothing about how people use them to make economic evaluations, or what kinds of evaluations are most important for political support decisions. To learn about these matters and, hence, to resolve some of the debates discussed above, variables measuring subjective economic evaluations must be incorporated into party popularity models.

Available evidence is fragmentary, but the importance of the subjective economy has been illustrated in the aforementioned debate about the impact of the Falklands war on the popularity of the governing Conservative Party in Britain. Sanders, Marsh and Ward (1987) argued that subjective economic evaluations rather than Britain's victory in the Falklands caused the resurgence of Tory support in 1982. Using more sophisticated analytic techniques Clarke, Mishler and Whiteley (1990) showed that subjective economic evaluations and the war both had significant effects, and the inclusion of the former actually strengthened the effects of objective economic conditions. Similarly, MacKuen, Erikson and Stimson (1989) have demonstrated that subjective economic judgments as measured by the well-known University of Michigan consumer confidence index influence the distribution of partisanship in the United States net of public evaluations of presidential performance and various noneconomic events and conditions.[2]

More generally, the lack of consensus concerning model specification is perhaps the single most important reason why there has been so much disagreement about the magnitude and stability of economic effects on voting behavior and party support between elections. Illustrative of such disagreements Hibbs (1982a) concluded that there were strong and enduring relationships between economic conditions and the popularity of American presidents. In a paper published only a year later, Norpoth and Yantek (1983) reported just the opposite was the case.

Although these disputes persist, many analysts continue to believe that economic variables frequently are influential and occasionally are critically important. Perhaps the strongest recent statement on behalf of economic variables is that by Lewis-Beck (1988a:155) who concludes that "macroeconomic indicators virtually always register a statistically significant effect in the numerous aggregate time series popularity or vote functions. . . . Furthermore, individual-level survey-based voting models . . . consistently demonstrate statistically significant effects from evaluations of economic performance and policy." Other analysts suggest (either implicitly or explicitly) that there is still much to learn. Paldam (1991:28), for example, notes that relationships between economic conditions and political support, while typically significant, are quite variable: "The whole argument . . . is that the V-P (voting and popularity) function is a function that is on the one hand unstable and, on the other hand, often highly significant." Schneider and Frey (1988:246) are less sanguine: "The results for a majority of the countries show that the economic situation has an important influence on the election outcome, but just how strong this influence is and which economic factors are most crucial is difficult to tell."

Overall, then, although most studies show that the economy influences political support, important "how?" "why?" and "when?" questions remain unanswered. We contend that to answer them we need to know more about the circumstances under which people attribute responsibility to government for economic conditions, and how the choices provided by competing parties affect political support decisions.

## Responsibility Attributions and Political Choice

When the economy worsens do voters automatically blame the government? When it improves do they automatically praise government? If blame and praise are contingent, under what conditions do they occur? Answering these questions is important because responsibility attributions constitute a crucial link between economic conditions and political behavior. V.O. Key's (1968) answer is that voters utilize a simple *reward-punishment* model of attribution. If the economy is doing well, such that inflation and unemployment rates are low or falling and income is rising, then the incumbent party and its leader will be rewarded with increased support, and opposition parties and their leaders will lose support. However, if the economy is faring poorly, then voters punish the government and reward the opposition.

This "Keysian" model is extremely popular. Monroe and Erickson (1986:619) note that its logic "is found in Down's original economic theory of voting (1957) and is tested by virtually every analyst in the field." However, its assumptions have not gone unchallenged. Note that it assumes a narrowly focused and retrospectively oriented electorate which concentrates its attention on the performance of the economy during a government's term in office. This image of the electorate is not universally accepted, and the possibility that prospective judgments are influential is indicated by a number of empirical analyses such as those by Chappell and Keech (1985), Kuklinski and West (1981) and Lewis-Beck (1988a). The image of the voter in the former study is considerably different from that articulated by Key and his followers. Chappell-Keech voters calculate the expected utility derived from an incumbent retaining office, deriving this measure by means of a sophisticated rule that uses retrospective evaluations of economic performance and ensures that incumbents are not penalized for errors committed by their predecessors. Analyses assuming a sophisticated prospectively oriented electorate explain political support as well as do those which assume voters are naive Keysians.

The reward-punishment model also ignores the context within which political choices are made. Contexts vary in a number of important ways. Structural differences between presidential and parliamentary systems inhibit or facilitate responsibility attributions. In the United States, the division of executive and legislative powers means that the president and congress constantly attempt to claim credit and assign blame to one another for the state of the economy. The results of this exercise are not foreordained. During the Reagan years, for example, the administration enjoyed considerable success in shrugging off responsibility for the burgeoning budget deficit by blaming it on Democratic spendthrifts on Capitol Hill (Kenski, 1989; Thomas, 1989). Such attribution gamesmanship between executive and legislative branches of government is impossible in a Westminster-model parliamentary system. Thus, Mrs. Thatcher's Conservative government could hardly shift blame to the Tory majority in parliament for Britain's growing balance-of-payments deficit in 1989.

Federal versus unitary forms of government also may influence the outcome of the attribution process. Canada is a case in point. The Canadian federal system is highly decentralized, and the subnational (provincial) governments have major fiscal powers and broad programmatic responsibilities. A national government under fire for its economic performance may attempt to escape responsibility for hard times by blaming the provinces. The Conservatives recently have tried this tactic, claiming that their deficit reduction plan is being undone by the irresponsible spending policies of the social democratic New Democratic Party that currently governs Ontario, the country's largest province. In contrast, Britain's highly centralized unitary form of government means that the national government in London cannot shift blame to any other government (or at least any other *domestic* government) for economic troubles. Other scapegoats must be found. In the Thatcher years, trade unions were an attractive and highly visible target (e.g., Jenkins, 1988:369–70).

Party systems differ as well. In multiparty systems, such as those in many Western European countries, coalition governments are common, and it may be difficult for voters to attach praise or blame to individual parties participating in such coalitions. Not all coalitions are the same, however, and parties are not passive partners in the attribution process. In situations of economic adversity, if the government contains small parties which are dominated by larger coalition partners, the former may be able to distance themselves from attributions of blame accruing to the dominant partner. For example, the Free Democratic Party in the Federal Republic of Germany was a member of a number of coalition governments dominated by the Christian Democrats and the Social Democrats. The FDP vote held up well during periods of declining support for its coalition partners, suggesting that the party was able to avoid much of the blame attached to its partners when times were bad.

Another important feature of party systems concerns the extent to which the parties have distinctive issue and policy priorities. According to an *issue-priority* model (e.g., Budge and Farlie, 1983; Clarke, Stewart and Zuk, 1986), when parties are seen as having different economic issue priorities, economic conditions influence political support by affecting the salience of various economic issues on the political agenda. In the United States, for example, in times of rising inflation, voters concerned about this problem would not punish a Republican administration because they believe that Republicans accord a higher priority to the battle against price increases than do Democrats. To abandon the GOP when inflation is a threat would be irrational—"a jump from the frying pan into the fire." Similarly, when unemployment is increasing, voters concerned with joblessness would not withdraw support from a Democratic administration because they believe that the Democrats assign a higher priority to this problem than do Republicans. Such perceptions are not unreasonable because historically Democratic and Republican administrations have tended to be associated with lower levels of unemployment and inflation, respectively (Hibbs, 1977, 1987a; Whiteley, 1988a). Such findings accord well with the more general observation that left-of-center parties are more unemployment-averse and less inflation-averse than are right-of-center parties (Alt, 1985; Hibbs, 1977, 1987a).

The issue-priority model has implications for the debate about the importance of retrospective and prospective economic evaluations. The model clearly requires prospective judgments about the intentions and capabilities of competing parties. Whereas a reward-punishment approach relies exclusively on retrospective judgments about the performance of a governing party, the issue-priority model requires voters to forecast what would happen if different parties were in office. Arguably, then, the issue-priority model requires voters to have more information and to use it in more sophisticated ways than does the reward-punishment model.

The issue-priority model also suggests the possibility that changes in the context within which economic evaluations are made will change the types of judgments made. Periods of severe economic distress such as those that characterized many Western countries during the "stagflated" 1970s heighten the salience of economic issues and encourage citizens to acquire information about the policy priorities of competing parties. Moreover, parties' issue priorities and policy preferences are not necessarily constant and, thus, the choices presented to the electorate may change over time. For example, the range of economic policy options available to the British electorate was greater during the Thatcher era than it had been during the heyday of "Butskellism" in the 1950s and 1960s when both Labour and the Conservatives agreed on the necessity of maintaining high levels of employment and believed in the efficacy of Keynesian demand-management techniques for controlling the economy. Changes in the place of economic issues on the political agenda and the kinds of economic policy alternatives presented to the electorate may encourage a shift from retrospective to prospective assessments or vice versa.

Yet another debatable assumption of the reward-punishment model is the notion of symmetric responsibility attributions. In one early study Bloom and Price (1975) hypothesized that in American congressional elections political parties are punished for bad economic performance, but not rewarded for good performance. Their analyses relied on aggregate data which, as noted above, are mute about psychological processes occurring at the level of the individual voter. Analyses of survey data have given mixed reviews to the asymmetry hypothesis. Kiewiet (1983:49), for example, does not find asymmetrical effects in his research on congressional voting, but Canadian studies (e.g., Clarke et al., 1991:ch. 2) are more encouraging.

The questions of responsibility attribution raised by the reward-punishment model suggest additional considerations. One of them is related to our earlier discussion of public perceptions of the economy. If voters follow a classic rational-choice strategy of optimization, then they will punish departures from their optimal or preferred performance, and reward the party which can bring the economy closer to this position. At first blush, it might be assumed that everyone would prefer zero inflation and unemployment as their optimal points, but possible tradeoffs between these two variables, plus differences in peoples' economic positions, can create differential "demands" for inflation and unemployment (Alt, 1979:ch. 1; Gordon, 1975; Hibbs, 1987a:chs. 2-4). For example, net borrowers logically will prefer a higher rate of inflation than net lenders since rising prices erode the cost of repaying loans. Again, since unemployment tends to affect working class persons more than those in the middle and upper classes, it is rational that the former would be willing to tolerate higher inflation if this will ward off the specter of rising joblessness.

But is the optimization assumption viable? A well-established literature dating from the seminal contribution by Simon (1959) on *satisficing* behavior in decisionmaking (see also Braybrooke and Lindblom, 1963) argues that because of uncertainty, the costs of information processing, and problems of collective action, individuals do not seek optimal solutions to choice problems. Rather, they are content to find "satisfactory" solutions. This is particularly true in situations where the decisions made have relatively low priority for the individual. Electoral choices may be a case in point. If voters satisfice rather than optimize, they would not respond to changes in the economy unless these exceed some threshold of significance. Thus, relatively small fluctuations in economic conditions, e.g., rates of inflation and unemployment, should not affect political support, although large changes would have an impact. This argument is consistent with Yantek's (1988) finding that the public responds negatively only to extreme deteriorations in economic performance, as well as with studies (e.g., Paldam, 1991; Schneider and Frey, 1988; Whiteley, 1984a, 1986b) which show that the influence of economic conditions on voting intentions is unstable over time.

Another factor which is likely to influence the extent to which people attribute responsibility for economic performance is the *international economy*, and the increasing interconnections between the economies of the advanced industrial countries. This important development has received little attention, although it is clear that governments in small open economies pursue different strategies than do governments in large, relatively closed ones, for reasons directly attributable to the former's vulnerability (Cameron, 1978; Katzenstein, 1976). The increasing integration of the economies of countries in the European Community scheduled to occur in the 1990s will present opportunities to ascertain if public perceptions of the locus of authority in economic policymaking shift from the national to the supranational level.

Another aspect of responsibility attribution deserving greater attention concerns the question of whether people focus on regional or local as opposed to national economic conditions when assessing government performance. Uneven development is a common characteristic of advanced capitalist societies, and this gives rise to spatial variations in economic conditions that may affect party support, much as fluctuations in national economic performance over time give rise to temporal variations in support. Although research on the point is limited, a recent study by Johnston et al. (1988) shows that regional economic disparities are a strong predictor of voting patterns in Britain. This finding is consistent with the notion that there may be a significant geographic component to responsibility attributions.

A final general issue which relates to perceptions of economic performance as well as to responsibility attributions concerns the question of whether governments can manipulate public perceptions of economic performance. We will consider the question of manipulating the economy for political advantage below, so the issue raised here is the extent to which governments can divert attention from economic failures to boost flagging popularity. It is clear that party support can be affected, in some cases quite radically, by political and economic events or "interventions" of various kinds (e.g., Clarke, Mishler and Whiteley, 1990; Clarke and Zuk, 1989; MacKuen, 1983; Mueller, 1970, 1973; Norpoth, 1987a, 1987b; Ostrom and Simon, 1985). The effects of such interventions are often temporary, but omitting them from party support models risks misestimating the economic effects of interest. In this regard, many early studies can be faulted for either ignoring political events and conditions completely or incorporating only a few very highly salient ones (see, e.g., Hibbs, 1977; Kernell, 1978).

Political events and conditions may be classified as "systemic," "strategic" or "one-off." Systemic events are integral to a particular political system, and they influence party popularity at frequent or regular intervals. By-elections and party conferences in parliamentary systems such as Britain or Canada, and midterm congressional elections and presidential nominating conventions in the United States are examples. Strategic interventions are engineered by parties and their leaders to enhance their visibility and popularity. These often are timed to build support when it matters most—in the run-up to a general election. For example, summit conferences which capture prime-time media attention are a favorite ploy of incumbent prime ministers or presidents seeking to boost their popularity. The third category of political interventions, "one-off shocks," are occurrences unanticipated by politicians and public alike. They are the unpredictable events of political life such as hostage crises, assassination attempts, scandals, or wars which can burst onto the political stage and alter the fortunes of parties and their leaders.

Governing and opposition parties are keenly aware of the potential importance of these various kinds of interventions. Party chieftains, along with their hired "media gurus" and "spin doctors," work assiduously to control how such events are presented to the public. Indeed, much that passes for day-to-day "politics" involves politicians' attempts to take maximum advantage of newsworthy events to enhance their support while diminishing that of the opposition. In addition to trying to manage the effects of political interventions, incumbent parties and their leaders also attempt to manipulate the economy for their benefit. As we will argue below, this is a difficult and unpredictable enterprise, but governments that are successful in accomplishing it will quickly claim responsibility for the happy state of affairs.

## Political Control of the Economy?

The extent to which governments can affect economic outcomes is one of the areas of sharpest controversy in contemporary political economy. This is because it takes in the whole of macroeconomic theory and, since a number of authors have tried to develop microeconomic foundations for macroeconomics, large areas of microeconomic theory as well. A full analysis of all of the debates in macroeconomic theory is beyond the scope of this book, but it is possible to highlight the key issues which concern analysts trying to explore the nature of political effects on economic policy (reaction functions) and political and economic policy effects on economic outcomes (outcome functions).

The central debate in studies of reaction functions concerns the existence of *political business cycles* (PBCs). The term "political business cycle" refers to an incumbent government manipulating policy instruments at its disposal to improve the performance of the economy in the period preceding an election. In its classic formulation (Nordhaus, 1975), the political business cycle involves Phillips-curve type tradeoffs (Phillips, 1958) between unemployment and inflation. A government desiring to implement a PBC will invoke policies to stimulate the economy to reduce unemployment and thereby increase its popularity. Increases in inflation will occur, but only with a lag such that they become apparent after the election, at which time the government can take measures to curb accelerating prices. These measures, in turn, will slow the economy and increase unemployment, but the loss of support that this entails can be remedied by invoking a new PBC in the run-up to the next election.

There are several preconditions that must be met for PBCs to be possible. First, voters must be willing to reward a government for good economic performance, in other words, economic conditions affect political support. In the absence of such effects, governments might attempt to invoke PBCs, but their efforts would be wasted. Relatedly, voters must be sufficiently sophisticated that they monitor the economy and detect changes in its performance, but not be so sophisticated that they perceive the government is attempting to use the economy to manipulate them. If voters can recognize PBCs, governments will hesitate to attempt them, fearing charges of cynicism and the attendant punishment that might be meted out by an irate electorate.

A second requirement for PBCs is that the government is able to manipulate the economy by using policy instruments such as monetary and fiscal policy to affect economic outcomes. Here we immediately confront key debates in macroeconomics about whether governments can control the economy and, more particularly, the debate about the efficacy of stabilization policies. The political business cycle requires that stabilization policies work, which means that a government must be able to stimulate growth and employment in a slump, and constrain inflation in a boom. Most macroeconomic theorists would accept that government can, to a significant extent, control the money economy which implies that it can limit inflation, although there are disagreements about how this can best be done. However, there are major disputes over whether government can influence the real economy of employment, productivity and growth; some would argue that the real economy cannot be controlled in the long run, and others, that it cannot be controlled even in the short run. Thus, theorists disagree whether government has enough control over economic outcomes to manipulate them for political benefit.

These debates are linked to very general controversies between neo-classical and neo-Keynesian economists. The neo-classical school argues that government intervention in the economy usually makes things worse. If this argument is coupled with the assumption that people have "rational expectations," i.e., they make no systematic errors in forecasting the future behavior of the economy, the possibility of a PBC is ruled out. This is because government manipulation would only worsen economic performance and, because voters would know this, they would punish a government which attempted to do it. Of course, if the rational-expectations assumption is applied to government as well as the electorate, incumbents would not even attempt a PBC, knowing that it is bound to fail. Theoretical attempts have been made to generate a PBC within a neo-classical framework of rational expectations (e.g., Alesina, 1989, Alesina and Rosenthal, 1989; Alesina and Sachs, 1988), but these theories do not work very well since they must introduce arbitrary rigidities into the economy in order to generate the cycle.

For neo-Keynesians, PBCs are not theoretically prohibited. Neo-Keynesians argue that stabilization policies can improve economic performance by moderating the "boom and bust" cycles that bedevil capitalist economies. Since such policies do not eliminate the trade cycle completely, economic policies presumably can be geared to the political calendar so as to make upturns in economic activity coincide with preelection periods, and downturns, with postelection periods. PBCs are thereby possible for neo-Keynesians, although their theoretical understanding of the characteristics of advanced capitalist economies indicates that PBCs will difficult to carry out in practice. These characteristics refer primarily to the responsiveness of the economy to fiscal and monetary stimuli. Generally, neo-Keynesians see the economy as a large-scale stochastic system which contains significant rigidities, and displays considerable inertia in response to external forces. This interia makes economic change slow and unpredictable, implying that PBCs will be difficult to implement, since governments cannot be sure that their policy interventions will operate in synchronization with the electoral calendar.

Thus, both neo-classical and neo-Keynesian economists are pessimistic, albeit for different reasons, about the likelihood of successful political business cycles. However, the temptation to try to effect a PBC may be very strong, particularly when a governing party finds itself behind in the polls and facing the possibility of electoral defeat. Even if the effort proves unsuccessful, the government can claim that its economic policy initiatives were motivated by considerations of the national welfare rather than partisan self-interest. In sum, controversies among political economists about political business cycles may mean little to ambitious politicians whose business is ultimately politics not economics, and attempts to practice the arts of the PBC should not be confused with success in doing so.

## Methodological Issues

One of the more contentious aspects of studies of political economy concerns questions of research methodology. Debates about how to specify and test models of political support, economic policy and economic outcomes have been integral to the field for many years, and important questions remain unresolved. Some of these topics are highly technical, and we will not address them in detail here. However, we will highlight the key issues.

One issue concerns questions of *measurement*. It is clear that voting behavior and party popularity in inter-election periods are different things. Studies of the former typically use data collected in national surveys conducted at the time of a national election; studies of the latter use data from commercial public opinion polls, most of which are carried when such a contest is months or years in the future. A poll question on vote intentions that do not have to be acted on for some time may solicit a different type of response than that given in the midst of an election campaign, or right after one. Both kinds of data are likely to contain random measurement error or "noise," but this will tend to be greater in commercial polls that use relatively small samples and crude sampling designs than in large and carefully executed academic election surveys. Moreover, Miller (1989) has suggested that polls may have systematic biases as well. Specifically, they may inflate support for opposition parties by providing respondents with an opportunity to register a "cheap protest" about a governing party without having to make a real decision about whether to cast a ballot for that party or one of its rivals.

A second area of methodological controversy focuses on *model specification*. One aspect of this debate concerns what econometricians call the "omitted variable" problem. Variables affecting political support often are intercorrelated, and statistical estimates of the impact of the one of theoretical interest to the political economist, for example, unemployment, are likely unreliable if the model being analyzed does not contain other influential variables as well. Above, we have noted two examples of the problem, namely the omission of subjective economic evaluations and important political events.

A related concern in specifying models of dynamic systems is the question of *lagged effects*. For example, party popularity is likely to respond to changes in unemployment only after a period of time has elapsed. The time lags can be conceptualized as proxying unobserved learning processes—the time it takes for the public to adjust to changes in the economy. But such lags also represent processes related to the diffusion and decay of information. The diffusion of economic information acquired through sources such as the mass media, the market and interpersonal communication networks is not instantaneous and, once acquired, such information is perishable. It may be replaced by additional incoming information, discounted, or simply forgotten. The time lag for a change in unemployment to affect aggregate levels of party popularity represents the net result of this information spreading among the public and hence affecting an increasing number of people, on the one hand, while dissipating in its impact, on the other. Although lagged effects are thus reasonable, the length of such lags is debatable, and data gathered at theoretically attractive lags may be unavailable.

Another related topic concerns *functional form*. Is the effect of unemployment on party popularity linear such that a given increment in joblessness always produces an X% change in popularity, or is the effect nonlinear such that the amount of change in popularity varies with the level of unemployment? Similar questions can be asked about political

# Introduction

events. Is the impact of an attempted assassination of a president or an international conflict such as the Falklands war temporary or permanent? If the effect is temporary, how long does it last, and does it terminate abruptly or only gradually?

All of these questions about model specification are methodological in the sense that answers to them will govern the statistical analyses that the researcher performs. It is crucial to note, however, that the answers ultimately must be provided by one's theoretical understanding of the phenomena under consideration. Model specification can be assisted by advanced statistical techniques, but such techniques do not guarantee that the results are theoretically sensible.

A final area of methodological controversy concerns problems of time series analysis. Much of the data of interest to the political economist are gathered over regular time intervals, for example, rates of inflation and unemployment and levels of party support measured monthly, quarterly or yearly. Such data are vital for investigating the dynamics of economic and political processes, but they raise knotty technical difficulties. Some of these problems are well-known. For example, using traditional ordinary least squares regression to analyze time series data often violates the assumptions of that procedure, most notably the requirement that error terms be uncorrelated. What has been less widely appreciated is that the standard diagnostic for this problem, the Durbin-Watson test, and standard corrections for it such as the Cochrane-Orcutt procedure and other pseudo-GLS regression methods, deal only with correlations between adjacent error terms (first-order autocorrelation) (Ostrom, 1990). Other possible time series dependencies are not dealt with by these techniques and, thus, the threats to inference that they pose are not controlled.

Another difficulty endemic to time series analyses is what is known as mean nonstationarity. A stationary time series will fluctuate around a constant value, whereas a nonstationary one will have a mean that increases or decreases systematically over time. It is very easy to draw misleading inferences in time series analysis when variables are modeled in nonstationary form. Since the variables being analyzed trend over time they can be highly correlated (positively or negatively) even though they are unrelated theoretically (Granger and Newbold, 1974). It is, then, important to use a model-building strategy which is sensitive to this problem. Typically, analysts have addressed it by "differencing" their data to ensure that they are stationary. The assumption underlying this approach is that if a causal relationship between two variables exists, then changes in one are going to produce changes in the other, independently of the fact that they may be increasing or decreasing over time.[3]

## Three Contexts of Controversy

The controversies discussed above guide the analyses presented in the succeeding chapters. Our fundamental general argument is politico-economic interactions do not take place in a void; rather, they are subject to a variety of contextual influences. Thus, it is important to outline significant contextual differences among the three Anglo-American democracies—Great Britain, Canada and the United States—that provide the settings for our empirical studies.

The three countries manifest a variety of important cultural and structural similarities and differences. The political cultures of all three have been heavily influenced by the liberal political tradition and, hence, are characterized by a concern for individual rights and liberties and political institutions which recognize the limited authority of the state (Hartz, 1955). This is not to say that the three political cultures are identical. Although broad agreement exists on the core elements of philosophic liberalism, in Britain and, to a lesser extent, in Canada liberal principles and beliefs coexist with significant strains of conservatism and socialism (Beer, 1965, 1982; Horowitz, 1966).

There are related, more specific, cultural differences as well. Perhaps the most important from the standpoint of the present study are those involving beliefs about government's role in economy and society. Closely related are differing beliefs about the extent to which individuals are responsible for their personal welfare. In the post–World War II era, government involvement in economy and society expanded greatly in all three countries, but the strongly individualistic strain in American political culture noted above is absent in Britain and Canada. The more elaborate development of the welfare state in the latter two countries testifies to these differing views concerning the proper balance of government and individual responsibility. Although Britain and the United States witnessed a resurgence of conservative ideologies and conservative parties enjoyed marked electoral successes in all three countries in the 1980s, there is evidence that the differences among them regarding public beliefs about government's proper economic and social roles remained essentially intact. Thus, national surveys indicate that British and Canadian citizens continue to believe that government can and should be deeply involved in economic and social life (Clarke et al., 1991:ch. 2; Clarke, Stewart and Zuk, 1988).

Similarly, it appears that the "Reagan revolution" in the United States had little influence on American public opinion about the proper role of government. For example, summarizing their analyses of voters' policy preferences circa 1988, Abramson, Aldrich and Rohde (1990:291) conclude: ". . . the Republicans are far to the right politically, and are far more conservative than the electorate." American voters favor less government involvement in economy and society than their British and Canadian counterparts, but their support for Reagan and his successor, George Bush, in the last three presidential elections did not constitute an endorsement for a neo-conservative policy agenda.

The three countries also exhibit important differences in their governmental structures. One such difference concerns federal versus unitary forms of government. Unlike Britain's unitary system, both Canada and the United States are characterized by federal political arrangements in which there exists a division, or sharing, of responsibilities and powers (Elazar, 1972; Grodzins, 1966). These arrangements have existed since the founding of the two countries, and the concept of federalism is deeply imbedded in their respective political cultures. An important feature of a federal system is that it devolves substantial policy-making and administrative responsibilities onto officials at the subnational levels of government. Such a dispersion of responsibility does not exist under unitary arrangements such as those in Britain.

Although both Canada and the United States are federal systems, there are important differences between them. The American states clearly have become relatively less important political entities during the 20th century and especially since the New Deal. The balance of power between national and subnational governments in Canada also has shifted, but in the opposite direction, such that the provinces have vital economic and social policy roles (Stevenson, 1989). As noted above, these differences in the American and Canadian federal systems may influence how citizens in the two countries attribute responsibility to government for economic policies and economic outcomes.

Another basic structural difference concerns parliamentary versus presidential forms of government. The Westminster-model parliamentary systems of Britain and Canada provide for a "fusion" of executive and legislative authority, with the prime minister and the cabinet sitting in parliament and being collectively and individually responsible to that body. In the United States, the president and the executive branch exist independently of the legislature (Congress). This separation-of-powers system can and does produce policy outcomes in which the inherent tensions created by countervailing institutional prerogatives and ambitions are exacerbated by the potential for the executive and legislature to be controlled, as it has for much of the post–World War II era, by different political parties. The Westminster system, in contrast, mandates that the "government" must have the support of the majority party or a majority coalition in parliament if it is to continue in office. As noted earlier, it can be argued that these different systems have consequences for responsibility attributions, with the Westminster-model system facilitating the public's ability to hold government accountable for (mis)deeds in office, and the presidential system inhibiting it.

A third important difference among the three countries concerns their political parties and party systems. In democratic theory and practice parties are charged with vital representational and policy-making functions. In performing them, parties affect the ability of citizens to express their preferences concerning economic (or other) policies and to hold governments responsible for their performance in office. Party systems delineate the range of policy options available to the public and, by so doing, define the logic of political choice.

It traditionally has been argued that Westminster-model parliamentary systems tend to produce "principled" parties with clearly demarcated policies, programs and ideologies, whereas presidential systems do just the opposite (e.g., APSA, 1950). The two major national Canadian parties, the Liberals and the Conservatives, historically have hewed very close to the center of the ideological spectrum. During election campaigns they typically eschew clearly defined policies and coherent programs in favor of brokerage electioneering strategies emphasizing "quick fixes" for salient economic and social problems and the personal and stylistic qualities of party leaders (Clarke et al., 1991). In contrast, in Britain, the Labour and Conservative parties have located themselves clearly on the left and right, respectively, of the ideological spectrum. However, the extent of their policy differences has varied over time. During the 1950s and 1960s the two parties shared a broad, albeit imperfect, *de facto* consensus on most major economic and social policies. This eroded during the 1970s, and by the 1980s both Mrs. Thatcher and her Labour opponents had espoused a politics of strident ideological "conviction" (e.g., Crewe and Searing, 1988; Jenkins, 1988).

The idea that the range of policy choices offered by the parties can change over time also is illustrated in the American case. While the Democratic and Republican parties traditionally have been characterized as quintessential brokerage organizations competing for the favor of a perceived "median voter" at the center of the ideological spectrum, this image was not accurate during the Reagan years. In the 1980s the Republicans attempted to effect a neo-conservative policy agenda, while the Democrats searched for an alternative that did not entail abandonment of their historic commitment to New Deal liberalism. As a result, the economic and policy choices offered by American parties became clearer than at any previous time in the post–World War II period.

The range of political choice offered by the three countries differs in another way as well. Although two parties have dominated the political stage in Britain and Canada, their party systems are characterized by the presence of long-lived "third" parties. In Britain, the Liberals ceased to be a major force after the 1920s. Although they enjoyed periodic surges in public support, they were never able to challenge for power, and were widely seen as a convenient centrist alternative for Conservative or Labour voters wishing to register a "safe protest" (Clarke and Zuk, 1989; Rasmussen, 1981). In the early 1980s it appeared that Liberal fortunes might change, when the party formed the "Alliance" with the new Social Democratic Party, which was led by several former Labour leaders disillusioned with Labour's leftward drift (Bradley, 1981). Although the new political formation enjoyed an initially strong surge in popularity, in the end the Liberals and their SDP allies failed to "break the mould" of the British party system.

In Canada, the most important minor party on the national stage is the New Democratic Party. The NDP's forerunner, the Cooperative Commonwealth Federation (CCF) was formed during the 1930s by an assortment of "left" and social democratic groups protesting the failure of the old-line Liberal and Conservative parties to deal with the severe economic and social dislocations brought about by the Great Depression (Young, 1969). In 1961, in an effort to strengthen its ties with organized labor, the CCF was reorganized as the NDP. In recent years the NDP has made occasional strong showings in public opinion polls, but like the British Liberals and the Alliance, it suffers from a "first-past-the-post" electoral system that makes it difficult for the party to translate popular support at the ballot box into seats in parliament.

The differences in the American, British and Canadian party systems combine with the structural and cultural differences among the three countries to define three different contexts of political choice. These contexts are not invariant; rather they can vary over time. We argue that these differing contexts and changes therein can have important effects on political-economic interactions of various kinds. In this volume, we pursue this argument with a series of investigations that address the major controversies in contemporary political economy discussed above.

## The Controversies Considered

We begin our empirical analyses in Chapter 2 by examining the dynamics of presidential approval in the United States during the Reagan years. Although media commentators have depicted Reagan as a highly popular figure with a "teflon" image impervious to the corrosive effects of economic and political adversity, this portrait is inaccurate. In fact, Reagan's approval ratings were not especially high in comparison with most post-war presidents and they reacted in predictable ways to economic conditions and political events. The effects of inflation and unemployment conformed to an issue-priority rather than a traditional reward-punishment model, a finding consistent with the increased ideological polarization of the American party system precipitated by Reagan's neo-conservative policy agenda. As for subjective economic evaluations, they were only weakly affected by objective economic conditions, and they exerted an independent impact on presidential approval. Political events also were important—indeed, they had stronger effects on Reagan's public standing than either objective economic conditions or subjective economic evaluations.

Relationships between subjective economic evaluations and objective economic realities are investigated in greater detail in Chapter 3. Consistent with our theoretical expectations and the analyses in Chapter 2, we find that the British electorate's evaluations of national and personal economic conditions were affected by objective economic conditions during the first eight years of the Thatcher era, but these effects were modest. Moreover, highly salient political events such as the Falklands war had major impacts on subjective economic evaluations. Finally, objective economic conditions, subjective economic judgments and political events all influenced support for the Thatcher government. Taken together, the findings suggest the existence of a genuine *political* economy of party support.

The theme of the interplay of economic and political influences on party popularity is pursued in Chapter 4 which focuses on public support for the British Liberal/SDP Alliance. Although the Alliance had been launched in a period of economic adversity and political turmoil that seemed especially auspicious for upending the existing party system, the new party failed to do so. Our analyses suggest an explanation. After articulating alternative theoretical perspectives on how economic conditions might influence support for minor parties in multiparty systems, we show that during the Thatcher years at least economic influences on support for the Liberal/SDP Alliance conformed to a traditional reward-punishment model, with increases in inflation and unemployment boosting Alliance popularity. National and personal economic evaluations also influenced Alliance popularity, as did a host of political events and conditions. The latter were particularly important for a third party such as the Alliance, which often found itself buffeted by political forces it could not control. These forces, together with the heavy penalties imposed on such parties by a single-member plurality electoral system, ultimately thwarted the Alliance's bid to overturn the longstanding Conservative-Labour duopoly.

In Chapter 5 we consider the impact of economic and political forces on party popularity in Canada. Unlike most previous studies that have ignored contextual effects, this chapter investigates how regional variations in unemployment and regional differences in public reactions to salient political events affected support for the national parties. Canada is an ideal locale for such an investigation because it long has been characterized by marked regional disparities in economic activity and party support. During the period under consideration, however, economic variables including regional-level unemployment had only minor effects. What mattered were political events, particularly an ongoing series of scandals and intraparty squabbles which diminished the popularity of the governing Conservatives and the Liberal opposition, respectively. Similar to the Alliance in Britain, the NDP also was strongly affected by political events and conditions, including a third-party squeeze that eroded its support in the run-up to the 1988 general election.

Regarding the weakness of economic effects in the Canadian analyses, it should be noted that between 1985 and 1988 the economy finally improved after a decade of distress which culminated in a serious recession in the early 1980s. If economic effects on party popularity are asymmetric, such that people blame governments for hard times but do not praise them for good times, the impact of the economy should be stronger in the former circumstance. Analyses of individual-level survey data enable us to investigate this and other hypotheses about subjective economic evaluations.

Chapters 6 and 7 present these analyses. Despite the protracted debates about the importance of national versus personal and retrospective versus prospective economic evaluations in political support models, there are remarkably few studies of how people actually organize their thinking about the economy. Accordingly, in Chapter 6 we consider alternative models of the structure of public economic evaluations in the contemporary United States. We find that economic judgments are organized in terms of a retrospective sociotropic factor, a retrospective egocentric factor, and a prospective factor that combines future-oriented national and personal evaluations. A causal model shows that retrospective sociotropic judgments have strong indirect effects on candidate preference in the 1988 presidential election. Retrospective egocentric evaluations are relevant too but, again, their effects are indirect. Prospective evaluations, in contrast, are insignificant, a finding which we believe reflects the context of electoral choice created by party strategies in the 1988 campaign. Recall that this contest was largely devoid of debates concerning the country's economic future (Farah and Klein, 1989:118–21).

Chapter 7 shows that, in fact, Canadians are strongly predisposed to make asymmetric responsibility attributions, blaming the government for national and personal economic adversity, but not crediting it for the country's or their own prosperity. Also, Canadian voters' economic evaluations are structured in terms of the same retrospective sociotropic, retrospective egocentric, and prospective factors found in the American case. However, all three types of economic evaluation influenced support for the governing Conservatives. Why? We argue the principal reason is that the context of Canadian politics circa 1990 was one in which two highly publicized government economic policy initiatives, a free trade agreement with the United States and a general goods and services tax, concentrated public attention on present and future economic conditions. Given tendencies toward asymmetrical economic evaluations and the presence of a serious recession, this focus magnified the impact of negative economic evaluations of all kinds, prospective as well as retrospective. The result was that government support eroded so precipitously that some observers quipped it might well fall below the prime interest rate!

Chapters 8 and 9 consider relationships between the economy and government support in terms of the much disputed political business cycle hypothesis. Chapter 8 begins by explicating the foundations of the dispute in neo-Keynesian and neo-classical macroeconomic theories. This is followed by a theoretical development of the political business cycle from a neo-Keynesian perspective and a critique of attempts to develop the logic of PBCs in terms of rational-expectations theory. The chapter concludes by testing a PBC model of economic policy and outcomes for Britain between 1983 and 1987. We argue that the Conservative government attempted to manipulate the money supply and other policy instruments to reduce unemployment and stimulate economic activity in the run-up to the 1987 general election. The analyses agree—in addition to reflecting changes in Tory support in public opinion polls, the money supply grew extraordinarily quickly beginning in early 1986 as the Conservatives began their "long campaign" for reelection. This, in turn, had the desired effect of creating a favorable trend in unemployment as the election approached. The Conservative PBC also boosted inflation, but the negative impact this had on the government's popularity was not felt until well after it had been returned to power.

Finally, Chapter 9 argues that the perplexities of political business cycles are understandable in terms of several developments in the international arena. Analyses show that factors tied to presidential politics, such as election periods and party priorities, have exerted weaker effects, while international political and economic developments such as major wars, oil-price fluctuations, and trade problems, have had stronger influences on inflation and unemployment rates over the 1947–85 period. These developments also have generated episodic relationships among presidential elections, party priorities, and macroeconomic conditions. These analyses suggest two conclusions. The first is that various administrations have sought to manipulate international politics for economic advantage but, in so doing, have undermined their ability to operate the domestic economy for political gain. The second is that contemporary electorates have held governments accountable for economic performance that is increasingly determined by international events and conditions. Current developments promise greater international constraints on domestic policy and, thus, fewer opportunities to engineer political business cycles.

## Notes

1. Useful reviews of the literature include Keech, Bates and Lange (1989); Lewis-Beck (1988a); Mansbridge (1990); Miller (1989); Monroe (1984, 1991); Ostrom (1991); Paldam (1981); Schneider and Frey (1988).

2. The vast majority of American studies of the impact of economic variables on political support in inter-election periods have investigated presidential approval as measured in monthly Gallup polls. The MacKuen, Erikson and Stimson partisanship variable, in contrast, is the Gallup measure of party support. Abramson and Ostrom (1991) have argued that this variable is not equivalent to the traditional party identification measure in the American national election studies.

3. Most of the statistical analyses in this book use the Box-Jenkins-Tiao approach to time series modeling (Box and Jenkins, 1976; Box and Tiao, 1975). This approach involves a systematic model-building strategy in which a good deal of preliminary work is done to identify the best univariate and multivariate models of a time series before the models are estimated. The strategy pays particular attention to diagnostic testing to ensure that all series are stationary, that the models have picked up all the systematic information available in the data, and that there are not relationships in the model residuals which are likely to distort the interpretation of the estimates. The Box-Jenkins-Tiao approach also facilitates the modeling of complex dynamic effects that may be associated with various political and economic events (McCleary and Hay, 1980:ch. 3). The several steps involved in developing and testing Box-Jenkins-Tiao models are described in Appendix A.

# 2

# The Economics and Politics of Presidential Approval: The Reagan Years

*Many analysts believe that Reagan's landslide reelection in 1984 confirmed that he is a phenomenally popular president. . . .*
—Ranney (1985:31)

*In recent years, the Republicans have had the good fortune to run during periods of economic expansion.*
—Abramson, Aldrich, and Rohde (1990:300)

Studying how the economy affects public support for American presidents is a thriving cottage industry in contemporary political economy. Although it is one of the most developed areas of the literature, it also is one characterized by a number of longstanding controversies. In this chapter we examine several of these controversies within the context of a model of support for President Reagan over the eight years of his presidency. Our principal concern is the impact of subjective assessments of the national economy and personal economic conditions on presidential approval. In addressing this topic, we also deal with two other important controversies, namely, the relative importance of economic variables and various noneconomic events and conditions in presidential approval models, and the nature of the effects of objective economic conditions in such models.

Most previous studies of public support for incumbent governments and their leaders have focused heavily, sometimes exclusively, on the influence of *objective* economic conditions, most notably, rates of inflation and unemployment. Model specifications which include only objective macroeconomic conditions make the often implicit assumption that the electorate's *subjective* judgments about national and personal economic conditions accurately reflect the state of the objective economy. In this chapter we will show that, although economic evaluations are influenced by objective economic factors, the fit is far from perfect, and that subjective economic variables also are affected by various noneconomic (political) events and conditions. Since subjective economic variables are not simply mirrors of what is transpiring in the objective economy, the failure to include them in political support models may result in specification problems. Relatedly, those few studies which have incorporated subjective measures of the economy (e.g., Sanders, Marsh and Ward, 1987; Clarke, Mishler and Whiteley, 1990; Clarke and Whiteley, 1990) have shown that objective macroeconomic conditions and subjective economic evaluations both influence political support. Consequently, we will test models of President Reagan's approval that include both types of variables.

A second controversy addressed in this chapter is the question of whether political support is based on the public's assessments of *personal* economic circumstances (egocentric evaluations) or, alternatively, on evaluations of *collective* economic well-being (sociotropic evaluations). To date, most of the empirical evidence addressing this controversy has been provided by individual-level analyses of cross-sectional survey data. Many of these studies indicate that political support is governed primarily by sociotropic concerns (e.g., Kinder and Kiewiet, 1979, 1981; Monroe, 1984). However, the adequacy of these individual-level survey findings has been challenged on methodological grounds (e.g., Kramer, 1983). Here, we join this controversy by investigating the effects of both egocentric and sociotropic evaluations in dynamic analyses of aggregate-level models of presidential approval.

A third, related, concern is whether the public is *retrospectively* or *prospectively* oriented. Do voters rely primarily upon judgments about past economic performance or anticipated future economic conditions when making their political decisions? Although there is a substantial literature supporting the hypothesis that retrospective judgments are more important (Monroe, 1984:chs. 1, 2), some research indicates that prospective evaluations may be influential as well (e.g., Chappell and Keech, 1985; Fiorina 1981; Kuklinski and West, 1981; Lewis-Beck, 1986, 1988a). Accordingly, we consider both retrospective and prospective subjective economic variables in our presidential approval analyses.

Many presidential approval models also can be faulted for ignoring salient noneconomic events and conditions, or for failing to model them appropriately. With regard to the latter, it is important to note that events may be simple and highly transient, and thus can be modeled as brief "pulses," or they may be complex and longer lived, requiring more elaborate specifications. A closely related consideration in analyses of the effects of such variables is the need to consider the time lags at which such interventions operate.

When modeling interventions, it is useful to distinguish between two basic types: systemic events and conditions that are integral features of a particular political system and consequently occur at regular intervals (e.g., presidential or congressional elections), and *nonsystemic* "one-off" shocks (e.g., international crises and wars, scandals involving high-ranking government officials). Although these nonsystemic interventions frequently are unanticipated by politicians and the electorate, they can have major effects on political support. While there is no *a priori* theoretical guidance for selecting particular interventions for consideration, and limited degrees of freedom impose a technical constraint on the number of possibilities that can be considered, efforts should be made to model those highly salient events which seem to have *prima facie* potential to affect the support series of interest.

Finally, we are concerned with the *nature* of the impact of objective economic variables. As noted in Chapter 1, the vast majority of presidential approval and party support studies have been guided by a simple "reward-punishment" hypothesis (Key, 1968) which specifies that voters reward incumbent parties and their leaders for good or improving economic conditions and punish them for bad or deteriorating ones (Monroe and Erickson, 1986:619). This hypothesis ignores the possibility that voters may perceive that parties have different issue priorities (Budge and Farlie, 1983). An alternative issue-priority hypothesis contends that the salience of economic issues, especially those associated with inflation and unemployment, varies according to levels and trends in such variables, and that voters offer or withdraw support depending upon the perceived priorities that competing parties and their leaders accord to the issue in question. In the American context, the expectation is that people concerned about inflation will not punish a Republican president for price increases because they perceive that the Republicans accord priority to this issue and will accept increases in unemployment if these are deemed necessary to check inflation. Similarly, persons concerned about unemployment will not punish a Democratic president because they believe that the Democrats accord higher priority to the fight against joblessness than do the Republicans. By the same logic, rising unemployment should have negative effects on support for Republican presidents, and increases in inflation, negative ones on support for Democratic presidents.[1]

## Measures and Methods

Data gathered by the monthly Gallup Poll question "Do you approve or disapprove of the way _____ is handling his job as President?" are used to measure presidential approval. Information on monthly rates of inflation and unemployment are obtained from the OECD *Main Economic Indicators*. Evaluations of past and future national (sociotropic) and personal (egocentric) economic conditions are ascertained using data from the monthly "Surveys of Consumers" studies conducted by the Survey Research Center, University of Michigan. Retrospective assessments of the national economy are measured with the following question: "Would you say that *at the present time* business conditions are better or worse than they were *a year ago?*" The question measuring retrospective assessments of personal economic conditions is: "We are interested in how people are getting along financially these days. Would you say that you (and your family living here) are *better off* or *worse off* than you were a year ago?" Assessments of the future of the national economy are tapped with the question "Now turning to business conditions in the country as a whole—do you think that during the next 12 months we'll have *good* times financially, or *bad* times, or what?" Forecasts of personal economic circumstances were ascertained with the question "Now looking ahead— do you think that *a year from now* you (and your family living here) will be *better off* financially, or *worse off,* or just about the same as now?" The Survey of Consumers constructs indices of subjective economic evaluations (ranging from 0 to 200) based on answers to these four questions by adding 100 to the percentage of positive responses minus the percentage of positive ones.[2] Information on the timing of various nonsystemic events that might have affected presidential approval net of changes in objective economic conditions and subjective economic evaluations are obtained from *Keesings Contemporary Archives*.

Box-Tiao (1975) and Box-Jenkins (1976) time series analysis procedures are employed to analyze how the several economic and noneconomic variables of interest affected presidential approval. These procedures provide an effective means of detecting and modeling lagged effects of independent variables, and they enable one to control for complex autoregressive and moving average processes that, if unattended, might confound the estimates. Box-Jenkins-Tiao modeling techniques involve an iterative process of model specification, testing and diagnosis. The several steps in this process are discussed in Appendix A.

We first describe the dynamics of presidential approval during the Reagan years, as well as trends in objective economic conditions and subjective evaluations of the national economy and personal economic circumstances during this period. Next, we provide a brief overview of the economic and political events during Reagan's presidency which are included in our presidential approval models. We then analyze these models and conclude by discussing the implications of our findings.

FIGURE 2.1 Presidential Approval, Eisenhower to Reagan

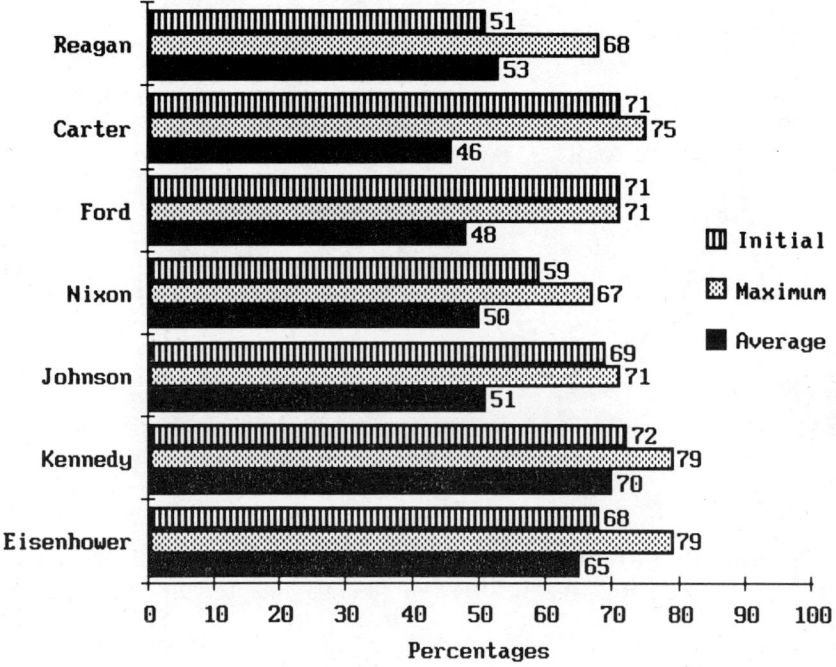

## Reagan's Presidential Approval Ratings

Notwithstanding the widespread belief that President Reagan was one of the nation's most popular chief executives, his initial approval rating (51% in January 1981) was substantially lower than those for any of his predecessors in the post-Truman era (Figure 2.1). However, it increased to 60% over the next two months, and then jumped to 68% following his attempted assassination on March 31, 1981 (Figure 2.2). Reagan's approval remained over 60% during June and July, a period which concluded with his dramatic tax cut victories in Congress and the nomination of the first woman Supreme Court Justice, Sandra Day O'Connor. It then gradually declined and, coincident with rising unemployment and a deepening recession, continued to drop throughout 1982, reaching a low of 39% in January of 1983. His approval then rebounded in the spring and summer of that year. Following the Grenada intervention in mid-October 1983, his rating increased to slightly over 50%, and then continued on a fairly level path until increasing at the time of the 1984 election.

Reagan began his second term with a solid 63% approval rating (Figure 2.1). It declined somewhat during the early spring of 1985, and then

FIGURE 2.2 Reagan's Presidential Approval Rating, January 1981–September 1988

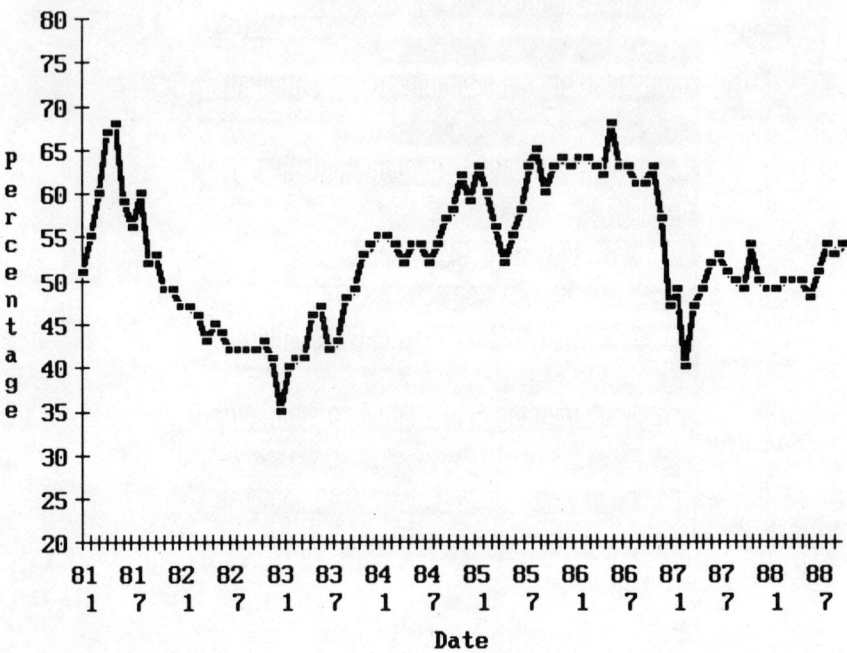

rebounded to 65% in early July of 1985. It subsequently remained very stable, jumping briefly to 68% in April of 1986 following the air strike against Libyan leader Qaddafi. In late fall 1986, however, following Republican setbacks in the midterm congressional elections and the Iran-Contra scandal, his support plummeted to 40%, the lowest level since the depths of the recession in early 1983. Reagan subsequently made a partial recovery, edging back over the 50% in May 1987. His support then leveled off, fluctuating in a relatively narrow band between the high 40's to low 50's. He finally closed out his presidency at 53%—2% above the level at which he had begun eight years earlier.

## Trends in Inflation and Unemployment

Inflation and unemployment are two of the most salient aspects of a nation's economic life and, as such, they have been the focal points of most previous studies of the political economy of presidential approval. During Reagan's first term in office trends in inflation and unemployment, when plotted together, reveal a fairly distinct "Phillips curve" pattern (Phillips, 1958) (Figure 2.3). The unemployment rate stood at 7.5% when

FIGURE 2.3 Inflation and Unemployment, January 1981–September 1988

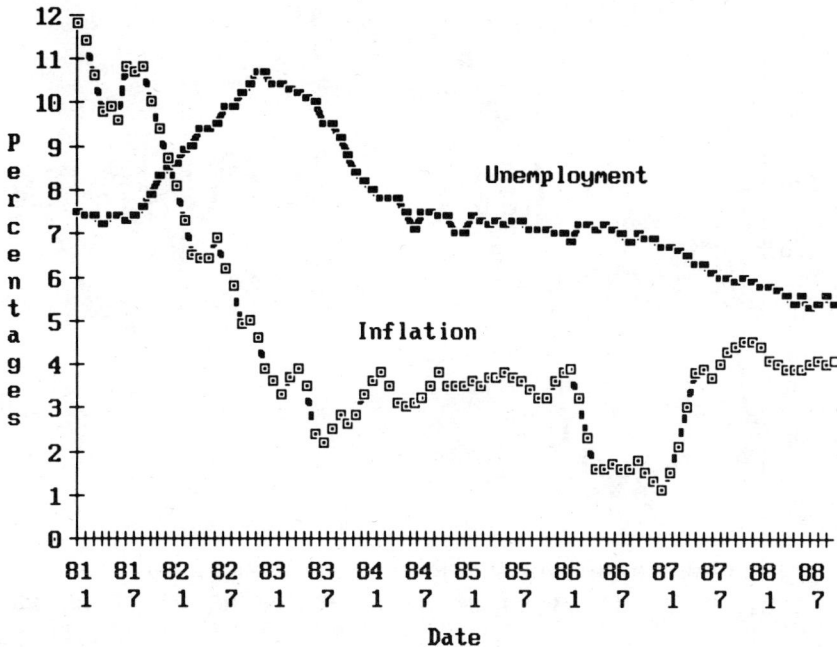

Reagan assumed office in January 1981. After the onset of the recession late in that year, it increased steadily until December 1982, when it reached a peak of 11.1%. However, in the spring of 1983 joblessness began to decline, and continued to do so throughout the remainder of his first term. By the time of the 1984 election, it had receded to 7.0%, the lowest level since Reagan became president. Although unemployment subsequently increased slightly, (to 7.3% in the summer of 1985), an overall downward trend operated throughout much of his second term.

The path for inflation was quite different. The rate of price increases, which was nearly 12% in January of 1981, varied in the 9–11% range for much of that year, but then began to decline as the economy slowed (Figure 2.3). Price increases subsequently fell precipitously, and reached a low of 2.2% per annum in July of 1983. They remained modest (less than 4%) for the rest of Reagan's first term. His entire second term also was characterized by relatively low inflation figures which stayed in the 3–4% range throughout 1985 before tapering off slightly in 1986. They then increased slightly in early 1987 (to 4.5%) before modestly declining again. At the end of Reagan's second term, the inflation rate was slightly over 4%.

FIGURE 2.4 Retrospective Economic Evaluation Indices, January 1981–September 1988

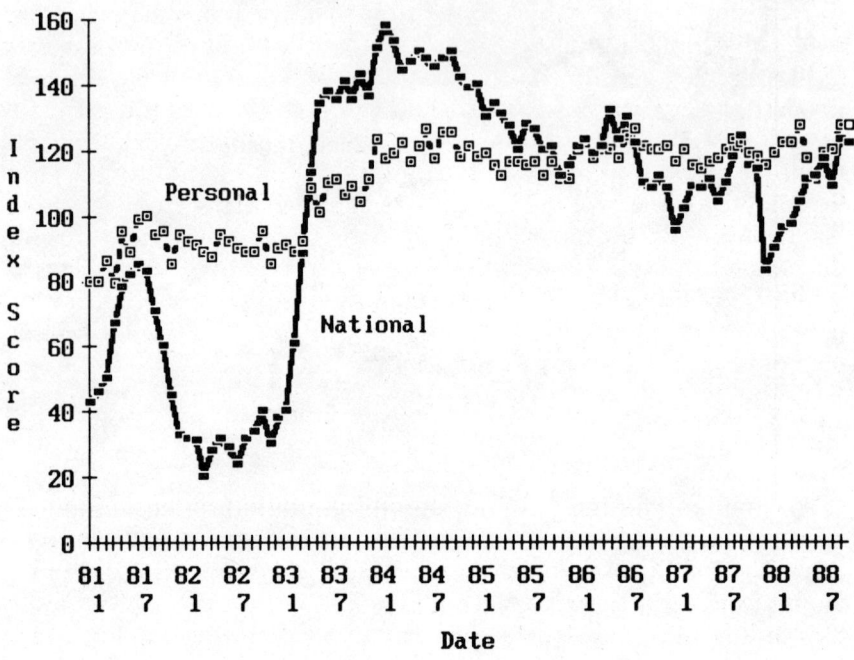

## The Subjective Economy

The data on retrospective evaluations of national and personal economic conditions displayed in Figure 2.4 indicate that they manifested parallel trends during Reagan's initial term, but that the former series was considerably more volatile than the latter. This is the case—the correlation (r) between the two series at zero lags is +.82, and the standard deviations are 38.8 and 13.7 for national and personal evaluations, respectively. A more detailed inspection of the data reveals that, with only one exception, negative responses to the two retrospectively oriented questions were more frequent than positive ones throughout the first 27 months of Reagan's first term. However, in keeping with their overall patterns, personal evaluations were more stable than national ones during this period. Both series moved into the positive (100+) range in April 1983 but, again, the increase in the latter was much more pronounced. Thereafter, and throughout Reagan's second term, retrospective personal evaluations remained positive and quite stable. Judgments about the performance of the national economy, however, declined substantially from a high point of 158 at the beginning of 1984, and dipped into the negative range in November 1987 following the stock market crash. They then gradually improved in the months preceding the 1988 election.

Trends in prospective sociotropic and egocentric economic judgments were very similar to those for retrospective ones. The two prospective series were strongly intercorrelated (r = +.85) and, again, national evaluations were much more variable than personal ones (the standard deviations being 27.10 and 7.10, respectively). Prospective judgments about the national economy were negative until the spring of 1983 when they improved markedly. They then remained positive until the stock market decline in the autumn of 1987. After being in negative range for three months, they again became positive and improved sharply in the run-up to the 1988 elections. In contrast, prospective assessments of personal economic circumstances were consistently positive throughout both of Reagan's terms in office.

## Political (and Economic) Interventions

A variety of systemic and idiosyncratic events and conditions may affect presidential approval net of economic conditions and public evaluations thereof. Systemic events included in the present analysis are: (1) the 1982 mid-term congressional election, modeled as a two-month pulse,[3] and (2) the 1984 presidential election, modeled as a one-month pulse. From the set of nonsystemic events and conditions, we selected the following: (1) the assassination attempt of March 31, 1981, modeled as a temporary two-month effect (pulse) beginning in April of that year; (2) Reagan's July 1981 tax cut victories combined with the appointment of Justice O'Connor to the Supreme Court, a one-month pulse; (3) the Grenada intervention of October 1983, a two-month pulse; (4) the bombing attack against Libya in April of 1986, a one-month pulse; (5) the Iran-Contra scandal which broke just prior to Thanksgiving, 1986. This was a complex effect, modeled as a temporary shock in December of that year, with another shock in the following February as additional information about the scandal was made public by the Tower Commission investigation. Since intensive media coverage of "Irangate" extended over several months, a decay parameter is included to capture lagged effects of the scandal; (6) the stock market crash of October, 1987, modeled as a permanent effect for the remainder of Reagan's second term.

## Models of Presidential Approval

The general Box-Jenkins model of presidential approval implied by our preceding discussion is:

$$(1-B)PA_t = \Sigma\omega_i(1-B)SUBEC_{t-k} +/- \omega_j(1-B)INF_{t-k} +/-\omega_k(1-B)UNEMP_{t-k}$$

$$+/-\Sigma\omega_l/(1-\delta B)(1-B)INT_{t-k} + \phi_i(B)/\theta_i(B)a_t$$

where:

$PA_t$ = presidential approval at time t

$SUBEC_{t-k}$ = subjective economic evaluations at time t - k

$INF_{t-k}$ = inflation rate at time t - k

$UNEMP_{t-k}$ = unemployment rate at time t - k

$INT_{t-k}$ = intervention effects at time t - k

$a_t$ = error term at time t

$\omega$ = impact parameter

$\delta$ = decay parameter

$\phi$ = autoregressive parameter

$\theta$ = moving average parameter

B = backshift operator

t-k = time lag

A number of variants of this model are analyzed to test the several hypotheses presented above.

The first set of analyses include the subjective economic evaluation variables and the various economic and political interventions, but not inflation or unemployment.[4] It was noted above that the two retrospective and the two prospective evaluation measures are strongly correlated. This is true more generally, with correlations (r) between the four subjective economic variables ranging from +.81 (retrospective and prospective egocentric judgments) to +.97 (retrospective and prospective sociotropic judgments). Given this extreme collinearity, the four variables were entered in separate models, with the time lag at which a variable was hypothesized to affect presidential approval being ascertained by the results of its cross-correlation with the approval series.[5] The analyses

Table 2.1. Effects of Retrospective Sociotropic Economic Evaluations and Political Interventions on President Reagan's Approval Rating, 1981-1988

| Predictor Variables | | Coefficient | t |
|---|---|---|---|
| Retrospective sociotropic evaluations | $\omega$ (B1) | 0.05 | 1.85b |
| Assassination attempt | $\omega$ (B1) | 9.54 | 2.70a |
|  | $\omega$ (B2) | 9.60 | 3.92a |
| Tax cut/Judge O'Connor | $\omega$ (B0) | 5.86 | 3.41a |
| Congressional election | $\omega$ (B0) | -3.17 | -1.84b |
| Presidential election | $\omega$ (B0) | 3.64 | 2.12b |
| Stock market crash | $\omega$ (B1) | -4.01 | -1.65b |
| Grenada invasion | $\omega$ (B0) | 1.69 | 0.98 |
| Libya bombing | $\omega$ (B1) | 4.95 | 2.84a |
| Iran-Contra affair | $\omega$ (B1) | -9.13 | -4.00a |
|  | $\omega$ (B3) | -11.42 | -5.21a |
|  | $\delta$ | 0.57 | 3.43a |

Residual mean square (RMS) = 5.90
Ljung-Box Q (df = 20) = 14

a  $p \leq .01$
b  $p \leq .05$
c  $p \leq .10$; one-tailed tests

show that retrospective and prospective sociotropic evaluations and prospective egocentric ones have statistically significant positive effects (p < .05) on presidential approval net of the impacts of the several interventions. Retrospective egocentric judgments, in contrast, do not have significant effects.

An example of these analyses using retrospective sociotropic evaluations is displayed in Table 2.1. As anticipated, the relationship between such evaluations and presidential approval is positive, signifying that increasingly favorable judgments about how the national economy had performed during the previous year were associated with heightened presidential approval ratings. The estimated size of the effect ($\omega = .05$) indicates that presidential approval increased by one-twentieth of 1% when the balance of positive versus negative retrospective judgments about the national economy changed by one point on the 200-point index. Although this does not appear to be a large amount, the wide variation in retrospective judgments about the national economy in Reagan's first term suggests that such judgments had nontrivial effects on his approval rating. Specifically, since scores on the retrospective sociotropic evaluation index ranged from a low of 20 in February 1983 to a high of 138 in January 1984, the $\omega$ coefficient suggests that, net of other considerations, improving judgments about national economic performance bolstered Reagan's support by approximately 8% over this period.

The model employing prospective sociotropic judgments yields a virtually identical estimate, whereas that using prospective egocentric judg-

Table 2.2. Effects of Subjective Economic Evaluation Index and Political Interventions on President Reagan's Approval Rating, 1981-1988

| Predictor Variables | | | Coefficient | t |
|---|---|---|---|---|
| Subjective economic evaluations index | $\omega$ | (B1) | 0.08 | 1.88b |
| Assassination attempt | $\omega$ | (B1) | 9.83 | 2.75a |
|  | $\omega$ | (B2) | 9.75 | 3.96a |
| Tax cut/Judge O'Connor | $\omega$ | (B0) | 6.25 | 3.63a |
| Congressional election | $\omega$ | (B0) | -3.33 | -1.94b |
| Presidential election | $\omega$ | (B0) | 3.74 | 2.17b |
| Stock market crash | $\omega$ | (B1) | -3.67 | 1.50c |
| Grenada invasion | $\omega$ | (B0) | 1.75 | 1.02 |
| Libya bombing | $\omega$ | (B1) | 5.10 | 2.95a |
| Iran-Contra affair | $\omega$ | (B1) | -8.95 | -3.93a |
|  | $\omega$ | (B3) | -11.70 | -5.32a |
|  | $\delta$ |  | 0.56 | 3.36a |

Residual mean square (RMS) = 5.89
Ljung-Box Q (df = 20) = 14

a $p \leq .01$
b $p \leq .05$
c $p \leq .10$; one-tailed tests

ments produces a larger one ($\omega = .11$). However, the total variation in the latter series was much smaller (from a low of 104 in March 1981 to a high of 137 in June 1983), thus indicating that increasingly favorable judgments about the future course of the national economy in the period boosted Reagan's approval by about 4%. Since the subjective economic judgments are highly correlated, their overall effects are estimated by combining the three (sociotropic retrospective, sociotropic prospective, egocentric prospective) that have significant effects on presidential approval into a summary index.[6] Estimating the overall impact of subjective economic judgments using this index yields an $\omega$ coefficient of .08, and the effects of other variables remain essentially undisturbed (Table 2.2).

Similar to the models using the individual subjective economic variables, this latter analysis shows that several of the political and economic interventions had significant effects, and that many of them were quite sizable. Particularly noteworthy are the March 1981 assassination attempt and the Iran-Contra affair. The coefficients for the former suggest that the assassination produced a temporary rally in favor of the president that enhanced his approval ratings by nearly 10% in each of the two months (April and May 1981) following the attack. The effects of the latter were equally profound, but negative—the initial Iran Contra revelations lowered Reagan's approval rating about 9%, and those coming three months later reduced it by nearly 12%. Moreover, the significant $\delta$ parameter (.56)

FIGURE 2.5 Impact of Iran-Contra Scandal on President Reagan's Approval Rating

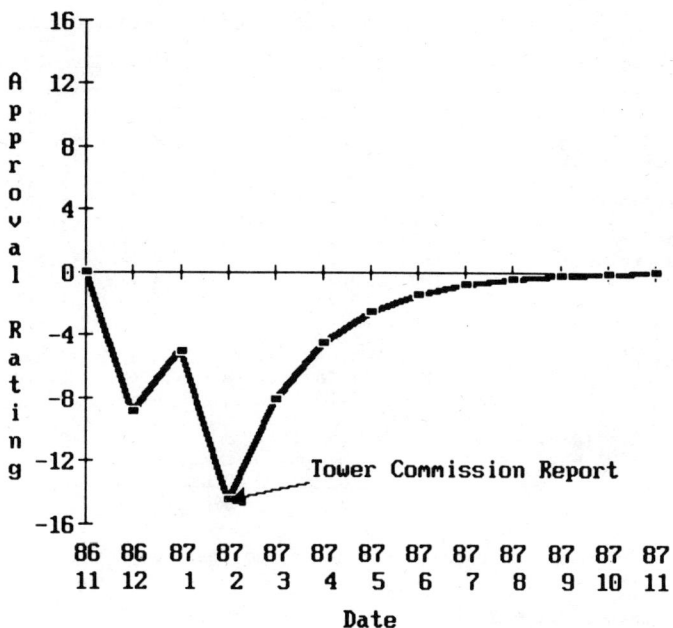

indicates that the impact of Irangate persisted, albeit with decreasing force, over the next several months (Figure 2.5).[7] However, it was then exhausted and did not affect presidential approval as the 1988 election approached.

Other political and economic interventions had smaller effects but, with the exception of the Grenada invasion, all were significant and operated as anticipated (Table 2.2). Thus, the summer 1981 combination of the tax cut and nomination of Judge O'Connor for the Supreme Court temporarily increased the president's approval rating by over 6%. Similarly, the Libyan bombing had a transient positive effect of five points, and Reagan's successful 1984 reelection bid boosted his support by nearly 4%. The Grenada invasion had a positive impact as well, but it was statistically insignificant (t = 1.02). Other significant negative effects included those associated with the 1982 congressional elections and the 1987 stock market crash. The 1982 elections produced a temporary downturn of slightly over 3%, and the crash, a permanent one of slightly less than 4%.

*Objective Economic Effects:* We next considered the impact of the two objective economic variables, inflation and unemployment.[8] We first analyzed a model which included these two variables and the several political and economic interventions, but not subjective economic expectations.

Table 2.3. Effects of Subjective Economic Evaluation Index, Inflation and Unemployment on President Reagan's Approval Rating, 1981-1988

|  |  | Model A | | Model B | |
|---|---|---|---|---|---|
| Predictor Variables |  | Coefficient | t | Coefficient | t |
| Inflation rate | $\omega$ (B1) | 0.99 | 1.45 | 0.86 | 1.25 |
| Unemployment rate | $\omega$ (B2) | -2.96 | -2.21b | -2.83 | -2.12b |
| Subjective economic evaluation index | $\omega$ (B1) | + | + | 0.06 | 1.45c |
| Assassination attempt | $\omega$ (B1) | 7.87 | 3.38a | 9.31 | 2.66a |
|  | $\omega$ (B2) | 9.67 | 2.36a | 10.19 | 4.30a |
| Tax cut/Judge O'Connor | $\omega$ (B0) | 5.53 | 3.21a | 5.79 | 3.37a |
| Congressional election | $\omega$ (B0) | -3.12 | -1.87b | -3.02 | -1.82b |
| Presidential election | $\omega$ (B0) | 3.39 | 2.04b | 3.57 | 2.16a |
| Stock market crash | $\omega$ (B1) | -4.52 | -1.92b | -4.19 | -1.78b |
| Grenada invasion | $\omega$ (B0) | 2.00 | 1.19 | 2.13 | 1.28c |
| Libya bombing | $\omega$ (B1) | 5.94 | 3.55a | 5.59 | 3.34a |
| Iran-Contra affair | $\omega$ (B1) | -8.78 | -3.96a | -8.63 | -3.94a |
|  | $\omega$ (B3) | -11.28 | -5.29a | -11.60 | -5.45a |
|  | $\delta$ | 0.55 | 3.27a | 0.53 | 3.15a |
| Residual mean square (RMS) = |  | 5.51 | | 5.43 | |
| Ljung-Box Q (df = 20) = |  | 15 | | 14 | |

a $p \leq .01$
b $p \leq .05$
c $p \leq .10$; two-tailed test for inflation; one-tailed tests for other predictors

+ Variable not included in model

The estimates (Table 2.3, Model A) show that the effects of the intervention variables are essentially unchanged from those described above. Unemployment is significant (t = -2.21) and, as expected according to both the traditional reward-punishment as well as the issue-priority hypotheses, the impact is negative. The size of the $\omega$ parameter (-2.96) indicates that a 1% increase in the unemployment rate decreased Reagan's approval rating by nearly 3%. Viewed in terms of the increase in the joblessness rate that occurred between 1981 and 1982 (from 7.2% in April 1981 to 10.7% in November 1982), this suggests that, *ceteris paribus,* the recession cost the president over 10% in public support.

Inflation behaved differently—net of other considerations, it had a small *positive,* although marginally insignificant, impact on presidential approval. The positive sign is consistent with an issue-priority rather than a reward-punishment hypothesis about how rising prices should affect public support for a *Republican* president in an era when the competing parties accord quite different priorities to the battles against inflation and unemployment.

The final presidential approval model includes inflation and unemployment as well as the subjective economic evaluation index. The estimates again show that unemployment has a significant negative impact ($\omega = -2.83$) on Reagan's approval, and inflation has a positive, but insignificant, one ($\omega = 0.86$) (Table 2.3, Model B). Subjective economic evaluations are significant and positive, although the size of the coefficient ($\omega = .06$) is somewhat smaller than that for the previous analysis that did not include the objective economic indicators. In this final model all of the political and economic interventions have significant effects similar to those described above.

*Economic Versus Political Effects:* Thus far, we have demonstrated that several economic and political variables influenced presidential approval during the Reagan years. To determine which of these variables had the largest effects we reestimated the models using various combinations of predictors. Following the typical practice of according pride of place to economic variables in political support models, we first included only inflation, unemployment and the subjective economic evaluation index. These variables collectively accounted for a 3.2% reduction in the residual mean square (RMS), the standard measure of goodness-of-fit in Box-Jenkins analyses (see Appendix A). Next, we added the two economic interventions, the tax cut and the stock market crash. Doing so produced a further 5.8% reduction in the RMS. We then added the several political interventions. At this stage the RMS was reduced by an additional 45.1%, thereby indicating political events and conditions rather than economic ones provide the bulk of the explanatory power in the approval models. An analysis including only the political interventions substantiates this conclusion—by themselves the political variables reduced the RMS by 46.9%.

## Models of Economic Evaluations

The preceding analyses suggest that objective indicators of macroeconomic performance such as inflation and unemployment rates are not simply surrogates for subjective economic evaluations, but that the two types of variables do convey some of the same information. This is not surprising; the mass media regularly emphasize inflation and unemployment rates when presenting economic news, and levels and trends therein are interpreted as indicators of the health of the nation's economy. Of course, people learn about the health of the economy in other ways as well. Markets continually supply data regarding prices and jobs, and interpersonal communication networks convey economic news of various kinds to family, friends and neighbors. Exposure to information supplied by these various channels of communication make it very plausible that rates of price increases and joblessness will influence the public's economic evaluations. Other, related, influences may be at work as well. Most

Table 2.4. Effects of Inflation, Unemployment and Economic and Political Interventions on Subjective Economic Evaluations, 1981-1988

| Predictor Variables | | | Coefficient | t |
|---|---|---|---|---|
| Inflation rate | ω | (B2) | -3.53 | -2.30b |
| Unemployment rate | ω | (B2) | -5.76 | -1.81b |
| Tax cut/Judge O'Connor | ω | (B1) | 4.34 | 1.08 |
| Stock market crash | ω | (B1) | -18.44 | -3.53a |
|  | δ |  | 0.63 | 2.24a |
| Assassination attempt | ω | (B1) | 6.88 | 1.52c |
|  | ω | (B2) | 8.92 | 1.98b |
| Congressional election | ω | (B1) | -3.37 | -0.85 |
| Presidential election | ω | (B1) | 1.51 | 0.38 |
| Grenada invasion | ω | (B1) | 5.36 | 1.36c |
| Libya bombing | ω | (B0) | 6.36 | 1.61c |
| Iran-Contra affair | ω | (B1) | -7.90 | -2.03b |

Residual mean square (RMS) = 30.23
Ljung-Box Q (df = 20) = 17

a $p \leq .01$
b $p \leq .05$
c $p \leq .10$; one-tailed tests

obviously, one would anticipate that highly salient economic events such as the 1987 stock market decline or Reagan's successful tax cut package would affect public economic judgments. Then, too, it is possible that political events such as the successful resolution of an international conflict, the attempted assassination of a president, or a highly publicized scandal such as the Iran-Contra affair will bolster or erode people's confidence in the economy as well as their forecasts about personal economic prospects.

We tested these hypotheses by employing the subjective economic evaluations index as a dependent variable in a model which included inflation and unemployment rates and the several political and economic events used in the Reagan approval analyses as predictor variables. Inflation and unemployment rates have the expected statistically significant, negative, effects on subjective assessments of the economy—as inflation and unemployment rates climbed, economic judgments became increasingly pessimistic (Table 2.4). Economic events also were influential, although Reagan's tax cut victory had only a small and insignificant positive impact on public economic judgments, the stock market crash had an immediate negative impact in excess of 18 points. The large and significant δ parameter (.63) indicates that the effect of the crash on public economic assessments continued to reverberate for several months, and was not totally extinguished until the end of the second quarter of 1988.

Finally, the estimates also reveal a *politics* of economic judgments. Events such Iran-Contra scandal, the Libyan bombing, the Grenada invasion and the assassination attempt all had temporary influences on the electorate's subjective economic evaluations.

How large were the several effects? We answered this question by reestimating the economic evaluation model employing various combinations of predictor variables. In the first analysis we entered only inflation and unemployment. Although both variables were statistically significant, the reduction in the residual mean square (RMS) was less than 1%. Adding the two economic events (the tax cut and stock market crash) produced a 11.4% reduction to the RMS. A further 6.7% reduction was achieved when the several political interventions were considered. These analyses thereby suggest that economic and political *events* had larger effects on changes in subjective economic assessments than did movements in rates of inflation and unemployment. The latter have statistically significant influences, but they leave much of the variance in the subjective economy unexplained. The model's performance improved discernibly when the economic and political events were included but, again, much variance remains unexplained. Thus, in the Reagan years at least, subjective economic evaluations had a substantial "life of their own"—they responded to but were not governed by changes in the objective economy and the many salient economic and political events that occurred during his presidency.

## Conclusion: A "Teflon" President?

This chapter has examined several longstanding controversies in the political support literature in the context of an analysis of the dynamics of public approval for Ronald Reagan during his eight years in office. Unlike most previous research on the political economy of presidential approval, the present inquiry has focused on the effects of the electorate's subjective economic evaluations. Using data gathered in the University of Michigan's monthly consumer confidence surveys, we investigated the effects of assessments of both national (sociotropic) and personal (egocentric) economic conditions over retrospective and prospective time horizons. Similar to the dominant findings of analyses of individual-level survey data, we found that retrospective judgments about the national economy affected presidential support, but that retrospective judgments about personal economic circumstances did not. Contrary to many of these studies, however, we also found that prospective sociotropic evaluations had significant effects, as did prospective egocentric judgments. Since all four types of subjective economic assessments were highly intercorrelated, it was impossible to model their effects simultaneously. Nevertheless, findings from this study do not provide grounds for concluding, as many previous studies have, that prospective and egocentric judgments do not matter. Untangling the skein of causality among the various aspects of the subjective economy remains a topic for future research.

It is clear that the subjective economic evaluations do not simply reflect monthly trends in the objective economy. Although subjective economic judgments were adversely affected by increases in the rates of inflation and unemployment, the effects were far from overwhelming. A major economic event, the stock market crash of 1987, and several political events had somewhat stronger, albeit temporary, effects on subjective economic evaluations, but they too left much of the variance in such evaluations unexplained. This suggests, in turn, that future research should pursue other lines of inquiry. As Mosley (1984) has argued, one of the most promising of these would seem to be the mass media. The media, in addition to reporting regularly on trends in the macroeconomy, *interpret* these trends for the public and present summary statements of what is happening. Thus, people are told, for example, that "times are getting worse," "the country is falling into recession," or "the economy is booming." Headlines such as these may well do more to determine the course of subjective economic judgments than does more finely grained reporting of the detailed movements of particular macroeconomic indicators.

The objective economy, however, does affect presidential approval, net of its effects via subjective economic assessments. As noted in the introduction, virtually all previous research on this topic has employed a simple reward-punishment model, i.e, the electorate rewards an incumbent party and its leader for good or improving economic conditions and punishes them for bad or deteriorating ones. An alternative issue-priority hypothesis argues that what matters are perceptions of competing parties macroeconomic priorities. In the case of a Republican president, this hypothesis suggests that rising unemployment and inflation should have negative and positive influences, respectively, on presidential approval. As anticipated by both hypotheses, increases in unemployment negatively affected Reagan's approval ratings net of subjective economic judgments as well as inflation. However, the impact of inflation was weaker and positive, thereby indicating that issue-priority processes were operative in the Reagan years.

Although both objective and subjective economic variables influenced Reagan's approval, the full impact of these variables only became apparent in analyses in which several important political events occurring during his presidency were considered. This finding indicates that previous studies which have ignored political interventions or concentrated on only a few extremely salient ones have worked with misspecified models. The importance of modeling political interventions also is reinforced by the observation that they have much stronger explanatory power in the presidential approval models than do the economic variables. Similar to other presidencies, the Reagan years were characterized by an ongoing series of highly publicized political events. Some of these had positive effects on people's feelings about the president, whereas others had negative ones. The strength of these effects suggests that future studies need to emphasize the politics and not only the economics of presidential approval.

Ronald Reagan was the first two-term president since Dwight Eisenhower. His successful 1980 and 1984 election campaigns have led numerous observers to conclude that he was a highly popular, even charismatic, figure whose support had a "teflon" coating that rendered it impervious to economic conditions and political events. These conclusions are wrong. Reagan entered the White House with the lowest level of public approval of any post–World War II president. Although his approval ratings subsequently improved, they never were atypically high and, as a glance back at Figure 2.1 shows, on average, Reagan was far less popular than Eisenhower or Kennedy, and only slightly more popular than Johnson and Nixon.[9] Moreover, he was not, as many have claimed, a teflon president; his approval ratings responded predictably to political events occurring during his two terms in office, and some of them had major effects. For example, the attempted assassination and the Iran-Contra scandal had large influences on his approval ratings and, in the case of Iran-Contra, the impact persisted for several months. The teflon argument does not hold even for the economy. Although, as noted, the effects of economic conditions and the public's economic assessments thereof were considerably less profound than those associated with political events, nevertheless, the former did influence Reagan's approval ratings. Moreover, given the range of variance in some of the economic variables, the substantive effects on public judgments of his performance were hardly trivial. Recall, for example, that the improvement in subjective economic evaluations after the 1982 recession were sufficient to bring about a sizable increase in approval. Like his predecessors, Reagan encountered a complex set of economic and political forces that had significant and, in some instances, marked effects on his standing with the American public.

## Notes

1. Although the size of the effect is disputed, previous analyses support the proposition that American parties have different macroeconomic priorities, with unemployment levels being significantly lower under Democratic presidents. See Beck (1982a); Hibbs (1977, 1983). As we shall see in Chapter 9, much of the difference may be a product of international conflicts and exogenous economic forces produced by the "oil shocks" of the 1970s.

2. See *Surveys of Consumers Monthly Time Series Data Base PC Disk Documentation,* Tables A, 4, 6, 12, 15.

3. No attempt is made to model the 1986 congressional election as a separate effect because it occurs in the same month as the initial report of Iran-Contra affair. Thus, the first estimated effect for the latter (see below) also *de facto* models the former.

4. Diagnostics provided by the autocorrelation (ACF) and partial autocorrelation (PACF) functions for the presidential approval series indicate that the series needs to be (first) differenced to attain mean stationarity. Doing so produces white noise residuals with an LBQ = 10 (p > .05) (Ljung-Box, 1978).

5. Following conventional Box-Jenkins procedures, noise models were identified for the input series (the four subjective economic evaluation variables), and these were used to filter ("pre-whiten") the output series (presidential approval). Then, cross-correlations were computed between the residuals for the input and output series. The noise models for the differenced subjective economic series were: retrospective egocentric – $\theta(B^1)$, $\theta(B^4)$; retrospective sociotropic – $\phi(B^1)$; prospective egocentric – $\theta(B^1)$, $\theta(B^3)$; prospective sociotropic – $\theta(B^2)$.

6. The subjective economic evaluations index is the mean score for the retrospective sociotropic, prospective egocentric and prospective sociotropic variables.

7. For an dynamic intervention that has a temporary effect, the size of the impact after n time periods is $Y_{t+n} = \delta^{n-1}\omega_t$ (McLeary and Hay, 1980:166). When such an intervention has multiple impacts, as in the case of Iran-Contra, the total effect after n time periods is the sum of this calculation for each impact.

8. The noise models for the differenced inflation and unemployment series were: $\phi(B^1)$, $\theta(B^1)$, $\theta(B^{12})$, and $\theta(B^3)$, $\theta(B^5)$, respectively.

9. For a more detailed analysis of this point see Yeric and Todd (1989:ch. 6).

# 3

# Through a Glass Darkly: Economic Evaluations and Governing Party Support in Mrs. Thatcher's Britain

*To us, as to all post-war governments, sound money may have seemed out of date: we were all dominated by the fear of unemployment. It was this which made us turn our back against our better judgment and try to spend out of unemployment.*
—Sir Keith Joseph, October 1974 Election Campaign Speech

*Labour isn't working.*
—Conservative 1979 Election Campaign Slogan

The proposition that economic conditions affect public feelings about political parties and their leaders is conventional wisdom for political scientists and political practitioners alike. Despite two decades of research, however, the nature and extent of the economy's influence on political support remains unclear. In some countries and at certain times inflation seems to be the principal factor influencing political support. In other countries or at different times, unemployment appears primary. In still other places or at other times, income, interest rates, taxation levels, exchange rates, and sundry other economic conditions seem important. In some cases, the evidence disputes the conventional wisdom and challenges the political importance of economic conditions altogether.

No doubt part of the confusion stems from the use of different economic and political support measures collected at different times and places and analyzed with diverse and sometimes inappropriate estimation procedures. However, it increasingly appears that a more important problem is that many political support models are seriously misspecified because

---

This chapter is coauthored by Roy Fitzgerald.

they omit critical variables. As is well known, the omission of theoretically relevant and empirically significant variables raises the possibility that observed relationships between a dependent variable and included explanatory variables are spurious or distorted and might be quite different if appropriate controls were introduced. In this regard Sanders, Ward and Marsh (1987) make a compelling case that correctly specified political support models should incorporate direct measures of the public's perceptions of, and future expectations about, the economy's performance.[1] Lewis-Beck (1988a:315–17) makes much the same case in arguing the need for extensive cross-sectional survey data on public economic evaluations to complement aggregate time series data on objective economic conditions.

Theoretically, there are good reasons for including measures of public economic perceptions and expectations in political support models. Although scholars continue to debate the relative merits of retrospective judgment versus prospective policy evaluation models, simple versus government mediated models, and affective versus cognitive models, there is a common, if frequently unstated assumption that the effects of macroeconomic conditions on political behavior are filtered through people's evaluations of the economy. Until very recently, however, the absence of suitable time series data on economic perceptions and expectations has forced scholars to ignore these variables and treat relationships between objective economic conditions and political behavior as direct and unmediated. This approach is justified to the extent that the linkages between the objective economy and economic evaluations, and those between evaluations and political behavior, are strong and direct. However, if either set of linkages is weak, mediated by intervening variables, or contingent upon exogenous ones, the use of objective economic indicators as surrogates for economic perceptions and expectations can produce inconsistent and contradictory results across different studies.

Empirically, evidence of the importance of subjective economic evaluations in time series models of political support is sparse but, recently, findings have begun to cumulate. Using data on government popularity in Britain, Sanders, Ward, and Marsh (1987) demonstrate that economic perceptions and expectations have powerful effects on governing party support. Using different model specifications and more sophisticated time series methods, Clarke, Mishler and Whiteley (1990) have confirmed these findings, and analyses presented in Chapter 4 in this volume show that economic evaluations affect support for opposition parties as well. The British findings are not unique. In Chapter 2 we demonstrated that economic judgments affected presidential approval during the Reagan years. MacKuen, Erikson, and Stimson (1989) report similar findings in their study of "macropartisanship" in the United States, as does Kirchgassner (1985) in an analysis of party popularity in West Germany. These results also are consistent with those obtained by Lewis-Beck (1986, 1988a) in analyses of the effects of economic evaluations on political support in Britain, France, West Germany, Italy, and Spain.

Anticipating these findings, Alt and Chrystal (1983:151–52) have stressed the importance of economic information in understanding the link between economic conditions and public economic evaluations:

> The fact that the relationship between economic conditions and political evaluation is unstable should not be a surprise. Look at the problem as one of information. What information about the economy is available? How is it obtained? How long are memories? How is conflicting information reconciled? . . . We need a theory of the demand for economic outcomes and a theory of *information* usage.

What is needed, in particular, is an understanding of the relationships among objective economic conditions, public economic perceptions and economic expectations—a theory of the dynamics of economic evaluations. This chapter contributes to such a theory by examining these relationships in Great Britain during Margaret Thatcher's first two governments. We begin with a discussion of some theoretical considerations that bear upon the processes of perception and expectation and the mechanisms by which the public acquires information about the economy. We then proceed to model the linkages between the objective economy and public economic evaluations, and those between evaluations and party support, using aggregate economic and public opinion data for the 1979–1987 period.

## Theoretical Considerations

Underlying the widespread use of objective indicators in political support models is an assumption, usually implicit, that economic conditions are widely and correctly perceived by the public.[2] The assumption is that the public is awash in economic information and that, collectively at least, its members behave as if they closely and continuously monitor the performance of the economy through reports in the media and personal experience. A further assumption of existing research is that the images people form about the economy are reasonably accurate and unbiased, again, at least in the aggregate (Kramer, 1983). Although any individual may miss the latest newspaper report on interest rates, misperceive a change in prices at the grocery store, or be misinformed by neighbors about layoffs at the mill, errors in individual perceptions are assumed to be distributed randomly so that aggregate perceptions are accurate and reliable.

With regard to public evaluations of future economic performance, retrospective voting models typically assume that current and past economic experiences influence economic expectations both directly and indirectly through the effects of perceptions on expectations (e.g., Downs, 1957; Fiorina, 1981; Kramer, 1971; Lewis-Beck, 1988a).[3] Although prospective voting models maintain that the effects of past economic conditions on future expectations are conditioned at least partly by more sophisticated public assessments of the future consequences of current policies, they typically place even greater faith in the accuracy and reliability of public perceptions of and expectations about an even wider and more subtle range of economic conditions (e.g., Chappell and Keech, 1985).

Empirical research on the availability of economic information and its diffusion through society raises serious doubts about all of these assumptions (see Alt, 1979:ch.6; Miller, 1989:143-72). It appears that voters often do not have easy access to a broad range reliable economic information and that the information available to them frequently is distorted in systematic ways. For example, although Mosley (1984) shows that unemployment and inflation statistics are reported regularly in Britain's three most popular daily newspapers, coverage of other aspects of the economy is episodic, limited, and less prominently displayed. Economic conditions other than employment and inflation are presented principally on the business pages of the high quality/low circulation papers, and are featured in the popular press only during periods of crisis, for example, when the stock market plummets or interest rates climb beyond some dramatic threshold. Mosley also notes that press coverage of economic conditions frequently is inconsistent with official government statistics. He offers several reasons for this. Government economic statistics are subject to repeated revision, often months after they are initially reported. Moreover, in an effort to make the news more interesting and accessible, the press often develops and reports its own indicators of economic conditions which can differ significantly from the official ones.

Of course, the public is not limited to media reports for information about the economy. Individuals acquire economic information in their daily lives, especially with respect to the economic conditions most salient to them. Shoppers learn about food prices at the grocery store; homebuyers learn about interest rates; individuals learn about unemployment when friends, neighbors or family members lose their jobs. However, the information acquired from experience tends to be narrow and is not easily— or at least reliably—generalized to broader economic trends or other economic conditions. Moreover, Whiteley (1986b) argues that economic information acquired through personal experience is likely to diffuse through the public more slowly than information acquired through the media. As a result, information acquired through the media will influence political attitudes and behavior contemporaneously or at very short lags, whereas that acquired through direct experience is likely to influence perceptions at longer lags. This is not only because the process of face-to-face communication is slow, but also, as Alt and Chrystal (1983) argue, people do not easily abandon their opinions and may require repeated exposure to news about the economy before their perceptions catch up to reality. By the time perceptions finally have changed, economic conditions may have altered, thus again rendering perceptions obsolete.

Public evaluations of the economy may be distorted in another way. Recent research in cognitive psychology suggests that people are "cognitive misers" (Fiske and Taylor, 1984). Because they have limited capacities to process information, they take shortcuts whenever possible. If they tried to give full consideration to every bit of information received, they would be unable to form stable, let alone accurate, perceptions, or to take action based on those beliefs. Precisely because economic information is multifaceted and complex (how many citizens, after all, really understand exchange rates or public sector borrowing requirements?), it is likely that the public will acquire and process it in ways that put a premium on simplicity and ease of access rather than accuracy. The fundamental tendency, then, is to adopt strategies that simplify inherent complexities. Such strategies "may not be normatively correct or produce normatively correct answers," but they are efficient (Fiske and Taylor, 1984:12). The cognitive miser theory lends force to the proposition that voters may perceive only the most dramatic economic conditions, or respond only to economic changes that are especially large, exceed some threshold of perception, or diverge sharply from conditions to which they have grown accustomed.

Finally, public perceptions of economic conditions may be influenced by political discourse and, specifically, by the efforts of self-interested actors to manipulate economic information in ways conducive to satisfying their political ambitions. Indeed, considerable evidence has accumulated that public opinion is influenced by information controlled both by government and the media (Edwards, 1983; Kernell, 1986; Iyengar and Kinder, 1987). For the government, this may involve withholding information about economic conditions, deemphasizing bad economic news, shifting blame to a previous administration or other convenient scapegoats (e.g., bankers, bureaucrats, corporations, the EEC, foreign countries, the IMF, OPEC, unions), releasing economic information at strategic times, manipulating economic statistics[4] or simply lying. Obviously, the images of the economy, past or future, that are created by such communications can be very different than the picture that would emerge were the public to undertake a thorough and dispassionate analysis of objective macroeconomic trends and conditions.

## Modeling the Subjective Economy

The preceding discussion suggests that, both individually and collectively, members of the public are likely to perceive the economy as "through a glass darkly," forming vague and imprecise images based on scraps of information, frequently biased or distorted, and acquired at irregular and infrequent intervals, often during periods of economic crisis. To consider this possibility, we developed and tested a series of models of the relationships between economic conditions and public economic perceptions and expectations in Britain between 1979 and 1987. In developing these models we focus on aspects of the economy that are relatively visible in the media and salient to people's daily lives. These are the conditions about which individuals are most likely to be informed and which are most likely to structure their evaluations of economic performance and influence the support they accord political parties and party leaders. Given their prominence in the media (Mosley, 1984) and their salience to voters (e.g., Sarlvik and Crewe, 1983:ch. 6), unemployment and inflation certainly meet these criteria and are included in our model along with two other macroeconomic indicators, interest rates and real income growth. Although less visible in the media, interest rates and real income levels have important impacts on people's everyday lives. Also, individuals can learn about them through personal experience, for example, when making a major purchase, depositing the weekly paycheck, or receiving notice of a salary raise. The specific economic variables in our model include: seasonally adjusted indicators of the number of unemployed[5] and retail prices; a measure of real income growth (based on average earnings adjusted for inflation); and interest rates (London clearing banks' base rate). All of the economic variables are measured monthly for the period May, 1979 through December, 1987.

Consonant with the possibility that economic perceptions may be influenced disproportionately by dramatic events as opposed to normal economic fluctuations, we followed a strategy suggested by Whiteley (1986b) and include in our models a measure designed to register major economic shocks. This is a dummy variable coded one in any month in which a major economic event occurred and zero for other months. Included are crises, such as the October 1987 stock market crash, as well as significant threshold events, such as unemployment reaching three million persons or inflation reaching 20% for the first time.

To test the hypothesis that economic evaluations also may be influenced by dramatic, noneconomic events, we focus on the Falklands war. Most previous research indicates that the war had profound effects on Conservative popularity and approval of Mrs. Thatcher's performance as prime minister (e.g., Norpoth, 1987a, 1987b; Clarke, Mishler and Whiteley, 1990) and, as documented in Chapter 4, it significantly influenced support for the then fledgling Liberal/SDP Alliance. Given the magnitude of these effects, it is reasonable to expect that the conflict also may have influenced other political and economic attitudes and beliefs including those concerning the economy and the government's ability to manage it successfully. To measure the Falklands effect we constructed a dummy variable coded one in the month (April 1982) that Argentina invaded the Falklands and zero otherwise.

With regard to the effects of political discourse on public perceptions of the economy, we created two additional dummy variables geared to periods when political discussion of the economy typically is high. The first is coded one during months in which a general election campaign is waged and zero for other months.[6] The assumption is that election campaigns are periods when voters are most attentive to the arguments, economic and otherwise, of the competing parties and their leaders. They also are periods when party leaders present their economic programs for the future and attempt most self-consciously and intensively to create public images of past economic conditions favorable to their parties and themselves. Although the parties can be expected to put their own "spin" on how the economy is doing, the resources of the government are considerably greater and provide it with distinct advantages. Thus, our expectation is that elections will influence public perceptions and expectations, and will tend, on balance, to bolster assessments of past and future economic conditions.

Another period when the media and, therefore, public attention is particularly focused on the economy is during the annual debate in parliament on the government's budget. Again, the economic signals received by the electorate at this time are likely to be mixed as government and opposition compete to portray past economic conditions and the future consequences of government policies very differently. However, the government enjoys significant advantages because it controls the proposed taxing and spending policies and their accompanying justifications. Because we expect budget debates to provide opportunities for the government to create favorable perceptions of the past performance of the economy and sanguine expectations about its future, our measure of budget debates is coded one during months in which the government tables its budget and zero otherwise.

Table 3.1. Crosscorrelations of Retail Prices, Unemployment, Real Income Growth and Interest Rates with Public Perceptions and Expectations of Prices, Household Finances and General Economic Conditions

A. Price Perceptions And:

| Lag | Prices | Unemployment | Income | Interest Rate |
|---|---|---|---|---|
| 0 | .13 | -.11 | -.16 | -.08 |
| 1 | .22 | .17 | -.21 | .30 |
| 2 | .09 | -.15 | -.22 | .13 |
| 3 | .13 | .01 | -.17 | -.02 |
| 4 | -.04 | .14 | -.05 | .09 |
| 5 | -.03 | .08 | -.12 | -.07 |
| 6 | -.06 | -.12 | .12 | .01 |

B. Price Expectations And:

| Lag | Prices | Unemployment | Income | Interest Rate |
|---|---|---|---|---|
| 0 | .18 | -.09 | -.18 | .19 |
| 1 | .10 | .09 | -.12 | .22 |
| 2 | -.09 | -.04 | .00 | -.11 |
| 3 | -.04 | .01 | -.05 | .03 |
| 4 | -.11 | -.03 | -.02 | .00 |
| 5 | .00 | .06 | -.04 | -.14 |
| 6 | -.04 | -.03 | .18 | .01 |

C. Household Finances Perceptions And:

| Lag | Prices | Unemployment | Income | Interest Rate |
|---|---|---|---|---|
| 0 | -.05 | .05 | .09 | -.05 |
| 1 | -.13 | .00 | .18 | -.15 |
| 2 | -.05 | .02 | -.09 | .06 |
| 3 | .05 | .10 | -.03 | -.12 |
| 4 | -.03 | -.16 | .15 | .07 |
| 5 | -.04 | .04 | .06 | .13 |
| 6 | .04 | .02 | -.10 | -.21 |

As indicators of public perceptions of the economy, we use aggregate responses to three questions asked monthly in Gallup surveys of the British electorate for the period May, 1979 to December 1987, 104 months, in all.[7] The specific questions asked were: (a) How do you think the *general economic situation* in this country has changed over the last 12 months? (b) How does the *financial situation of your household* compare with what it was 12 months ago? and (c) By comparison to what is happening now do you think that over the past twelve months *prices* have increased sharply, moderately, remained the same or fallen? Three similarly worded

Table 3.1. continued

**D. Household Finance Expectations And:**

| Lag | Prices | Unemployment | Income | Interest Rate |
|---|---|---|---|---|
| 0 | -.04 | .12 | -.03 | <u>-.26</u> |
| 1 | -.10 | <u>-.22</u> | .06 | .06 |
| 2 | .12 | .12 | .10 | .05 |
| 3 | -.01 | .13 | .07 | -.12 |
| 4 | .02 | -.07 | .08 | .16 |
| 5 | -.06 | -.05 | .11 | .11 |
| 6 | .03 | .06 | -.17 | .06 |

**E. General Economic Perceptions And:**

| Lag | Prices | Unemployment | Income | Interest Rate |
|---|---|---|---|---|
| 0 | .06 | -.08 | .01 | <u>-.23</u> |
| 1 | -.10 | -.10 | .05 | -.10 |
| 2 | -.01 | .14 | -.02 | -.01 |
| 3 | -.03 | .13 | .04 | -.04 |
| 4 | -.04 | -.07 | .04 | -.12 |
| 5 | .05 | -.17 | -.03 | -.06 |
| 6 | .11 | -.04 | -.09 | .11 |

**F. General Economic Expectations And:**

| Lag | Prices | Unemployment | Income | Interest Rate |
|---|---|---|---|---|
| 0 | -.02 | -.07 | .05 | <u>-.26</u> |
| 1 | -.08 | -.14 | .02 | -.05 |
| 2 | .03 | <u>.21</u> | -.05 | .13 |
| 3 | -.04 | .07 | .10 | .00 |
| 4 | .11 | -.11 | .09 | .02 |
| 5 | .06 | .02 | -.03 | -.01 |
| 6 | -.04 | -.09 | .12 | .07 |

Note: Perceptions and expectation variables prewhitened prior to analysis; underlined correlations $p < .05$.

questions about the likely performance of the general economy, household finances, and prices over the next twelve months are employed to measure economic expectations. The measures of the general economic situation and household finances are constructed as the percentage of respondents in any month thinking the overall economy (or household finances) had improved during the year minus the percentage thinking it had deteriorated. Prices are measured as the percentage thinking prices have "increased a lot" minus the percentage thinking they have "remained the same" or "fallen."

Although vital for understanding the dynamics of economic evaluations, the analysis of time series data is complicated by the tendency of time-related observations to be autocorrelated. This is very much the case for macroeconomic conditions and public evaluations thereof. To deal with this problem we use Box-Jenkins transfer function modelling procedures (see Appendix A).[8]

## From the Objective to the Subjective Economy

To begin our investigation of relationships between economic conditions and public evaluations of the economy, the economic perception and expectation series were correlated with the four macroeconomic series at lags from zero to six months.[9] Perhaps the most striking observation to be drawn from these analyses is the small size of most of the correlations—of nearly 150 coefficients only 16 are statistically significant, and all of these are quite modest in magnitude (Table 3.1). Predictably, the strongest correlations occur where the logical connection between economic conditions and evaluations is most direct. The concept of retail prices arguably is more tangible and less vague than those of general economic conditions or household finances. Thus, presumably, retail prices are easier for the public to evaluate. Perhaps as a result, evaluations of prices are more strongly related to a variety of economic conditions. Perceptions of price changes over the previous year respond positively, significantly and at short lags to changes in retail prices and interest rates, and negatively to changes in the growth of real income (Table 3.1, Panel A). Objective retail prices and interest rates also are related significantly to expectations about future price levels (Table 3.1, Panel B). Only unemployment appears to be entirely unrelated to price evaluations.

In contrast, evaluations of general economic conditions appear to be almost entirely unrelated to objective economic conditions. Only interest rates appear to have appreciable effects on general economic perceptions and expectations (Table 3.1, Panels E and F). Although unemployment levels are significantly related to general economic expectations, the sign of the relationship runs contrary to prevailing theories.[10] Given that the coefficient is small and occurs at a moderately long lag of three months, the likelihood is that the relationship is spurious—a possibility we explore in the multivariate analyses below.

Specific information about changes in household finances over the previous year is less directly discernible from objective economic information than is the case for retail prices. However, individuals have access to more and more reliable information about their personal financial situations than they do about the state of the economy as a whole. It is not surprising, therefore, that public evaluations of household finances appear to fall midway between price evaluations and general economic evaluations in terms of their sensitivity to economic conditions. Perceptions of household finances over the past year are related at short lags to real income change and at longer lags to interest rates, and expectations about future household finances are related to interest rates and unemployment levels at lags of one and two months, respectively (Table 3.1, Panels C and D).

Although useful for obtaining an initial overview of possible relationships, bivariate correlations must be interpreted cautiously. Without appropriate controls, true relationships can be masked, and observed ones can be spurious. Consequently, the information from the bivariate correlations presented above was used to specify multivariate models for each of the perception and expectation variables. These models included the most promising specifications for each of the four objective economic indicators (unemployment, inflation, real income growth, interest rates), plus the most plausible specifications for our measures of economic shocks and salient political events (the Falklands war, election campaigns, budget debates). The general form of the models is as follows:

$$(1-B)SUBEC_t = \omega_i(1-B)INF_{t-k} + \omega_j(1-B)UNEMP_{t-k} + \omega_k(1-B)INCOME_{t-k}$$

$$+ \omega_{t-k}(1-B)INTEREST_{t-k} + \omega_l(1-\delta B)(1-B)ECS_{t-k}$$

$$+ \Sigma \omega_{m-o}(1-\delta B)(1-B)POL_{t-k} + \theta(B)a_t$$

where:

SUBEC = subjective economic perceptions/expectations at time t

INF = inflation rate

UNEMP = number unemployed, in thousands

INCOME = growth in real income

INTEREST = interest rates

ECS = economic shocks

POL = political events

$a_t$ = error term at time t

$\omega$ = impact parameter

$\delta$ = decay parameter

$\theta$ = moving average parameter

B = backshift parameter

t-k = time lag

The initial models were estimated, revised based on standard diagnostics, and reestimated through several iterations until the best fitting models were obtained. Consistent with the patterns observed in the bivariate correlations, the results clearly demonstrate the weak connection between objective economic conditions and the public's retrospective evaluations of the national economy and personal financial circumstances. Overall, objective economic conditions have their greatest impact on perceptions of inflation, somewhat smaller effects of perceptions of household finances, and only minimal effects on general economic perceptions.

As we have argued, prices are more specific than either household finances or the general economic situation and, therefore, information about prices should be derived more easily from personal economic experiences or reports in the media. Interest rates, income, and unemployment all affect price perceptions at short lags. The estimated effects of interest rates and income growth on price perceptions indicate that every 1% increase in interest rates produces an immediate swing of slightly over one and one-half points in the percentage of people who perceive inflation to be getting worse (Table 3.2). This is followed by a second 1% increase in price perceptions at a lag of two months. The effects of income are nearly as strong but, predictably, they operate in the opposite direction. A one-point increase in the growth of real income dampens perceptions of inflation by about .5% in the month the gain occurs and by more than 1.5% over the next two months. The overall explanatory power of the model can be assessed by comparing the residual mean square (RMS) statistic for the analysis with that for the univariate moving average model of price perceptions (see Note 8 and Appendix A). Since none of the political variables bear significantly on price perceptions, the 32% improvement in the RMS of the price perception model is entirely attributable to objective economic conditions.

Household financial perceptions also appear to be driven exclusively by economic conditions. Perhaps, however, because voters tend to see their individual financial situations as being influenced disproportionately by personal and idiosyncratic forces (see Chapter 1), the reduction in RMS

Table 3.2. Effects of Economic and Political Variables on Public Perceptions of Prices, Household Finances, and General Economic Situation

| | | | Perceptions | | | |
|---|---|---|---|---|---|---|
| Predictor Variables | Prices | | Household Finances | | Economy | |
| Inflation rate | $\omega$ (B0) | 0.92 | + | | + | |
| | $\omega$ (B1) | 1.07 | + | | + | |
| Unemployment | $\omega$ (B0) | 0.02 | $\omega$ (B0) | -0.01 | $\omega$ (B0) | -0.02 |
| Real income growth | $\omega$ (B0) | -0.60 | $\omega$ (B1) | 0.50 | + | |
| | $\omega$ (B1) | -0.75 | + | | + | |
| | $\omega$ (B2) | -0.91 | + | | + | |
| Interest rates | $\omega$ (B1) | 1.65 | $\omega$ (B1) | -1.31 | $\omega$ (B0) | -4.39 |
| | $\omega$ (B2) | 1.16 | + | | + | |
| Economic shocks | + | | + | | + | |
| Budget debates | + | | + | | $\omega$ (B1) | 4.41 |
| Election campaigns | + | | + | | $\omega$ (B1) | 20.62 |
| | | | | | $\delta$ | 0.83 |
| Falklands war | + | | + | | $\omega$ (B1) | 18.12 |
| | + | | + | | $\omega$ (B2) | 29.10 |
| | + | | + | | $\omega$ (B3) | 31.73 |
| | + | | + | | $\delta$ | 0.39 |
| Noise model | $\theta$ (B1) | 0.50 | $\theta$ (B1) | 0.48 | $\theta$ (B1) | 0.57 |
| | | | | | $\theta$ (B2) | -0.22 |
| Residual mean square (RMS) = | 25.2 | | 14.8 | | 84.4 | |
| Ljung-Box Q (df = 20) | 15 | | 14 | | 16 | |

Note: All coefficients $p \leq .05$

+ Variable not included in model

indicates that the total impact of economic conditions on perceptions of household finances is not especially strong. Interest rates, income growth, and unemployment levels all have significant effects but, together, increase our ability to explain perceptions of personal economic circumstances by only 14%.

Economic conditions also influence perceptions of the general economy, but their collective impact is dwarfed by those associated with various political events including election campaigns, the Falklands war, and the annual budget debate in parliament. The effects of the 1983 and 1987 elections are especially dramatic. Elections were modeled as having abrupt effects which gradually decay over time.[11] The Conservative Party generally is credited with running a far superior campaign to Labour in 1983, but in 1987 the situation was reversed (Butler and Kavanagh, 1984, 1988). Nevertheless, although the Conservatives formed the government when both elections were held, the estimates indicate that public perceptions of general economic conditions improved by more than 20% in the month following the two campaigns. Moreover, the large $\delta$ parameter (.83) associated with the campaign variable indicates that the upsurge in economic confidence produced by the two elections declined only gradually over the ensuing year.

The Falklands war also had strong effects on public evaluations of the health of the economy. Judgments of past economic conditions rose for three straight months following the Argentine invasion in April 1982—by 18%, 29% and 32%, respectively. However, the modest δ (.39) indicates that the impact of the Falklands on people's economic judgments eroded quickly in the following months. The effects of the budget debates on evaluations of national economic conditions are significant as well, albeit more modest and short-lived. Nevertheless, the positive spin the government puts on its economic record in its annual presentation of the budget was sufficient to tilt the balance of favorable versus unfavorable perceptions of economic conditions by an average of nearly 4.5% in the following month.

Interestingly, despite the attention usually focused on them, neither unemployment nor inflation appears to have particularly strong influences on any of the three economic perception series. Unemployment is significant in all of the perception models, but its effects are modest—an increase in unemployment of 100,000 individuals produces a negative swing of only 1 to 2% (Table 3.2). However, these are initial effects and, if the increase in unemployment continues, its *cumulative* impact can be substantial in the long run. For example, other factors being equal, our estimates suggest that the growth in the number of unemployed of almost two million persons which occurred between September 1979 and July 1986 was sufficient to move public perceptions of the economy in a negative direction by nearly 40% over this period.

Inflation's effects on economic evaluations are smaller. Variations in retail prices did not significantly influence any of the three perception series. There are two reasons, however, that lead us to suspect the impact of inflation may be underestimated in these models. First, retail prices are closely related to other economic conditions including interest rates, unemployment and, especially, real income growth. As a result, income and interest rates substantially overlap with inflation and tend to diminish its effects in our models. When income and interest rates are removed from the price perception model, prices register larger effects than those indicated by the figures presented in Table 3.2. The estimates indicate that a 1% rise in inflation produces a negative swing of nearly 3% in price perceptions. Similar patterns obtain when prices are substituted for income and/or interest rates in the household finances and general economic perceptions models.

A second and related reason for the weak showing of inflation is that, for most of the period encompassed by this study, the rate of price increases was either declining rapidly or fluctuating at modest levels. As a result, inflation simply was not a visible or pressing problem, and public attention was focused on the explosive growth and subsequently very high

Table 3.3. Effects of Economic and Political Variables on Public Expectations of Prices, Household Finances and General Economy

|  |  | Expectations | | |
|---|---|---|---|---|
| Predictor Variables | | Prices | Household Finances | Economy |
| Inflation rate | (B0) | 1.23 | + | + |
|  | ω (B1) | 1.02 | + | + |
| Unemployment (in thousands) | ω (B0) | 0.02 | + | + |
| Real income growth | ω (B0) | -0.75 | + | + |
| Interest rates | ω (B1) | 2.38 | ω (B0) -1.46 | ω (B0) -2.15 |
| Economic shocks | ω (B2) | 2.12 | ω (B2) -2.28 | + |
| Budget debates |  | + | ω (B1) 2.64 | ω (B1) 8.06 |
| Election campaigns |  | + | ω (B1) 9.96 | ω (B1) 20.62 |
|  |  | + | δ 0.65 | δ 0.73 |
| Falklands war |  | + | + | ω (B1) 23.75 |
|  |  | + | + | δ 0.72 |
| Noise model | θ (B1) | 0.33 | θ (B1) 0.45 | θ (B1) 0.70 |
| Residual mean square (RMS) = | | 33.4 | 16.0 | 71.3 |
| Ljung-Box Q (df = 20) = | | 14 | 17 | 13 |

Note: All coefficients p ≤ .05

+ Variable not included in model

levels of unemployment that plagued the country during most of the era. Consistent with this interpretation, Gallup data on public perceptions of the "most urgent problem" facing the country show that from the end of 1981 until the June 1983 general election, large majorities consistently cited unemployment, and only very small minorities mentioned inflation. The pattern persisted thereafter, with the average percentages mentioning joblessness and prices between June 1983 and June 1987 being 73% and 3%, respectively. Our suspicion is that in periods of rapidly rising or high inflation such as those in Britain during much of the 1970s, the effects of inflation on subjective economic evaluations would be considerably stronger, and that inflation might replace income, interest rates, or both in our models.

Although public perceptions of economic conditions are shaped in predictable ways by objective economic trends, there clearly is considerable slippage between the objective economy and perceptions of it, and political events can intervene to produce major, if temporary, changes in such perceptions. This is very much the case with public expectations about future economic trends as well (Table 3.3). Moreover, because expectations are generally more vague and abstract than perceptions, it is not surprising that the connections between objective economic conditions and prospective economic evaluations are even more tenuous.

As we observed with respect to perceptions, price expectations are driven exclusively by economic conditions including income growth, interest rates, and unemployment. Economic shocks also have a significant impact, driving up inflation expectations by slightly over 2%. As in the price perception models, the RMS statistic indicates that economic conditions leave much of the variance in price expectations unexplained. The modest effects of economic conditions are even more apparent with respect to household finances. Although public forecasts about personal financial prospects respond significantly both to interest rates and economic shocks, they are not affected by inflation, unemployment or income growth. Moreover, they also are highly susceptible to political discourse in ways that price perceptions are not. The influence of election campaigns on personal financial expectations is particularly strong. Public optimism about household finances jumped an average of almost 10% in the month following each of the two elections in our study. Moreover, the dynamic coefficient ($\delta$ = .65) for the election variable indicates that its effects persisted for several months.

Finally, the weakest economic effects are observed, as expected, in the model of general economic expectations. Among the objective economic variables only interest rates have a significant impact, and this is less than half the size (-2.15 v. -4.39) of that exerted on general economic perceptions. Even more than was the case with perceptions, political variables drive the model of general economic expectations. Budget debates, election campaigns and the Falklands war all have strong effects. The annual budgets produced a positive swing in expectations about the performance of the national economy by slightly over 8%, whereas elections and the Falklands each had a positive impact over 20%. Moreover, both of these variables have large dynamic coefficients ($\delta$'s = .73 and .72, respectively), thereby indicating that their effects continued to color people's forecasts about the health of the national economy for many months after they occurred.[12]

## Do Subjective Economic Evaluations Matter?

To determine if economic evaluations affect party support, we conducted a series of analyses in which the governing Conservative party's share of major party support is the dependent variable.[13] The first models considered are bivariate ones which employ each of the six perception and expectation variables in turn as predictors. These show that the Conservative share of public support is significantly affected by perceptions and expectations of general economic conditions and by price perceptions (Table 3.4). However, expectations about future prices and evaluations of past and future personal finances have little or no effects. The

Table 3.4. Bivariate Models of the Effects of Subjective Economic Evaluations on Conservative Share of Major Party Support, 1979-1987

| Predictor Variables | | | Coefficient | LBQ* | RMS | Percent Reduction in RMS** |
|---|---|---|---|---|---|---|
| General economic expectations | ω | (B0) | 0.10a | 23 | 11.9 | 11.7 |
| | δ | | 0.66a | | | |
| Personal financial expectations | ω | (B1) | 0.10 | 15 | 13.5 | 0.0 |
| Retail price expectations | ω | (B1) | -0.02 | 18 | 13.6 | 0.0 |
| General economic perceptions | ω | (B0) | 0.09a | 14 | 12.6 | 6.8 |
| | δ | | 0.37b | | | |
| Personal financial perceptions | ω | (B2) | 0.03 | 17 | 13.6 | 0.0 |
| Retail price perceptions | ω | (B1) | -0.12 | 17 | 13.1 | 2.4 |

* df = 20

** Comparison with univariate noise model, θ (B1)

a p ≤.01
b p ≤.05
c p ≤.10; one-tailed tests

size of the coefficients indicates, at first blush, that the magnitudes of even the significant variables are modest. For example, a 10% increase in those believing that prices have held steady or increased only moderately over the past year produces only about a 1% swing in support in favor of the Conservatives. What this overlooks, however, is that price perceptions were extremely volatile in the period under consideration. Between January 1980 and May 1983 public expectations of sharp price hikes fell by more than 75%, an improvement that, *ceteris paribus,* would have produced a nearly 10% swing to the Conservatives from Labour.

The effects of evaluations of the general economy are more powerful. In addition to significant impact coefficients at a lag of one month, both general economic evaluation variables have significant dynamic (δ) parameters which indicate that their effects on the balance of major party support persisted over time. The estimates indicate that a 10% increase in public confidence in future economic conditions produces a 1% swing to the government after a lag of one month and an additional 2% swing over six months. Given that general economic expectations are even more volatile than price perceptions, this means that the impact of such expectations on the balance of major party support is approximately twice as strong as that of general economic perceptions and nearly three times greater than that associated with changing price perceptions. Note also that general economic expectations produce a much larger reduction in RMS (11.7%) than do price perceptions (2.4%) or any of the other subjective economic variables.

Although these analyses suggest that general economic expectations had strong positive effects on the balance of Conservative versus Labour support between 1979 and 1987, a stronger test involves the use of multivariate models that control for other pertinent economic and political factors. The latter set is potentially large, but here we include three highly salient events: the Falklands invasion of April 1982, the attempted assassination of Prime Minister Thatcher at Brighton in October 1984, and the use of British bases by the Americans for their raid on Libya in April 1986.[14] The first two are hypothesized to have temporary positive effects on the Conservative support share, and the third, a temporary negative one. To capture the impact of the minor-party support and more particularly, the formation and subsequent presence of the Liberal/SDP Alliance, support for these parties also is included as a predictor variable. The economic variables included are those used in our previous analyses, namely, inflation, interest rates, real income growth, and unemployment. Two analyses are performed. In the first, we include general economic expectations and the political variables; in the second, we add the objective economic variables.

The results of the first analysis show general economic expectations have a significant influence net of controls for political variables, with the size of the estimates being essentially unchanged from those for the bivariate model reported above. As in that model, forecasts about the health of the economy have an immediate impact on Conservative support which is supplemented by additional ones over several subsequent months (Table 3.5, Model A). All of the political variables also exert significant effects and, in the cases of the Falklands and the Brighton bombing, these are quite large. Thus, the war is estimated to have increased the Conservative share of major party support by approximately 10% in May and June 1982 and by over 7% in July. Moreover, as indicated by the large $\delta$ parameter (.88), the war's impact decayed very slowly in subsequent months. The Brighton incident's effects were also quite large (approximately 10% for two months and 5% for a third month), but they then evaporated. The Libyan raid had similarly short-lived effects, but these were smaller, reducing the Conservative share by 4 to 5% over a two-month period. Finally, the positive coefficient for the Alliance variable indicates that public support for the SDP and its Liberal ally was achieved

Table 3.5. Multivariate Models of the Effects of Objective Economic Conditions, Political Events and General Economic Expectations on Conservative Share of Major Party Support, 1979-1987

| Predictor Variables | | Model A | | | Model B |
|---|---|---|---|---|---|
| General economic expectations | ω (B0) | 0.11a | | ω (B0) | 0.14a |
| | δ | 0.68a | | δ | 0.63a |
| Liberal and Alliance support | ω (B0) | 0.18a | | ω (B0) | 0.20a |
| Brighton bombing | ω (B0) | 9.80a | | ω (B0) | 11.51a |
| | ω (B1) | 9.93a | | ω (B1) | 11.71a |
| | ω (B2) | 5.19b | | ω (B2) | 6.91a |
| Libya raid | ω (B0) | -4.89b | | ω (B0) | -5.73a |
| | ω (B1) | -4.30b | | ω (B1) | -4.91a |
| Falklands war | ω (B1) | 9.57a | | ω (B1) | 10.56a |
| | ω (B2) | 10.17a | | ω (B2) | 11.22a |
| | ω (B3) | 7.41a | | ω (B3) | 9.48a |
| | δ | 0.88a | | δ | 0.92a |
| Unemployment | | + | | ω (B0) | -0.01a |
| Real income growth | | + | | ω (B2) | 0.00 |
| Interest rates | | + | | ω (B2) | 0.01 |
| Retail price index | | + | | ω (B3) | -0.08 |
| Noise model | θ (B1) | 0.45a | | θ (B1) | 0.84a |
| Residual mean square (RMS) = | | 9.4 | | | 8.7 |
| Percent improvement in RMS = | | 30.1 | | | 35.4 |
| Ljung-Box Q (df = 20) = | | 10 | | | 15 |

a p ≤.01
b p ≤.05
c p ≤.10; one-tailed tests

+ Variable not included in model

disproportionately at the expense of Labour and thus benefitted the Tories on balance.

Estimates for the second model which includes objective economic conditions as controls are very similar to those just described. Importantly, general economic expectations continue to have significant effects, with the estimates indicating that a 10 point swing in such expectations immediately affected the Conservative support share by 1.4%, with the total impact ultimately being 3.8%. The potential importance of this effect may be appreciated by noting that between June 1979 and June 1987 the total variation in such expectations was 49 points, thus indicating that, other things being equal, they would have produced an 18.5% swing in major party support.

Of course, other things were not equal; in particular, unemployment increased greatly. The estimates indicate that unemployment was the only objective economic variable with a significant impact. Its coefficient indicates that an increase in joblessness of 100,000 would reduce the Conservative support share by less than 1%. However, given that unemployment increased by almost two million across the period means that its total impact, in the absence of countervailing forces, would have shifted public support almost 20% from the Conservatives to Labour. Overall, however, public confidence in the economy's prospects combined with the presence of the Alliance and various fortuitous political events were more than sufficient to offset the corrosive influence of unemployment on Conservative support.

Finally, to appreciate the relative strength of economic expectations and the several other variables, we focus on the reduction in RMS achieved by various specifications. Recall that by itself the expectations variable reduces the RMS by 11.7%. When the political variables are added, the reduction is 30.1%. Notwithstanding the impact of unemployment, the addition of the four objective economic variables reduces the RMS by only an additional 5.3%. Note also that a model using only the four objective economic variables fails to reduce the RMS, and none of the variables has a statistically significant impact. Taken together, these results clearly suggest the relative importance of the effects that economic expectations and political variables exerted on the Conservative share of major party support between 1979 and 1987.

## Conclusion: Through a Glass Darkly

The results of two decades of research show that objective economic conditions have inconsistent and sometimes insignificant effects on mass political attitudes and behavior. The evidence presented in this chapter helps to explain these findings. Our analyses strongly indicate that public economic evaluations are poorly informed by information about the objective economy and frequently distorted by the impact of salient political events. As a result, changing economic conditions have only moderate effects on perceptions of the performance of the national economy and one's personal economic circumstances, and even smaller ones on expectations about future national and personal economic trends.

Part of the reason that economic conditions have modest effects in structuring public evaluations is that systematic and reliable economic information is not always readily available either from personal experience, the mass media or other sources. In order for personal experience to yield accurate information of macroeconomic conditions individuals must: (a) correctly interpret the economic meaning of discrete events (e.g., they must be correct in thinking that a pair of shoes costs more this year than last, and they must be comparing equivalent shoes); (b) correctly weigh and aggregate diverse experiences (did the cost of shoes go up more this year than the price of gasoline went down, and by how much?); and

(c) have experiences that constitute a representative sample of economic reality.

Information acquired from the media or elsewhere also is subject to bias. As noted, even the best government statistics are subject to revision long after they have been published, and governments may deliberately manipulate such statistics, hoping to gain political advantage. For their part, the media may report economic news inaccurately, or simply fail to report important aspects of it at all. Of course, individuals can misread or misinterpret media reports and official statistics. In general, then, the costs of acquiring and processing accurate economic information can easily exceed what many people are able or willing to pay.

Logically, when economic information is unavailable or acquisition and processing costs are expensive, a cognitively impecunious electorate is likely to turn to other sources—including the political arena—where such information is more readily available, less expensive or both. Given the importance of public economic evaluations for political support, it is in the interest of political parties and leaders to wholesale information in such a way that they can manipulate such evaluations to their advantage. The evidence presented above indicates that governing parties enjoy inherent advantages in this enterprise and can be quite successful in their efforts to put a positive spin on economic news.

When economic information is limited or expensive the public also is likely to rely on cues that have little or nothing to do with the economy *per se* simply because they are readily available and, hence, cheap. Indeed, we interpret the evidence that the Falklands war had profound effects on public economic evaluations as demonstrating that noneconomic events can strongly influence economic evaluations in ways that may have little to do with objective economic conditions. Their country's victory in the South Atlantic created a sense of optimism and self-confidence in the British electorate which significantly colored voters' perceptions of past economic conditions as well as their expectations about the future. Moreover, because the discount rate on such a dramatic political event is much lower than on ordinary economic information, its impact persists for several months after it has occurred.

Finally, logic suggests and our analyses confirm that the effects of noneconomic information on economic evaluations and attempts to manipulate such information for political advantage are greatest where reliable economic information is least available. The supply of reliable economic information also varies directly with the specificity of the economic condition under consideration. It is greater with respect to prices than to the general health of the national economy, and greater with respect to past conditions than to future trends. Taken together, these findings suggest that the possibilities for political manipulation increase to the extent that prospectively oriented evaluations of the national economy drive party support and, indeed, our models of the Conservative share of major party support between 1979 and 1987 show that such evaluations had the strongest effects of any of the subjective economic evaluation variables. Moreover, these effects persisted in the presence of controls for objective economic variables and salient political events and conditions that obtained during the period. Although economic evaluations and economic realities are related, the former have important influences on party support and they are not simply mirror images of the latter. Such effects and inaccurate reflections, in combination, generate a genuine *political* economy of party support.

## Notes

1. This criticism, of course, applies only to aggregate time series models of political support. It does not apply to the equally numerous, micro-level, cross-sectional analyses which use survey data to focus explicitly on public economic perceptions and expectations. Cross-sectional studies are limited, however, in that they do not include direct measures of objective macroeconomic conditions since national economic conditions are constant across individuals in a national survey. Although the experience of national economic conditions may vary across individuals or sub-groups in a survey, we have yet to develop direct measures of such individual-level experiences independent of individual perceptions or recall. Thus, although it may be possible to examine the effects of both objective and perceived economic conditions using cross-sectional data, the limits of available data suggest that the incorporation of perceptual data in aggregate time series studies is a more promising way to proceed.

2. Such assumptions are not unique to political science. They are even more prevalent in economics which typically assumes that the public's perceptions of, for example, past inflation rates are identical to the actual historical rates. Similarly, rational expectations theories typically assume that individuals utilize all available information in formulating economic expectations, and that their expectations constitute unbiased estimates of the economic condition in question. Notwithstanding the centrality of these assumptions, economists have made little effort to test them empirically. Moreover, the results from the few studies which have been undertaken are mixed, at best (see, e.g., Carlson and Parkin, 1975; Darby, 1976, de Menil and Bhalla, 1975; Jonung, 1981; Jonung and Laidler, 1988; Watchel, 1977).

3. In economics as well, Jonung (1981:961) points out, "economists have used past (weighted) inflation rates to construct proxy measures for the expected rate. This common approach proceeds as if all relevant economic units have the same perceptions of past inflation rates and as if past inflation rates are identical to actually registered historical rates."

4. William Miller (1989:161) notes, for example, that since British unemployment levels began to rise in the late 1960s, "there have been at least sixteen

adjustments to the official method of calculating the unemployment rate, all designed to reduce it."

5. We decided to use the number of unemployed rather than the unemployment rate because the former is the more commonly reported statistic in the British press. However, the substitution of the unemployment rate for the number of unemployed has little effect on the results and none on their interpretation.

6. British election campaigns are quite short and are limited, by law, to 17 working days following the election proclamation. Although the dates of elections frequently are anticipated and considerable campaigning takes place before the formal campaign begins, it still is the case that the most intensive part of the campaign, and the part attended more closely by the public, is the period of approximately one month leading up to the election. Since our data encompasses the first two Thatcher governments, they include the two election campaigns occurring in May 1983 and May 1987.

7. The analysis extends six months beyond the June 1987 general election in order to be able to estimate the effects of economic conditions and political events occurring near the end of the second Conservative government.

8. Box-Jenkins procedures require that all variables be stationary both in mean and variance. Preliminary analyses indicated that the four macroeconomic variables and the six economic perception and expectation variables are all nonstationary in their means (i.e., the series trend or drift systematically upwards or downwards over extended periods). Therefore, all series were differenced prior to the identification of univariate ARIMA models. The unemployment and price series also exhibited variance nonstationarity. Thus they were log transformed prior to analysis. However, because these transformations complicate interpretation of results, we repeated all analyses using the untransformed versions of unemployment and prices. The results of the transformed and untransformed analyses were virtually identical. Since the untransformed results are easier to interpret, they are the only ones we report.

All six of the economic perception and expectation series were identified as simple first order, moving average ($\theta B^1$) processes. Among the macroeconomic variables, inflation, interest rates and real income also were identified as relatively simple, albeit somewhat different, moving average processes. Unemployment was identified as a second order, autoregressive ($\phi B^1$, $\phi B^2$) process.

9. Following conventional Box-Jenkins procedures (Appendix A), the economic perception and expectation series were prewhitened prior to computing the cross-correlations reported in Table 3.1.

10. Although the observation that rising unemployment levels appear to increase public confidence in future economic conditions can be reconciled with a rational expectations theory of political economy (see, for example, Chappell and Keech, 1985), the fit is not an especially good one in our data, not only because the relationship is modest and occurs as a moderately long lag, but also because of the absence of other evidence that would support a rational expectations interpretation.

11. Exploration of alternative dynamic specifications and lag structures indicated that our election terms are best modelled as abrupt, temporary effects which

are fully realized in the month following an election and decline gradually over the following year. Unfortunately, by specifying a lag of one month in the effects of election campaigns, we necessarily confound preelection campaign effects and postelection honeymoon effects. We attempted to address this problem by creating separate preelection (campaign effect) and postelection (honeymoon effect) variables. However, we were unable to identify plausible specifications that did not produce extreme correlations among the estimates.

Although the confounding of election and honeymoon effects undoubtedly means that our estimates of both the initial impact and the persistence of election campaign effects are somewhat exaggerated, the problem is not a serious one from our perspective. If, as we suspect, a primary function of the honeymoon effect is to increase the public credibility of the government's pronouncements (both in absolute terms and especially in comparison to the defeated opposition), then honeymoon effects can be interpreted as reflecting in part the greater ability of the government through ordinary political discourse to manipulate public opinion about the economy in ways favorable to itself. In other words, honeymoon effects may be as much a consequence of political discourse as election campaign effects are reflections of independent and unbiased assessments of objective economic conditions.

12. There may be good reasons for public expectations about future economic conditions to be influenced by wars and elections. Even relatively minor wars, such as the Falklands, have numerous and frequently substantial economic consequences which can bear significantly upon future unemployment and inflation levels, real income growth, and interest rates, among other effects. Recognizing this, it is reasonable for the public to adjust their expectations about future economic conditions in light of the outbreak or progress of a war. Similarly, because political parties typically are committed to different economic policies, knowledge of the outcome of an election can provide valuable information to individuals about the nature of future economic policies and, thus, about their likely consequences for economic conditions. In contrast, we cannot imagine the circumstances under which the outbreak of war or the outcome of an election will influence past economic conditions. This is not to suggest, however, that the effects of war and elections on future economic expectations are rational whereas their effects on past perceptions are not. Rather, what we would suggest is that both perceptions and expectations about the economy are manipulated by the political discourse attendant to campaigns and the emotional fervor that surrounds the outbreak of wars. That expectations are even more influenced by such events may be because there is a rational basis for such influence which reinforces nonrational effects.

13. Conservative party share is calculated as: Conservative Share = Conservative support/(Conservative support + Labour support). ARIMA diagnostics indicate that the variable needed to be differenced to achieve mean stationarity. The differenced series was modelled at a first order, moving average ($\theta B^1$) process.

14. These variables are scored 1 in the months in which the events occurred, and 0 in other months.

# 4

## The Dynamics of Third-Party Support: The British Liberals and the Alliance, 1979–1987

*Unfortunately for the Alliance, its future may lie not so much with its own efforts as with the behavior of others....*
—Jorgen Rasmussen (1985:107)

Like voters in American congressional elections, analysts of the political economy of party support manifest a strong "incumbency bias." Opposition parties, especially those in disadvantageous competitive positions, generally have been ignored. This is unfortunate because in multiparty systems the flow of support to and from smaller "third" parties may do much to determine the outcome of particular national elections, as well as the longer run dynamics of party fortunes. In this chapter we examine support for two such parties in contemporary Britain—the Liberals and the Social Democrats. Operating as the "Alliance" during the first eight years of the Thatcher era, these parties threatened to overturn the long-standing pattern of Conservative-Labour dominance.

The salience of the Liberals during the 1980s represented a dramatic reversal of political fortune. For much of the twentieth century, the party had been a quintessential "also ran" (see, e.g., Bogdanor, 1983; Rasmussen, 1981). Although periodic surges in popularity excited the party faithful, these always proved ephemeral, and the Liberals found it impossible to remove their minor-party yoke. Indeed, it can be argued that the Liberals' third-party image helped to create forces that perpetuated their minor-party status. Thus, when the political stakes were high, as they were whenever a general election loomed, potential Liberal supporters were confronted with the prospect of "wasting their vote" because the party was widely perceived as having no serious chance of forming a government. The Liberals were basically an interelection vehicle for safe protest, a means by which voters could register their displeasure with an incum-

FIGURE 4.1 Liberal-Alliance and Conservative Support, June 1979–June 1987

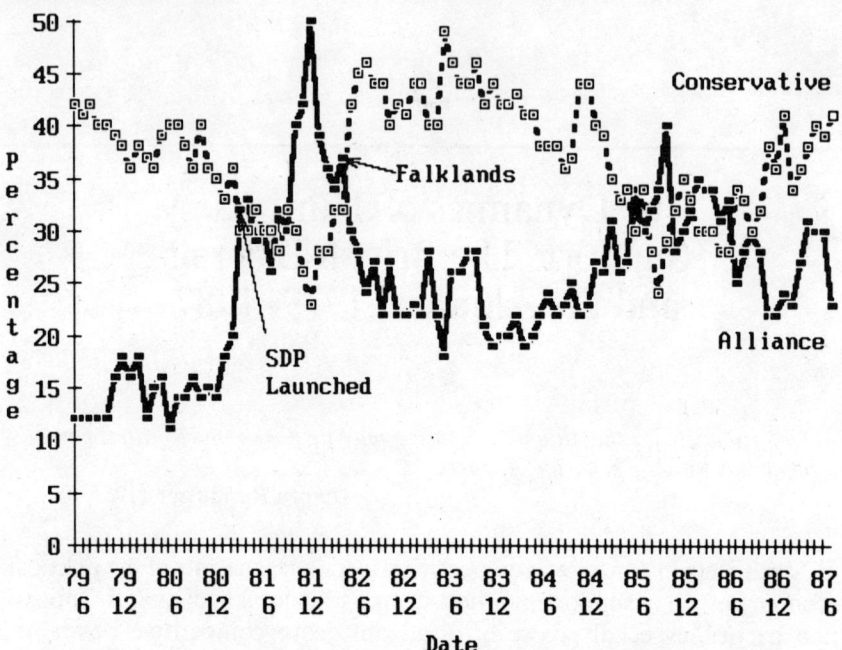

bent government by "parking their vote" with the party until a forthcoming general election forced them to decide which major party would better serve their interests.

In the early 1980s it appeared that the Liberals' status in British politics had changed profoundly. The party's 1981 pact with the new Social Democratic Party (SDP) and the Alliance's meteoric rise in the polls gave rise to widespread speculation that the fledgling "third force" might have "broken the mould" of British party politics and become a serious contender for political power (Bradley, 1981). By December 1981, the Alliance had soared to 51% in the Gallup Poll and it enjoyed a substantial lead over both of its major party rivals (Figure 4.1). Alliance support then began to wane in reaction to internecine disputes between the Liberals and their SDP allies and lukewarm public reaction to Alliance leader Roy Jenkins. Shortly thereafter, Britain's victory in the Falklands war led to a precipitous drop in the party's standing (to 28% in June 1982). After the cessation of hostilities, Alliance support dropped even further and reached a low of 18% one month prior to the June 1983 general election. Although the Alliance was able to capture 25% of the popular vote in that contest, only 23 Liberals and Social Democrats were elected to parliament. In the post-1983 period, Alliance popularity temporarily increased again, briefly reaching 40% in September 1985, before receding to the 25-35% range. In the 1987 general election the party again failed to make a breakthrough, receiving 23% of the popular vote, but electing only 22 of 650 MPs.

In the immediate aftermath of this election, the SDP split over the issue of a formal merger with the Liberals. One faction joined with the Liberals to form the new Liberal Democratic Party; another, led by David Owen, remained organizationally separate as the SDP. After a disastrous showing in the 1989 elections for the European parliament and disappointing by-election performances, the Owenites decided to disband what was left of their party. The SDP experiment had failed, and the mold of British party politics remained unbroken.

The Liberal-SDP experience in the 1980s provides an excellent case study of factors governing the dynamics of support for a small party attempting to enhance its competitive position in a multiparty system long dominated by two larger rivals. Investigating the economic and political forces affecting Liberal/SDP support between 1979 and 1987 will help us to understand why minor parties, even those operating in seemingly auspicious economic and political circumstances such as those enjoyed by the Alliance in the early 1980s, find it extremely difficult to change the contours of an ongoing party system.

## Theoretical Perspectives on Party Support

As noted in Chapter 1, most existing models of the aggregate dynamics of party support are open to challenge. In terms of model specification, the preeminence of objective macroeconomic variables, especially inflation and unemployment rates, in such models is readily apparent. In contrast, voters' subjective evaluations of national and personal economic conditions have received much less attention. In part, this neglect has been caused by a lack of adequate data and, in part, by an often implicit assumption that objective economic conditions accurately proxy subjective economic evaluations. Moreover, political events and conditions usually either have been omitted from support functions, or treated as theoretically uninteresting random shocks that are included in models only to achieve proper estimates of the impact of economic variables.

Researchers also generally have taken for granted that the electorate is incumbency oriented, assigns responsibility to the government for economic management, and behaves according to a simple reward-punishment process whereby a governing party either is rewarded for good or improving economic conditions, or is punished for bad or deteriorating ones. To paraphrase a familiar aphorism, "economics is the fate of *governing* politicians" (Norpoth, 1984:253). If opposition parties are investigated at all, it is assumed that macroeconomic variables have *symmetrical* effects on party support. Thus, the rising rates of inflation or unemployment that erode the standing of the governing party simultaneously boost support for all of its competitors, and the improving economic conditions that help the former hurt all of the latter.

These several assumptions need to be reexamined. Most basically, the supposition that the state of the economy *always* has an impact on levels of public support for parties and their leaders is problematic. Rather, macroeconomic effects are governed by political cultural beliefs about the proper functions of government (e.g., Schlozman and Verba, 1979; Sniderman and Brody, 1977), and such beliefs may change in the face of perceptions of repeated failures by government to alleviate longstanding economic distress (Alt, 1979:ch. 1). Economic effects also may reflect the outcomes of debates between a governing party and its critics. For example, the negative impact of a worsening economy on support for a governing party may be muted if elected political leaders and their hired "spin doctors" can convince an electorate that responsibility for the nation's economic affairs lies elsewhere.

The nature and impact of subjective judgments about economic conditions also are problematic. For example, even during periods of protracted economic malaise, sizable segments of the electorate may continue to believe that national or personal economic conditions are "better than they were" or will become "better than they are," and so they continue to support the party in power and its leader. Also, as noted, the prevailing political culture may be such that voters do not attribute responsibility to a governing party for the state of the economy or their personal economic circumstances. Relatedly, even if voters generally make such responsibility attributions, it does not follow that they do so in all cases.

The assumption that macroeconomic effects on support for governing and all opposition parties are symmetric and are mediated at the individual level by a reward-punishment process can be questioned as well. In circumstances where a country's economic condition is ratcheting from bad to worse, for example, the expectation according to this hypothesis is that opposition parties will see their support increase as discontented voters desert the governing party for its opposition rivals. It is plausible, however, that *minor* parties are by-passed in this process, i.e., reward-punishment-prompted voter exchanges involve only the major parties. In Great Britain, for example, the Conservatives and Labour always are seen by sizable segments of the electorate as having some chance of winning a forthcoming general election, but the prospects of third parties, such as the Liberals and their SDP allies, may not be taken seriously, regardless of their current standing in the polls.[1] Thus, voters who are exercised about a deteriorating economy and wish to bring about a change in government may be tempted to move to whichever of the two larger parties is in opposition rather than to one of the smaller parties that seemingly are proven losers. Accordingly, if a minor party can change its also-ran image and convince voters that it has a realistic opportunity to capture power, then it too may benefit from economically motivated disaffection with the incumbent government.

A second possibility arises if an *issue priority* rather than a reward-punishment model of macroeconomic effects is operative. According to this model, the popularity of ideologically centrist parties such as the Liberal/SDP Alliance[2] should always suffer in a period of economic adversity. Labour, as the principal party of the left and the self-styled champion of the working class, should benefit from increases in unemployment regardless of its government-opposition status because it is most closely associated in the public mind with concern about this issue. Similarly, the Conservatives' middle-class base, their often-repeated concern about price increases and more general right-of-center ideology help them to forge a strong link with inflation as an economic priority. Adverse trends in prices and unemployment thereby may create a double bind for a center party such as the Alliance: voters worried about inflation move to the right-of-center party, whereas those preoccupied with rising joblessness opt for the clearly defined left-of-center alternative.

A third possibility is a hybrid of the reward-punishment and issue-priority models. This hybrid model holds that the effects of inflation and unemployment on support for parties such as the Alliance vary according to which major power is in power. During periods of Conservative rule, price increases should benefit the Alliance, whose centrist ideological position implies that the party will accord greater priority to this issue than does Labour. Increases in joblessness, in contrast, should undercut support for the Alliance since the major opposition party, Labour, is most strongly identified with this issue. Conversely, when Labour is in power, rising prices should dampen Alliance popularity given that the major opposition party, the Tories, has made combatting inflation its chief goal. An increase in unemployment, however, should serve to boost support for the centrist Alliance when Labour is in office.

However economic forces affect party support, they are not the whole story. Noneconomic aspects of government and politics regularly receive extensive media coverage, and their impact on public feelings about parties and their leaders can be important. It is well documented, for example, that during periods of national emergency, such as during a war or crisis when a country's interests clearly are at stake, the public often rallies around the government as it did in Britain during the Falklands war (e.g., MacKuen, 1983; Mueller, 1970, 1973; Norpoth, 1987a, 1987b). We can anticipate that opposition parties, such as the Alliance, would lose support in such circumstances. Indeed, even if a crisis, war or scandal were not quickly resolved, or divided the public, a minor party like the Alliance might stand little chance of benefitting politically. In such a situation it might suffer issue-priority type effects similar to those discussed above regarding the economy. Voters applauding the way in which the situation was being handled would (continue to) rally behind the government, whereas those who did not would switch to the chief opposition party, which is apt to be the most salient critic of government policy, and is the likely alternative government.

Another instance in which a smaller opposition party might expect to see an erosion of support would be during national election campaigns. As argued above, when an election appears imminent, many backers of minor parties might be expected to begin to take their options seriously, and to move to one of the two larger parties to avoid wasting their vote. The timing of such a third-party "squeeze" is difficult to gauge. When an election is postponed until the fifth and final year of a government's term in office, the slide could begin almost anytime during that year since voters realize that an election is necessarily forthcoming. However, in more typical situations such as those considered here, national elections were called by the ruling party a year prior to the expiration of its mandate. In each case voters were alerted to the prospect of an election by the media well before the writs were issued (see Butler and Kavanagh, 1984, 1988). Given these circumstances, it is reasonable to expect a preelection skid in minor-party support in the quarter prior to polling day.

Three other political factors can influence party popularity in Britain and need to be considered in the context of modeling support for the Alliance: by-elections; the selection of new party leaders; and internecine disputes among party leaders and leading party activists. By-elections may be conceptualized as systemic political interventions—they are integral to the ongoing political process, and typically several of them are held during a government's term in office. Their importance in the support process is two-fold: first, they are commonly viewed as a barometer of public support for the party in power (Butler, 1973) and, as such, a dramatic by-election success or failure can affect a party's public standing. Second, and relatedly, by-elections receive considerable media coverage, and they thereby can help to focus public attention on smaller opposition parties, particularly when one of them is making a serious bid to capture a seat. By-elections thus may be particularly important for parties such as the Alliance which normally find it difficult to maintain a high public profile.

Leaders can have a variety of influences on support for their parties. In the interims between elections the leaders of minor parties generally receive much less media attention than the prime minister and the leader of the principal opposition party. One circumstance in which minor-party leaders do capture public attention is when they are initially selected for their posts. The leadership selection process thus provides minor parties with an occasion in which they can share the political limelight, if only temporarily, with their larger rivals. However, since the new minor-party leader is not taken seriously as a possible prime minister, the effect of his or her selection on party popularity should be brief.

Parties, major and minor alike, also can temporarily capture the headlines and the attention of voters for many other reasons as well. Such publicity is not always positive. Intraparty disputes are a case in point. In Britain, internecine disputes concerning leadership or policy questions typically are treated by press and public as evidence that a party's fitness to govern is problematic. The Alliance, by its virtue of its status as a pact between two organizationally separate parties, was susceptible to such disagreements and the attendant negative publicity they evoke. Although the Alliance had not been free from controversies before the 1983 election, those occurring afterwards were more serious. Widely publicized squabbles between and among Liberal/SDP leaders and party activists, such as the flaps concerning defence policy, tarnished the Alliance's image and undercut attempts to portray it as free from the quarrels that long had beset its major party rivals.[3] These squabbles, then, can be expected to have negatively affected Alliance support.

## Measures

Levels of public support for the Liberal/SDP Alliance are assessed using responses to the vote intention question asked in monthly Gallup public opinion polls for the period June 1979 to June 1987.[4] This variable is the percentage of respondents saying they would vote Liberal, SDP or Alliance were an election held at the time the survey was conducted. Inflation and unemployment data are gleaned from *Economic Trends* and the Department of Employment *Gazette,* respectively. Inflation is measured as the percentage change in the retail price index from month-to-month expressed as a yearly rate. Unemployment is the number of wholly unemployed in thousands.

The measures of retrospective national (sociotropic) and personal (egocentric) economic evaluations are based on responses to the following Gallup Poll questions: "How do you think the general economic situation in this country has changed over the last 12 months?" "How does the financial situation of your household compare now with what it was 12 months ago?" The measures of prospective economic judgments are based on responses to similarly worded questions concerning the general economy and household finances over the next 12 months. Variables measuring national retrospective, national prospective, personal retrospective and personal prospective economic evaluation are constructed by computing the difference between the percentage thinking conditions had improved (would improve) minus the percentage of those thinking that had deteriorated (would deteriorate). The four subjective economic variables thus indicate the balance of optimists and pessimists in a given month regarding the past and future performance of the national economy and personal finances.

The political interventions included in the analyses are dichotomous (0–1) measures geared to the occurrence and duration of the following nine events: the initial launching of the SDP; the relaunching of the Alliance in early 1987; Liberal/SDP leadership changes; disputes within or between the Liberals and the SDP; Liberal/SDP by-election victories; government (Conservative) by-election victories; the three-month periods preceding the 1983 and 1987 general elections; the Falklands war.[5]

## Economic Conditions and Economic Evaluations

As argued above, objective economic conditions constitute one theoretically important set of factors influencing Liberal and then Alliance support between June 1979 and June 1987. Here we focus on two of the most widely publicized aspects of the economy—inflation and unemployment. These macroeconomic indicators are widely reported in the mass media, and their potential to influence party support is suggested by the large movements in prices and joblessness that occurred during the period. During Mrs. Thatcher's first term in office the number of wholly unemployed grew dramatically from slightly over one million in June 1979 to some three million by February 1983, the largest number since the depression of the 1930s (Figure 4.2). Unemployment remained very high during her second term, although it started to decline during the eight months preceding the 1987 election. When the 1987 campaign began, the number out of work was slightly less than three million, which translated into a 10.4% unemployment rate.

Price movements over the 1979–87 period were equally profound. At the start of Mrs. Thatcher's first term, inflation was growing at an annual rate of 11.4%. Although she had come to power promising to quell the fires of inflation (Whiteley, 1986:ch. 5), she had no immediate success; on the contrary, by June 1980 prices were rising at a whopping 21.9%. Thereafter, however, inflation fell precipitously, and by the time of the June 1983 election it was less than 4% (Figure 4.2). After the election, it fluctuated between 4 and 5% before jumping to 7% in the summer of 1985. The spurt in prices proved temporary, and by the spring of 1987, inflation was again in the 4% range.

FIGURE 4.2  Inflation and Unemployment, June 1979–June 1987

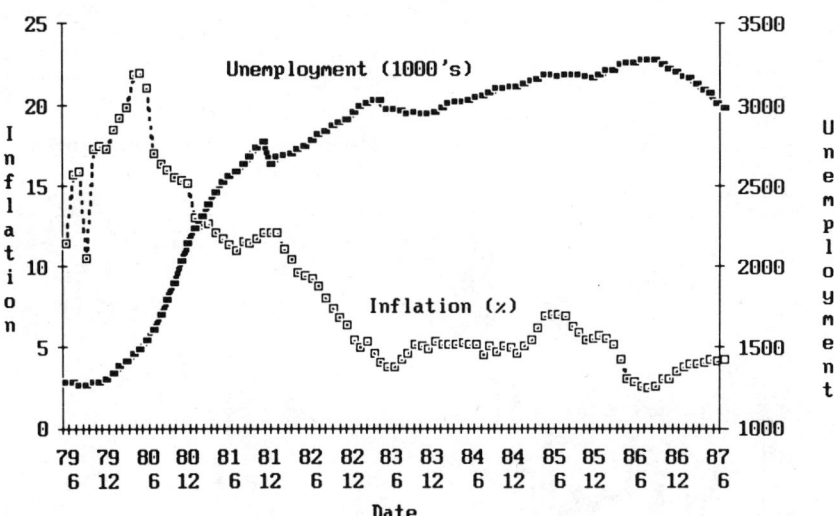

The subjective economic measures indicate that pessimistic assessments of national and personal economic conditions exceeded optimistic ones throughout much of the 1979–87 period. This was particularly the case for retrospective judgments about the performance of the national economy. As Figure 4.3 shows, the percentage believing that conditions had deteriorated exceeded that believing they had improved for all but four of 97 months. This is not to say that opinion was stable; rather, in the spring of 1982, and in the run-ups to the 1983 and 1987 general elections, it moved sharply in a positive direction. Retrospective assessments of personal economic conditions behaved similarly and were strongly correlated with national evaluations ($r = +.65$), although as Figure 4.3 reveals, the variance in the former was much smaller than that in the latter.

Prospective evaluations of the national economy also closely paralleled their retrospective counterparts ($r = +.80$). However, opinion was tilted more strongly in an optimistic direction, and in 21 months, the percentage of positive appraisals exceeded the percentage of negative ones (Figure 4.4). Similarly, prospective personal evaluations were strongly correlated with their retrospective counterparts ($r = +.75$), but again there was less volatility than in national prospective assessments, and optimistic forecasts about one's economic future were more frequent. Indeed, the percentage of positive assessments of personal economic prospects was greater than the percentage of negative ones during 40 of the 97 months under consideration. Most of these cases occurred between 1983 and 1987, and

FIGURE 4.3 Retrospective Economic Evaluation Indices, June 1979–June 1987

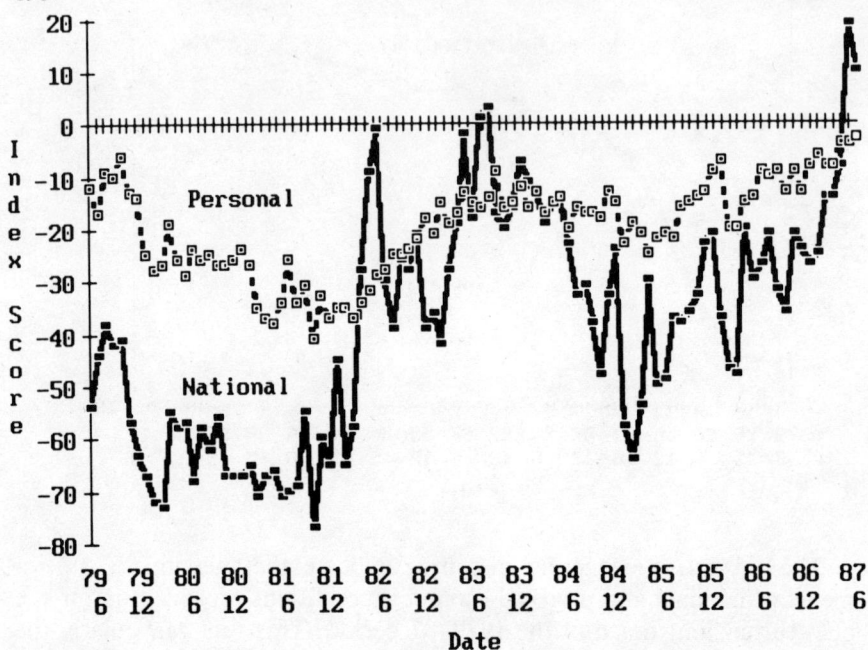

16 of them were concentrated in the 18 months preceding the 1987 election (Figure 4.4).

In sum, both the objective and subjective economic variables displayed characteristics that suggest that they might have significant effects on party support in the 1979–87 period. Inflation and unemployment varied sharply, as first prices and then joblessness escalated rapidly. Paralleling the ongoing economic adversity, economic issues dominated the issue agenda throughout the period,[6] and while public evaluations of national and personal economic conditions varied, pessimistic appraisals typically outnumbered optimistic ones. Specifying how these economic conditions and evaluations might have affected Alliance support is our next topic.

## A Model of Alliance Support

What kinds of economic effects on Alliance support might be anticipated? Before answering this question it should be noted that survey evidence indicates the assumption that British voters attribute responsibility to government for the management of the country's economic affairs is well-founded. In the 1987 national election survey, for example, 78% of those interviewed believed that government could "do a lot" to control

FIGURE 4.4 Prospective Economic Evaluation Indices, June 1979–June 1987

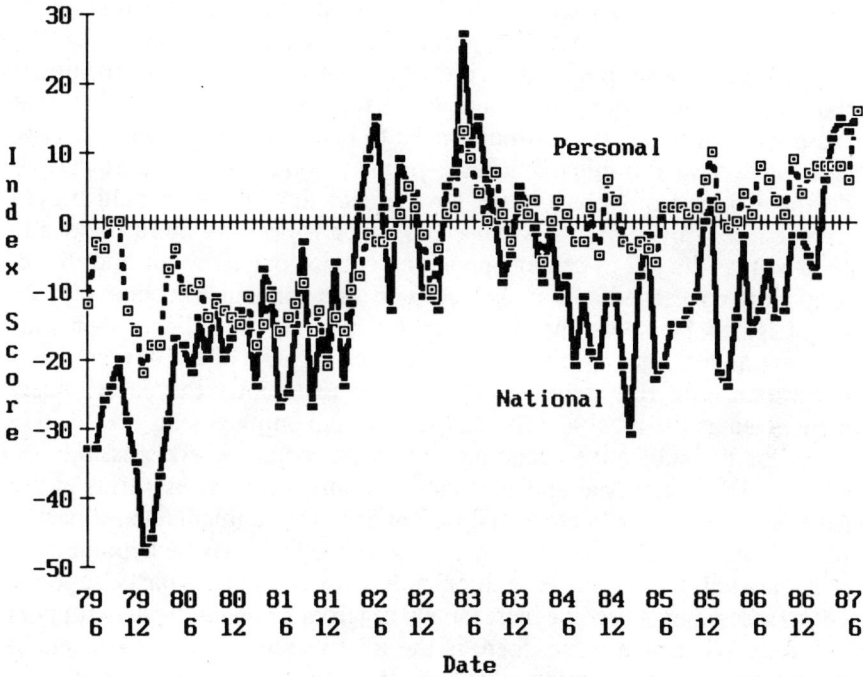

inflation, and 73% felt this way about unemployment. Data gathered in the 1983 election study similarly reveal that over 70% believed government could control wage increases, improve the standard of living, reduce taxes, and prevent strikes. Neither ongoing economic adversity nor Mrs. Thatcher's strident neo-conservative rhetoric prompted the British public to conclude that government could or should not play a large role in fostering national economic well-being.

As for the possible effects of inflation and unemployment, a conventional reward-punishment model would predict that these adverse economic conditions and generally pessimistic economic evaluations would help the standing of opposition parties, including the Alliance. However, as argued above, it is possible that reward-punishment processes do not influence support for smaller opposition parties. Such parties may not benefit from negative economic conditions and evaluations because they are not seen as being in a position to challenge successfully for political power, and hence, are not seen as being able to do anything to alleviate the economic problems exercising the electorate.

The basic issue-priority model, rooted as it is in public perceptions of parties' differential concerns with various types of economic problems, would predict that the Alliance would suffer from both rising unemployment and rising prices. Labour and the Conservatives had firmly established their *bona fides* regarding jobs and prices, respectively, whereas the Alliance's economic policy priorities were not as clear cut. Accordingly, those concerned about jobs would move to (stay with) Labour, whereas those worried about prices would move to (stay with) the Conservatives. A hybrid reward-punishment/issue-priority model would predict that during a period of Conservative government the Alliance would benefit from concern over prices because the party is seen as more politically centrist than its left-of-center opposition counterpart, Labour and, therefore, more concerned and associated with this particular economic problem. Rising joblessness, in contrast, would not help the Alliance—persons desiring an alternative to the Conservatives because of the government's performance on this issue would gravitate to Labour, the party widely recognized as the most forceful advocate of full employment.

As for the subjective economic variables, there are two possibilities. First, since the national and personal economic assessment variables are general "pro-con" indicators that do not involve judgments about particular aspects of the economy such as prices or jobs, it may be hypothesized that they will have inverse relationships with opposition party support, i.e., as assessments become increasingly negative, opposition party support will rise. What is at issue, then, is the relative strength of the effects of different types of economic evaluations. Previous research with individual-level survey data generally has found that retrospective evaluations of national economic conditions (retrospective sociotropic evaluations) are most important (e.g., Kinder and Kiewiet, 1979, 1981). However, some of these studies have made the case for prospective sociotropic assessments (e.g., Kuklinski and West, 1981; Lewis-Beck, 1986, 1988a:ch. 8), and some analysts (e.g., Kramer, 1983) have argued on methodological grounds that aggregate time series analyses are required to show the effects of personal (egocentric) economic judgments.

The second possibility harkens back to the competitive status of opposition parties. As with the impact of objective economic variables, it is possible that third parties will not benefit from negative national or personal economic judgments because such parties are not considered to be viable alternative governments. Persons making negative judgments and wishing to replace an incumbent government because of its perceived poor economic performance will move to a major opposition party because it has a realistic chance of coming to power and alleviating the problem.

The impact of the various political interventions discussed above should be more straightforward. The most obvious positive effect is the genesis of the SDP in March 1981, and the concomitant *de facto* launching of the Alliance. The enormous and highly favorable publicity surrounding the birth of the SDP should have had an immediate, permanent and positive impact on Alliance support. Relatedly, the reformation of the Alliance in January 1987 in the wake of severe intraparty disputes over the question of whether Britain should continue to deploy nuclear weapons may have helped to lift the party out of the political doldrums. However, Conservative preelection maneuvers, including a tax-cutting budget which presented the nation's economy in a very positive light and Prime Minister Thatcher's summit meeting with Soviet leader Gorbachev, as well as the calling of the 1987 election, may have combined to offset any increase in Alliance support caused by its "relaunching."

Other positive political effects should have been at work as well. Previous studies have demonstrated leadership selection effects for the Conservatives and Labour, as well as the Liberals in their pre-Alliance days (Clarke, Stewart and Zuk, 1986; Clarke and Zuk, 1989). Here, the selection of new Liberal or SDP party leaders, i.e., Roy Jenkins in July 1982, and David Owen in June 1983, should have generated favorable publicity that translated into temporary gains in Alliance support. Likewise, periodic by-election victories by Liberal or SDP candidates should have prompted surges in Alliance support that gradually dissipated in subsequent months as these events faded in the public memory.

On the negative side of the ledger, disputes among Alliance party leaders and between leaders and party activists, especially the widely covered and much discussed squabbles of September 1983 and June and September 1986, should have extracted a toll on the Alliance in the polls. As noted above, such disputes would undermine the public's image of the party and its leaders as cohesive and competent, and somehow "nicer" than the two older parties. Government (Conservative) by-election victories also should have temporary negative influences on Alliance support. The Falklands war almost certainly had an even larger negative effect on Alliance fortunes. The conflict proved to be a public relations bonanza for Prime Minister Thatcher and her party (e.g., Clarke, Mishler and Whiteley, 1990; Norpoth, 1987a, 1987b), and it can be hypothesized that Tory gains in the polls that occurred at this time came at the expense of the Alliance as well as Labour.

Finally, to break the mold of British party politics, the Alliance had to convince the electorate that it was a serious contender for power, and not merely a "Mark II" Liberal Party. To the extent that the Alliance continued to be seen as an "also ran," such perceptions should have had adverse effects on its support, especially in the months preceding the 1983 and 1987 general elections. As noted above, the timing of such a third-party squeeze should depend upon public perceptions of the likelihood of a forthcoming election. Here, we model the effect for the quarters preceding these two elections.

The models of Alliance support incorporating the several economic and political variables discussed above are estimated using ARIMA techniques developed by Box and Jenkins (1976) and Box and Tiao (1975). These techniques enable one to evaluate the effects of both interval-level variables (the economic measures) and dichotomous variables (political events) on a time series of interest (Alliance party support) (see Appendix A). Following conventional Box-Jenkins procedures, trends in the economic variables and Alliance support were removed by taking first differences. Diagnostic analyses of the differenced Alliance support series indicated the presence of time series dependencies which were controlled using a moving average parameter operating at a lag of one month.[7] The general multivariate Alliance support model is:

$$(1-B)ALL_t = \Sigma\omega_i(1-B)SUBEC_{t-k} + \omega_j(1-B)INF_{t-k} + \omega_k(1-B)UNEMP_{t-k}$$

$$+ \Sigma\omega_m(1-\delta B)(1-B)INT_{t-k} + \theta(B)a_t$$

where:

$ALL_t$ = Liberal/Alliance support at time t

$SUBEC_{t-k}$ = subjective economic evaluations/expectations at time t

$INF_{t-k}$ = inflation rate at time t

$UNEMP_{t-k}$ = number unemployed, in thousands

$INT_{t-k}$ = intervention effects at time t-k

$a_t$ = error term at time t

$\omega$ = impact parameter

$\delta$ = decay parameter

$\theta$ = moving average parameter

B = backshift operator

t-k = time lag

Table 4.1. Effects of Retrospective Sociotropic Economic Evaluations, Prospective Egocentric Economic Evaluations and Political Interventions on Liberal/Alliance Support, 1979-1987

| Predictor Variables | | Model A Coefficient | t | Model B Coefficient | t |
|---|---|---|---|---|---|
| Retrospective sociotropic evaluations | ω (B0) | -0.04 | -1.66b | + | + |
| Prospective egocentric evaluations | ω (B0) | + | + | -0.17 | -2.23a |
| SDP launched | ω (B0) | 13.00 | 4.53a | 12.75 | 4.52a |
| Alliance relaunched | ω (B1) | 1.04 | 0.33 | 0.88 | 0.29 |
| Leadership selection/change | ω (B0) | 3.65 | 1.59c | 4.26 | 1.94b |
| Internicine conflict | ω (B1) | -2.38 | -1.61c | -2.34 | -1.61c |
| Alliance by-election victories | ω (B0) | 5.55 | 4.35a | 5.34 | 4.24a |
| | δ | 0.78 | 5.60a | 0.77 | 5.45a |
| Conservative by-election victories | ω (B0) | -1.94 | -0.62 | -1.53 | -0.51 |
| Falklands war | ω (B1) | -3.62 | -1.44c | -3.84 | -1.49c |
| | δ | 0.64 | 2.19b | 0.57 | 1.73b |
| General election campaigns: 1983 | ω (B1) | -5.65 | -2.38a | -4.83 | -2.04b |
| 1987 | ω (B1) | 2.17 | 0.70 | 1.51 | 0.50 |
| Noise model | θ (B1) | 0.52 | 5.14a | 0.53 | 5.21a |
| Residual mean square (RMS) = | | 10.82 | | 10.53 | |
| Ljung-Box Q (df = 20) | | 26 | | 20 | |

a  $p \leq .01$
b  $p \leq .05$
c  $p \leq .10$; one-tailed tests
+ Variable not included in model

## The Economics and Politics of Alliance Support

Since the objective and subjective economic variables might tap substantially overlapping sets of information about public reactions to national and personal economic conditions, only the latter were employed in the initial analyses. As noted, the subjective economic evaluations are strongly intercorrelated and, accordingly, each was considered in a separate analysis. The results show that all four types of economic evaluations had immediate, statistically significant, negative effects on Alliance support. For example, the ω coefficient for retrospective sociotropic evaluations is -.04 (Table 4.1, Model A), indicating that a one-point shift in these evaluations depressed Alliance support by slightly less than .5%. The range of movement in such evaluations (87 points) suggests that, *ceteris paribus,* shifting evaluations of the national economy would have altered Alliance popularity by 3.5% between 1979 and 1987. The ω for prospective egocentric judgments is larger (-.17) (Table 4.1, Model B). Given that this series varied by 37 points, it appears that changing forecasts about one's personal economic circumstances would have changed Alliance support by just over 6%. Analyses of prospective sociotropic and retrospective

FIGURE 4.5  Liberal-Alliance Support and Economic Evaluations, June 1979–June 1987

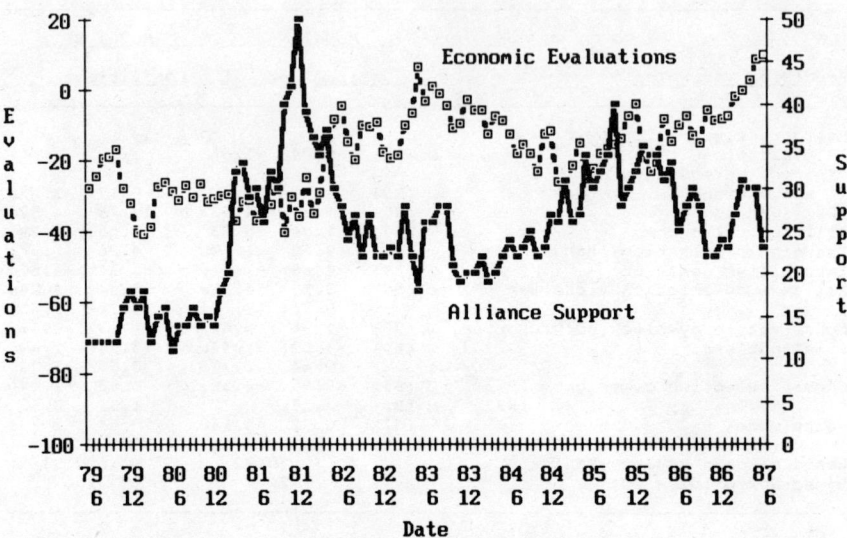

egocentric judgments suggest that their effects were of the same order of magnitude (data not shown). Since the subjective economic evaluations were highly intercorrelated, we summarized their effects by combining them into an overall additive index.[8] Figure 4.5 suggests that this index had the expected inverse relationship with Alliance support. Analyzing the index in the Alliance support model confirms this—the $\omega$ parameter is statistically significant ($p < .05$) and negative (-.11) (Table 4.2).

Do the effects of subjective economic evaluations operate net of variations in the objective economy? To answer this question a final model including inflation and unemployment,[9] as well the subjective economic evaluation index and the several political interventions was analyzed. The results show that inflation, unemployment and subjective economic evaluations all have significant effects (Table 4.3). The inclusion of inflation and unemployment changes the estimated impact of the latter variable only marginally. Given that the subjective economic evaluations index varied by 51 points, it appears that, controlling for other factors, such evaluations would have prompted a net movement of slightly over 5% in Alliance support.

Regarding inflation and unemployment, note first that their effects both are positive, a finding consonant with a traditional reward-punishment model of how economic conditions influence support for opposition parties. As for the size of the effects, since the two series have been (natural)

Table 4.2. Effects of Subjective Economic Evaluations Index and Political Interventions on Liberal/Alliance Support, 1979-1987

| Predictor Variables | | | Coefficient | t |
|---|---|---|---|---|
| Subjective economic evaluations index | $\omega$ | $(B0)$ | -0.11 | -2.04b |
| SDP launched | $\omega$ | $(B0)$ | 12.61 | 4.42a |
| Alliance relaunched | $\omega$ | $(B1)$ | 1.37 | 0.44 |
| Leadership selection/change | $\omega$ | $(B0)$ | 3.49 | 1.54c |
| Internicine conflict | $\omega$ | $(B1)$ | -2.41 | -1.65b |
| Alliance by-election victories | $\omega$ | $(B0)$ | 5.43 | 4.29a |
|  | $\delta$ | | 0.79 | 5.69a |
| Conservative by-election victories | $\omega$ | $(B0)$ | -1.93 | -0.63 |
| Falklands war | $\omega$ | $(B1)$ | -3.49 | -1.40c |
|  | $\delta$ | | 0.63 | 2.04b |
| General election campaigns: 1983 | $\omega$ | $(B1)$ | -5.13 | -2.16b |
| 1987 | $\omega$ | $(B1)$ | 2.06 | 0.67 |
| Noise model: | $\theta$ | $(B1)$ | 0.52 | 5.10a |
| Residual mean square (RMS) = | | | 10.62 | |
| Ljung-Box Q (df = 20) = | | | 24 | |

a  p ≤.01
b  p ≤.05
c  p ≤.10; one-tailed tests

log transformed prior to analysis, we interpret the estimates as (variable) elasticity coefficients.[10] Evaluated at the series mean (8.47%), a 1% increase in inflation boosted Alliance support by .19%. In keeping with its salience during much of the period under consideration, the impact of unemployment was larger—at the series mean (2,681,680 unemployed), a 1% rise in joblessness (26,817 more out of work) increased Alliance support by .7%.

All of the models presented above also indicate that several political interventions had significant influences on Alliance popularity. Since the model in Table 4.3 is the most comprehensive specification, it provides the best indication of the magnitude of these effects, net of controls for economic conditions and evaluations. As hypothesized, some of the political interventions had positive impacts. The launching of the SDP in March 1981 was greeted by a permanent increase of nearly 11 points in the then nascent Alliance's popularity. By-election victories also had sizable effects—on average, they led to an immediate increase of 5.6% in Alliance support (Figure 4.6). Such popularity gains were temporary, but they did not evaporate immediately. Rather, as signified by the large δ parameter (.82), they faded slowly, such that after six months, the Alliance still enjoyed a 2.1% increase in support due to its last by-election success.[11] The erosion was progressive, however, and after a year, the impact was virtually extinguished (Figure 4.6). Leadership effects also were at work—

Table 4.3. Effects of Inflation, Unemployment, Subjective Economic Evaluations Index and Political Interventions on Liberal/Alliance Support, 1979-1987

| Predictor Variables | | | Coefficient | t |
|---|---|---|---|---|
| Inflation rate+ | $\omega$ | (B0) | 4.78 | 1.75c |
| Unemployment (in thousands)+ | $\omega$ | (B1) | 17.57 | 1.91c |
| Subjective economic evaluations index | $\omega$ | (B0) | -0.10 | -2.00b |
| SDP launched | $\omega$ | (B0) | 10.96 | 3.72a |
| Alliance relaunched | $\omega$ | (B1) | 1.05 | 0.34 |
| Leadership selection/change | $\omega$ | (B0) | 3.49 | 1.55c |
| Internicine conflict | $\omega$ | (B1) | -2.34 | -1.60c |
| Alliance by-election victories | $\omega$ | (B0) | 5.63 | 4.50a |
|  | $\delta$ |  | 0.82 | 7.16a |
| Conservative by-election victories | $\omega$ | (B0) | -2.17 | -0.71 |
| Falklands war | $\omega$ | (B1) | -3.49 | -1.33c |
|  | $\delta$ |  | 0.55 | 1.41c |
| General election campaigns: 1983 | $\omega$ | (B1) | -4.33 | -1.85b |
| 1987 | $\omega$ | (B1) | 2.18 | 0.74 |
| Noise model: | $\theta$ | (B1) | 0.58 | 5.80a |
| Residual mean square (RMS) = | | | | 10.19 |
| Ljung-Box Q (df = 20) = | | | | 25 |

a $p \leq .01$
b $p \leq .05$
c $p \leq .10$; two-tailed tests for inflation and unemployment; one-tailed tests for other variables

+ Natural log transformed

the selection of Roy Jenkins and David Owen each provided the Alliance with a temporary boost in support of about 3.5%.

Much of the increase in support attributable to the launching of the Alliance, its periodic by-election successes, and leadership renewal, was undercut by the Falklands war. The outbreak of war in April 1982 led to a drop of 3.5% in the Alliance's standing in the following month (Table 4.3). This effect was permanent, and it grew with the news of victory. As shown by the $\delta$ parameter (.55), the eventual loss of support was nearly 8%. The calling of a general election the following year occasioned a further slide in the polls by the Alliance of over four points in the three months preceding the June 1983 election. However, no such third-party squeeze was evident in the run-up to the subsequent June 1987 election, perhaps because it was largely canceled by positive publicity generated by the relaunching of the party in January of that year. Finally, as anticipated, the Alliance suffered because of periodic internecine conflicts—on average, each of them reduced its popularity by over two points.

In sum, modeling political effects on Alliance support reveals that the birth of the SDP, by-election victories and, to a lesser extent, the selection of party leaders produced gains in support. The outbreak of the Falklands

FIGURE 4.6  Impact of By-Election Victories on Alliance Support

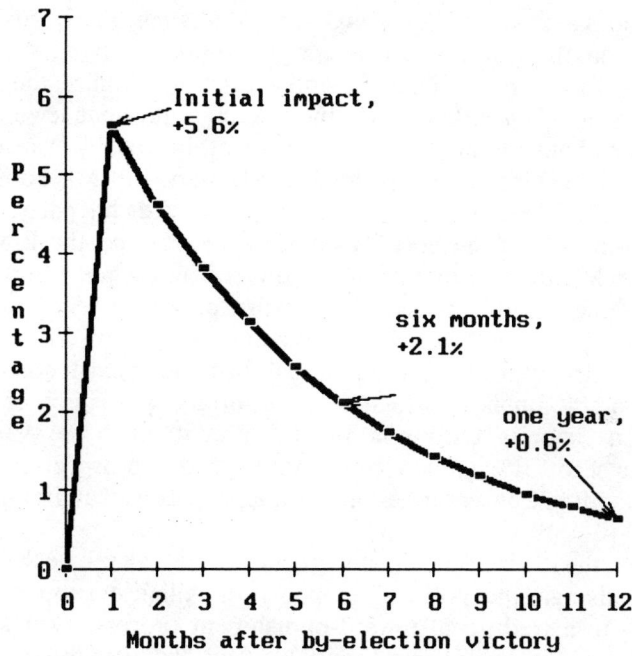

war and the public's strong, positive response to the government's handling of it, in contrast, cut deeply into the Alliance's standing in the polls. The calling of a general election in 1983 likewise eroded its popularity as did periodic infighting between party leaders and party members. Support for the Alliance, then, ebbed and flowed in predictable ways to major political events occurring during the 1979–83 period.

### Conclusion: The British Party System—Bent, Not Broken

The tempestuous economic and political climates of the late 1970s and early 1980s seemed especially propitious for the formation of a new "third force" in British politics. After the Conservative victory in May 1979 the economy was buffeted first by sharp hikes in inflation and then, as price increases abated, by skyrocketing unemployment. Public evaluations of the country's economic performance and its future prospects were massively negative and, although assessments of personal economic circumstances were not as bleak, pessimism was common. At the same time satisfaction with Mrs. Thatcher's prime ministerial performance plummeted from a high of 46% four months into her first term to 24% in

December 1981—the lowest level ever registered for a prime minister (Butler and Kavanagh, 1984). Moreover, Labour was poorly positioned to capitalize on the growing discontent. Discredited during the 1978–79 "winter of discontent" and subsequently voted out of office, the party and its new leader, Michael Foot, gave the electorate precious few reasons for enthusiasm about another Labour government. Indeed, by December 1981 only 19% of the electorate expressed satisfaction with Mr. Foot's leadership, and only 24% were positively disposed towards his party.

The formation of the Social Democratic Party and the Liberal/SDP Alliance in March 1981 immediately captured public fancy, and considerable excitement was expressed at the prospect of a truly competitive multiparty system with a viable alternative to the two old-line parties. During the first year of the new political formation's existence, it enjoyed much favorable publicity which was reinforced by a clutch of dramatic by-election victories. Only nine months after its birth the Alliance had achieved a heady 51% public approval rating, and its prospects for breaking the longstanding Conservative-Labour duopoly seemed an imminent reality.

And yet, the Liberal Party's noncompetitive past was to be the Alliance's future. Although the political economy of Alliance support operated according to a traditional reward-punishment process, even unemployment figures not seen since the 1930s and the pessimistic economic evaluations that accompanied them during most of Mrs. Thatcher's first term were not sufficient to sustain Alliance strength in the polls. By July 1982 it trailed both the Conservatives and Labour, and its support had fallen to 24%—only half what it had been six months earlier. Moreover, and unfortunately for the Alliance's long-term prospects, most of the benefit realized from growing unemployment and negative public reactions to the economy probably was concentrated in Mrs. Thatcher's first term. As we have seen, most of the dramatic surge in joblessness in the Thatcher years happened before the 1983 election. Also, inflation, increases in which enhanced Alliance support, had already sharply abated by this time, and subsequent price hikes were comparatively modest. In sum, economic developments between 1983 and 1987 were not geared to give the Alliance the boost it needed to make further gains in public support.

And if these economic trends were not problematic enough, political events and conditions—some of which were unanticipated by all concerned—helped to squelch the party's dream of power. The Falklands war was the first such intervention and, arguably, the most important. The war gave the ruling Conservatives and their unpopular leader an unexpected, much needed, opportunity to demonstrate leadership during a time of national emergency, and Mrs. Thatcher capitalized on the situation. Britain rallied behind the prime minister and her party when hostilities broke out, and Conservative support surged again with news that the Falklands had been recaptured and the Argentines defeated. A sizable portion of the recovery in Tory fortunes came at the Alliance's expense and, as our model estimates indicate, the losses (on the order of 8% after six months) were permanent.

The calling of a general election the following year brought another decline in party fortunes. Although the negative impact of the campaign *per se* was temporary, it can be argued that the election outcome had more longlasting effects. In what had become a familiar story during the pre-Alliance era, the British electoral system worked strongly to the new party's disadvantage. Like the Liberals before it, the Alliance was unable to translate votes into parliamentary seats and, thus, it found itself vulnerable to the stigma of being a "can't win" party rather than a serious contender for power. After 1983, many commentators speculated that a strong Alliance showing in the next general election might create a "hung parliament," but few believed that it could actually win on its own.

Political events and conditions continued to affect Alliance support between 1983 and 1987. Although it scored occasional by-election victories which temporarily bolstered its support, its appeal diminished in the wake of nasty intraparty squabbles which called into question the claim that somehow the new party was "different" than its old-line rivals. Also, the attempted relaunch of the Alliance in the run-up to the 1987 election did little to revive party fortunes. Once more, international developments worked against the Alliance. This time, however, it was news about the prospects for peace and disarmament which followed Mrs. Thatcher's well-timed meeting in Moscow with Soviet leader Gorbachev in March 1987. The public again applauded her leadership, and support for the Alliance again faded. The prime minister adroitly took further advantage of her opposition party counterparts at this time by introducing a preelection budget that suggested that the economy was on a sharp upward curve. Arguing that they had brought the country "peace, prosperity and leadership," the Tories called a general election in which they asked for a mandate to "take the next steps forward." During the ensuing campaign the Alliance quickly fell behind Labour in the polls and, for the second time in four years, finished a disappointing third when the ballots were counted.

Despite a very auspicious beginning, then, the SDP and their Liberal allies were unable to break the mold of British party politics. Ultimately, the Alliance's inability to stake out an issue concern of its own, be it national security, the economy or the environment, coupled with its lack of a sizable base of committed partisans,[12] proved its undoing. Given these factors, Alliance support, unlike Labour's, was very soft, and this, in combination with its opposition status, meant that the new party was highly vulnerable to political events and conditions over which it had no control. The Conservatives, in contrast, had the advantages of incumbency. As the government they were positioned to respond forcefully to unexpected developments such as the Falklands invasion and, thereby, to bolster their image in the public mind. Similarly, they were able to generate a positive impression among the electorate by engaging in expansionary economic policies in the year before the 1987 election (see Chapter 8), and by publicizing the good economic news in their March 1987 preelection budget. They also ensured that the prime minister received favorable publicity in the run-up to that contest. Again, the Conservatives' tactical advantages over their opposition opponents were particularly damaging to the Alliance since, unlike Labour, its support depended heavily on volatile short-term forces rather than more durable ones generated by longstanding partisan allegiances.

Lastly, the electoral system played a role in the Alliance's demise as well. Britain's single-member plurality scheme of representation strongly penalizes opposition parties such as the Alliance and their Liberal predecessors that lack a geographically concentrated base of support. In 1983, for example, the Alliance received only 2% fewer votes than Labour but elected only 23 of 650 MPs. Labour, in contrast, elected 209. Equally vast discrepancies in Alliance and Labour vote/seat ratios occurred four years later. The electoral system, then, made it very difficult for the Alliance to shed its third-party image. Since neither the Conservatives nor Labour have any incentive to change Britain's electoral system, and the Alliance's successor, the Liberal Democratic Party, continues to suffer from the widely dispersed and unstable support base of its predecessors, the new party's prospects for shedding the "also ran" label that bedeviled the Liberals and then the Alliance are hardly encouraging. In the end, the Alliance experience strongly suggests that the existing party system is very resilient. Adverse economic and political conditions may bend it, but structural factors make it extremely difficult to break.

## Notes

1. From January 1981 to June 1987 there were only four months (November 1981 [39%], December 1981 [43%], January 1982 [37%] and April 1982 [26%]) when as many as one-quarter of the British electorate thought that the Alliance might win a forthcoming election. After the latter date, no more than 14% thought so, and the average for the June 1983–June 1987 period was only 5%.

2. Although the fact that the SDP was founded by four former senior Labour politicians suggested that voters likely would see it as a moderate "Mark II" Labour Party, public perceptions of the ideological proclivities of the Alliance undoubtedly were blurred by the SDP-Liberal pact. Thus, data from the 1983

British election study show that 49% believed that the SDP was closer to Labour, and 22% thought it was closer to the Conservatives. For the Liberals, the pattern was reversed: 48% and 31% thought the Liberals were closer to the Conservatives and Labour, respectively. Poll data also indicated that there was considerably uncertainty re: Alliance policies on economic and other issues (Rasmussen, 1985:100). Similarly, when respondents in the 1983 election study were asked if Alliance policies were "clear" or "vague," 50% said "vague," and an additional 15% said they "didn't know."

3. When the Alliance was formed, the Liberals and SDP strived to created an image "of niceness, of friendliness, of two parties prepared to work in the national interest" (King, 1985:28).

4. In the British Gallup Poll party support is measured using the following questions: "If there were a general election tomorrow, which party would you support?" Respondents answering "don't know" are asked: "Which would you be most inclined to vote for?"

5. The initial launching and subsequent relaunching of the SDP and the Falklands war are modeled as permanent effects; the other political events are modeled as temporary (pulse) effects.

6. Gallup data show that the mix of inflation and unemployment concerns shifted sharply as joblessness mounted and price increases slowed. For example, in June 1979 the percentage stating inflation was the country's "most urgent problem" was 45%, and 19% mentioned unemployment. In sharp contrast, in December 1980 inflation references had fallen to 13% and unemployment ones had risen to 68%. At the time of the June 1983 election, unemployment was mentioned by 82% and inflation, by only 3%. The perceived importance of joblessness remained high afterwards as well—across the June 1983–June 1987 period the average percentages citing unemployment and inflation were 73% and 3%, respectively.

7. The value of $\theta(B^1)$ is 0.26 (t = 2.57, p < .01). An analysis of model residuals indicates that they are white noise (LBQ = 18, p > .05). The residual mean square (RMS) is 16.11.

8. The subjective economic evaluation index is the mean score on the retrospective sociotropic, prospective sociotropic, retrospective egocentric and prospective egocentric variables.

9. The inflation and unemployment series are (natural) log transformed and differenced to control for variance and mean nonstationarity. The noise model for inflation was $\theta(B^3)$, whereas that for unemployment was $\phi(B^1)$, $\phi(B^2)$. Box-Jenkins diagnostics (see Appendix A) suggested that inflation had a positive impact on Alliance support at zero lags, whereas unemployment had a positive impact with a lag of one month.

10. The elasticity coefficient for a "lin-log" model (i.e., a model in which the independent but not the dependent variable is logged) is $\omega(1/Y)$, where Y is the value of the dependent variable. See Gujarati (1988:154).

11. The size of the impact after n time periods is $Y_{t+n} = \delta^{n-1}\omega_t$ (McCleary and Hay, 1980:166).

12. As a new party the SDP did not have a base of party identifiers. Moreover, the cohort of Liberal partisans was both small and unstable (Clarke and Zuk,

1989:201-02). After its formation, the Alliance was spectacularly unsuccessful in attracting party identifiers. At the time of the 1983 election, for example, only 12%, 4% and 2% identified with the Liberals, SDP and Alliance, respectively. The Liberal figure was precisely the same as it had been in 1979 and, indeed, the same as that in 1964. See Clarke and Stewart (1984:692). The situation did not improve afterwards—the 1987 national election survey shows that 12% were Liberal identifiers, 5% were SDP, and 1%, Alliance.

# 5

# Regional Political-Economic Contexts and Party Support in Canada, 1985-1988

*The fact is that the Mulroney administration had racked up the finest economic record of any government in recent history. Unemployment was down, and the dollar was up; we were making inroads on the deficit; inflation had been brought under control, interest rates were down, and investment soared. Canada's export trade was booming, and the central part of the country was booming in response. While there were difficulties in other regions, we were doing more to rectify them than any predecessor government. Why couldn't we get credit for this?*

—Gratton (1988:233-34)

One of the most pervasive, but seldom acknowledged, assumptions in studies of the political economy of party support is that "context doesn't matter." The consequences of this assumption are manifested in several ways. Economic influences typically are hypothesized to be national in scope—party support is analyzed for entire electorates using data on national economic conditions. Studies of support among various subgroups are rare (e.g., Hibbs, 1982a, 1982b), and studies that employ group-specific rather than national macroeconomic indicators (see, e.g., Monroe, 1984) are rarer still. The neglect of context also is reflected in the proclivity of most researchers to analyze support over lengthy time intervals, and to ignore or downplay the significance of political events and conditions that may be a work during particular periods. The failure to recognize the possible importance of such contextual variations risks confounding our understanding of how economic and political forces affect party fortunes.

In this chapter we analyze support for national (federal) political parties in Canada, a country long characterized by highly salient regionally based cultural, economic and political divisions (Kornberg, 1970; Smiley, 1980; Stevenson, 1989). The centrality of regional cleavages in the Canadian political experience makes this country an ideal setting for investigating contextual effects. To analyze how economic conditions and political events affected support for the federal Conservative (PC), Liberal, and New Democratic (NDP) parties in various regions, we conduct pooled cross-sectional time series analyses of data gathered between February, 1985 and November, 1988.[1] By confining our attention to this period, we control for slowly paced changes in socioeconomic and political cultural variables that might have significant consequences over an extended time interval. In particular, we can reasonably ignore secular trends in the long-term determinants of party support in various regions, as well as evolutionary changes in public standards of acceptable government performance for social and economic well-being.

## The Canadian Political Context

Canada has a Westminster-model parliamentary system and, by tradition, the party receiving the most seats in a national election, even if not a majority, will form the government-of-the-day. This tradition, coupled with widespread public expectations that government will assume a broad range of economic and social responsibilities, help ensure that a governing party's performance is closely scrutinized (Clarke et al., 1991:ch. 2). The ability of national governments to carry out these responsibilities is constrained by a highly decentralized federal system in which the subnational governments (provinces) have important fiscal powers, functional duties, and constitutional prerogatives (Jackson and Jackson, 1990:ch. 6). Such decentralization reinforces and, in turn, is reinforced by strong ethnolinguistic and regional cleavages that characterize the Canadian economy and society.

These societal cleavages coupled with a decentralized federal system have influenced the evolution of Canadian political parties and patterns of competition among them. The federal and provincial party systems in the several provinces differ, with the discrepancies being especially pronounced in Quebec and British Columbia (Clarke, Kornberg and Stewart, 1992). At the national level the party system long has been dominated by the Liberal and Progressive Conservative parties. Both have avoided rigid ideological programs in favor of brokerage practices designed to maximize public support (Brodie and Jenson, 1990; Clarke et al., 1991:ch. 1). During their lengthy sojourn in office during the post-World War II era the federal Liberals gradually implemented an extensive panoply of social welfare programs (Landes, 1983:15–17) which was largely endorsed by the major national opposition party, the Conservatives. Of the minor federal parties, Social Credit and the New Democratic Party (NDP), only the latter now has a viable national presence. The NDP long has been committed to a social-democratic agenda. Although it has enjoyed periodic surges in popularity, it has not been able to break the "two-party plus" mold of the national party system (Epstein, 1964). However, the NDP has been an important actor in provincial politics in some areas of the country, and has formed governments in Ontario and three of the four western provinces.

Given the two major national parties' blurred ideological images, the substantial differences between federal and provincial party systems in several provinces, and the weakness of the social-structural bases of party support (Clarke and Stewart, 1992), it is not surprising that many Canadians' party identifications are weak, unstable, and inconsistent across levels of the federal system. These individual-level properties of party identification are conducive to rapid aggregate changes in party support. For example, at the national level, the Conservative Party's share of party identifiers declined from 40% to 30% within a year after its victory in the 1984 election, and to 24% in 1987, before rebounding to 39% at the time of the 1988 federal election (Clarke and Kornberg, 1992). Such partisan volatility over short periods of time suggests, in turn, that party support in Canada may respond strongly to changing economic conditions and the onward march of political events.

The 1985–88 period is an interesting one in which to investigate the economic and political determinants of party support in Canada. In the September 1984 federal election the governing Liberal Party was soundly rejected by a disgruntled electorate, and a massive "Tory tide" swept the Progressive Conservatives into office. The PCs subsequently won a second consecutive parliamentary majority in the November 1988 election. This outcome, however, was not foreordained. Concomitant with their loss of party identifiers noted above, soon after their 1984 triumph the PCs vote intention share skidded precipitously in public opinion polls (Figure 5.1). By 1987, they trailed both the Liberals and the NDP, but then they recovered as the 1988 election approached. The opposition parties' standings in the polls exhibited similarly high levels of instability. Both started with low ratings but then gained popularity and surpassed the Tories. The Liberal and NDP rallies did not last, however, and, although party support was highly fluid during the 1988 campaign, the PCs ultimately proved victorious.

Trends in party support at the national level between 1984 and 1988 were not mirrored in the various regions. Rather, although party support was highly unstable at both the national and regional levels, movements therein assumed different trajectories in different parts of the country. The central tendencies in the three parties' support in the five regions reflect, in part at least, longstanding regional discrepancies in their competitive statuses. Thus, despite the fluctuations in PC popularity in the Prairies, the party remained well ahead of the Liberals and the NDP in

FIGURE 5.1 Federal Party Support in Canada, February 1985–November 1988

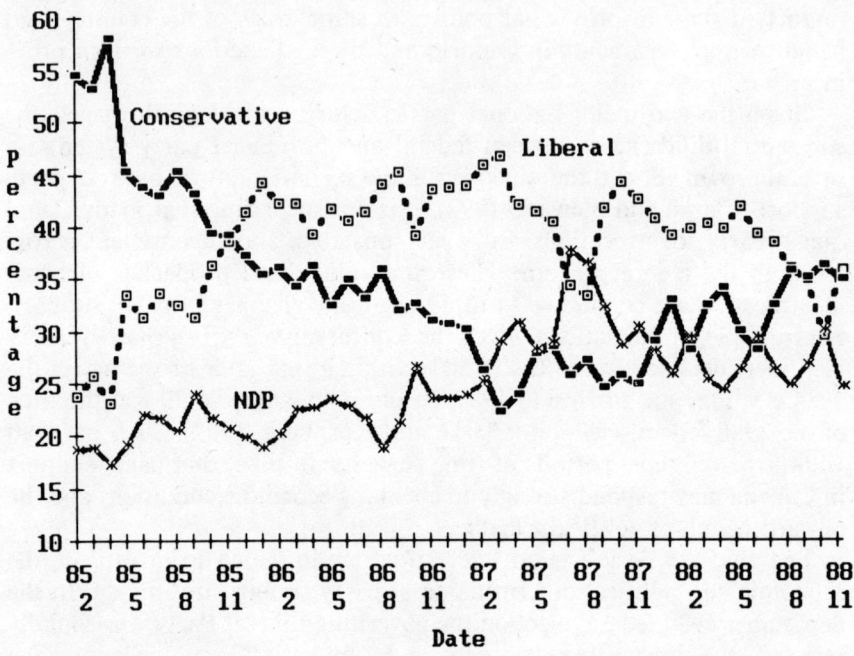

this region (Figure 5.2). In Ontario and Quebec, in contrast, the Tories' popularity share dropped quickly after their 1984 victory. In the former region the PCs continued to run well behind the Liberals and close to the NDP until the 1988 election. In the latter, the Conservatives remained below, then edged towards, and finally overtook the Liberals in the run-up to the election (Figure 5.3). The situation in the Atlantic provinces was extremely volatile. PC popularity moved downwards until early 1987, then surged and declined, and ultimately surpassed the Liberals immediately before voters went to the polls. Finally, in British Columbia PC support shifted downwards and ran close to that of the Liberals, but both parties' ratings remained below those of the NDP from early 1987 onwards.

The volatility in support for Canada's national parties between 1984 and 1988, and their differing patterns of popularity across the country during this period, suggest that public feelings about the parties reflected a complex mixture of long-and short-term forces. As noted above, region provides a convenient proxy for many of the more enduring aspects of Canada's society, economy and polity that collectively define the contexts within which more proximate determinants of party support operate. Two

FIGURE 5.2 Federal Party Support in the Prairies, February 1985–November 1988

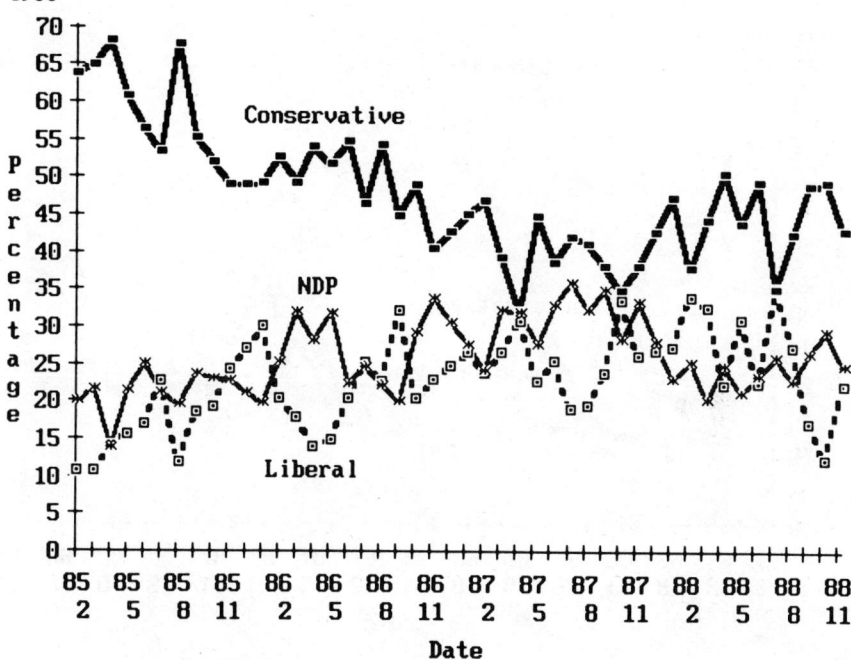

of the most important such determinants are economic conditions and political events.

## The Economics and Politics of Party Support

### *The Economy*

After a decade of economic distress which culminated in a serious recession in the early 1980s, the Canadian economy finally rebounded after 1984. Nationally, inflation, which had been largely wrung out of the economy by the recession, remained relatively low, averaging 4.1% and fluctuating between 3.7% and 4.7%. Regionally, the story was the same, as average levels of inflation in major cities varied from a low of 3.3% in British Columbia to a high of 4.2% in Ontario.[2] The bigger news was unemployment. Joblessness, which had soared to nearly 12% in 1983 began a gradual downward trend which continued throughout all but a few months during the 1984–88 period. By the time of the November 1988 election the unemployment rate stood at 7.8%. However, reflecting regional economic differences, levels of joblessness varied across the country. The Atlantic provinces, which historically have been especially prone to sharp

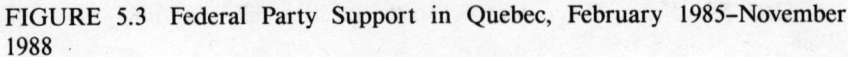

FIGURE 5.3 Federal Party Support in Quebec, February 1985–November 1988

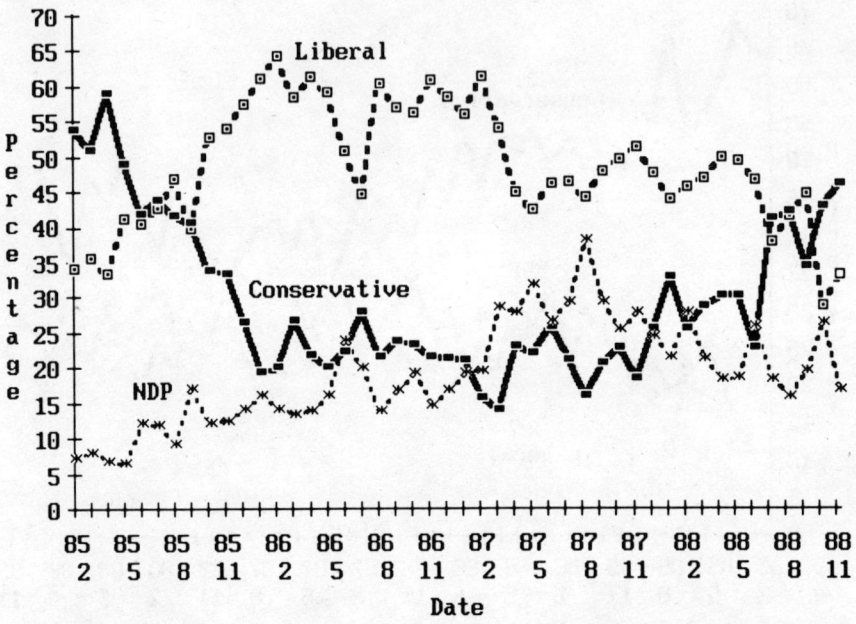

seasonal fluctuations in unemployment, as well as Quebec and British Columbia, reported unemployment averages (14.8%, 10.7%, and 12.3%, respectively) that exceeded the national figure. In contrast, in Ontario and the Prairies, joblessness figures (averaging 6.5% and 8.6%, respectively) were below the national level. These differences notwithstanding, unemployment receded in every region after 1984. As Figure 5.4 shows, the steepest declines occurred in the Atlantic region, British Columbia, and Ontario, with more gradual ones taking place in Quebec and the Prairies.

Were these regional differences in unemployment important? As noted, most studies of party support have focused on national economic conditions and ignored subnational effects. Doing so is problematic. One might argue that public reactions to the governing Conservatives and two opposition parties, the Liberals and the NDP, should have been less sensitive to national unemployment than to its regional counterpart. This argument is grounded in the reasoning that, although the national and regional economies were improving throughout the period under consideration, the rate of improvement diverged, and levels of unemployment differed as well. These variations suggest that joblessness may have been a more salient issue in some regions than in others.

This possibility is consistent with the existence of localized influences on economic information processing. In this regard, the subnational media

FIGURE 5.4 Regional Trends in Unemployment, February 1985–November 1988

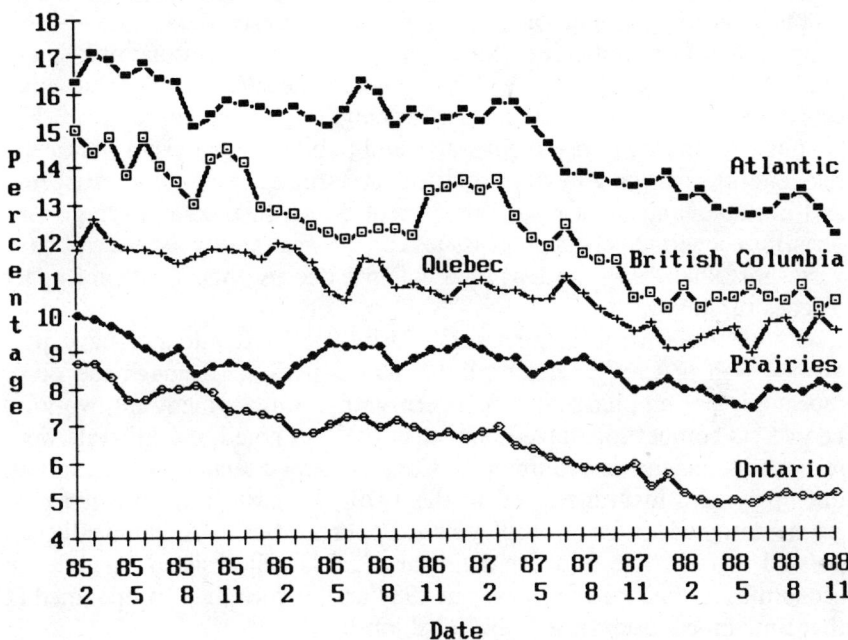

and interpersonal communication processes tend to personify and thereby heighten the visibility of local economic conditions (Kinder and Mebane, 1983; Mebane, 1988; Stimson, 1989). The importance of such information may be magnified by "efficient decision rules" which emphasize the monitoring of only highly visible conditions (Chappell and Keech, 1985; Entman, 1989; Phlips, 1988:1–13; Yantek, 1988). As a result, regional unemployment conditions may be perceived more accurately and have greater salience than those which characterize the country as a whole (Conover, Feldman and Knight, 1986). The quick projection and ready reception of economic information and the heightened visibility of economic issues, in turn, are important determinants of economic evaluations and associated political attitudes (Weatherford, 1983b, 1983c). These several factors should contribute to the enhanced salience of regional rather than national economic conditions and, hence, to the stronger impact of regional unemployment on party support.

What type of effects might be anticipated? The familiar reward-punishment model (see Chapter 1) posits that the incumbent party is held responsible for economic performance, credited (blamed) for improving (deteriorating) conditions, and rewarded (punished) by a vigilant electorate. An alternative, issue-priority, model proposes that parties' issue concerns are more important than incumbency status in determining party support. The party that assigns priority to a particular economic problem receives support from people most concerned about it. Accordingly, left-and right-of-center parties tend to benefit from unemployment and inflation, respectively. A third, political debate, model argues that economic effects on political support are highly "context contingent." The parties' presentation, media coverage, and public acceptance of politically relevant information govern party support. Issue agendas are multifaceted and mutable, and, as a result, the extent to which media coverage emphasizes economic versus other issues can change rapidly. Issues can have very short "half-lives" and, as their salience decays, their political impact recedes rapidly.

Of the three models, the issue-priority model should not have performed well in Canada during the 1985–88 period. Although the NDP repeatedly has emphasized its concern with unemployment and working people, its competitors have done so as well. As noted, the Liberals were responsible for the development of Canada's social security net including unemployment insurance, and in the 1970s the party implemented programs designed to foster employment opportunities in economically depressed regions. The PCs, for their part, had largely resisted Thatcherite economics in their run for power in 1984 and, indeed, had campaigned at that time on a platform of "jobs! jobs! jobs!"

The reward-punishment and political debate models, in contrast, are consistent with both national and regional economic influences on party support. With respect to the former model, however, it is possible that effects are asymmetric, i.e., the electorate assigns blame for economic adversity, but does not praise economic success. Survey data gathered over the past decade indicate that Canadians are indeed prone to make such asymmetric responsibility attributions (see Chapter 7). Thus, the generally improving economic conditions that prevailed between 1984 and 1988 may not have produced a popularity benefit for the governing PCs. A similar possibility obtains if the political debate model was operative during this period. Since political discussion occurred in a context of generally improving economy, this may have sharply reduced the salience of economic issues and thereby bolstered the visibility of other events and conditions. Party support reacted to the changing mixture of issues and events that dominated the political agenda at various points in time.

## *Political Events*

The 1985–88 period was an turbulent time in Canadian politics. Soon after assuming office, the new Conservative government was beset by a series of cabinet scandals which led to the resignations of, *inter alia*, Fisheries Minister Fraser in September, 1985 ("Tunagate"), Environment Minister Blais-Grenier in January, 1986, House Speaker Bosley in September, 1986, and Transport Minister Bissonnette in January, 1987 (the "Oerlikon Affair") (Gratton, 1988). The timing of the scandals was such that just as one was moving off the front page, another one took its place. They thus served as a more or less continuous reminder of the PCs' inexperience and apparent violation of their widely publicized campaign pledge to restore probity to government in Ottawa after the Liberals' lengthy and allegedly corrupt tenure. Accordingly, the scandals should have permanently and negatively affected Tory support and boosted support for the Liberals and the NDP.

Other events also threatened to jeopardize Conservative fortunes in the polls. Finance Minister Wilson's May 1985 budget included a provision to de-index old-age pensions. This proposal was widely seen as a major breach of Prime Minister Mulroney's widely publicized "sacred trust" pledge to protect universal social benefits, and it ran contrary to the aforementioned broad public consensus regarding government's social responsibilities. The pension scheme provoked a storm of controversy and was withdrawn by the government in June, 1985. The de-indexation proposal should have had a negative effect on Tory popularity but, since it was hastily withdrawn, the effect should have been temporary. It also should have had a positive impact on support for the Liberal Party, which had been responsible for the implementation of many social welfare programs, and the NDP, a longtime champion of such programs.

Other events promised to bolster Conservative fortunes in the polls. The earliest was the "Shamrock Summit" between Prime Minister Mulroney and President Reagan in Quebec City in March, 1985. The summit was promoted as an important meeting between Canada's new prime minister and the leader of the country's largest defense and trading partner. It also was widely publicized as a jocular meeting in which two media-savvy Irishmen established a personal rapport. By elevating the prime minister's political stature, the summit should have temporarily increased his party's standing at the expense of the Liberals and the New Democrats.

The Conservatives should have enjoyed an additional benefit from ongoing internecine conflict within the Liberal Party. Although John Turner made a seemingly triumphant return from private life when he assumed the Liberal leadership mantle in the spring of 1984, he quickly became highly unpopular among Canadians and his own party's activists. Intraparty intrigue against Turner broke into open revolt in the summer of 1987, and culminated in a serious caucus rebellion in December of that year. Although these insurrections failed, discontent with Turner did not abate, and speculation that his party might remove him as leader continued into the opening days of the 1988 election campaign. Media coverage of Turner's difficulties with his party repeatedly reminded the public of the questions that had been raised about Turner's leadership abilities during the 1984 campaign, and also displayed the party's incapacity to perform as a well-disciplined "government in waiting." The Liberals' leadership problems, then, should have adversely and permanently affected their support while providing popularity gains for their opponents.

It is possible, however, that the NDP may have gained little from the Liberals' rancor and, in fact, it may actually have had adverse effects. Liberal revolts dramatized concerns about Turner's inability to lead his party in the next election campaign, but they also reminded voters that another election would soon be in the offing. Although Canadian election campaigns officially are conducted over a span of eight to nine weeks, speculation that an election is imminent typically begins several months before the writs are issued. Such speculation can have adverse effects on minor parties such as the NDP which have no realistic prospects of forming a national government. In such a situation minor parties are apt to experience a "third-party squeeze," as erstwhile supporters reconsider their options concerning who they would like best (or least) to hold the reins of power (Clarke, Stewart and Zuk, 1986; Clarke and Zuk, 1987). Also, and relatedly, as election fever builds in the run-up to a campaign, the media and the public increasingly focus on the emerging race for power between the major parties and their leaders. A minor party and its leader thus are at risk of being left at the publicity "starting gate."

Expectations about a 1988 campaign and the campaign itself did, in fact, consign the NDP and its leader, Ed Broadbent, to the political sidelines. As Liberal leader Turner sought to recover from intraparty revolts, to galvanize his party organization, and to restore his party's and his own popularity, he embraced the free trade issue. The free trade agreement was concluded between the Conservative Government and the United States in October, 1987, but the Liberal-dominated Senate subsequently refused to ratify it. The Senate's unwillingness to accept the agreement, in turn, precipitated the prime minister's decision to call an election and handed the Liberal leader a much-needed campaign issue. By seizing the initiative on a classic "pro-con" issue such as free trade, the Liberals effectively marginalized their opposition rival, the NDP. The campaign period itself, then, should have temporarily reduced NDP popularity in the polls.

The effect of the campaign on Liberal support might have been expected to have been positive given the great publicity generated by their strident opposition to free trade. However, much of the impact occurred after nationally televised debates among the party leaders in late October gave Turner an opportunity to dramatize his opposition to the pact. Poll data suggest that Liberal gains attendant upon the debates was profound, but quite transitory (Frizzell, Pammett and Westell, 1989:95). The monthly data at our disposal are ill-suited to capture such extremely short-term fluctuations in party support. It is more likely that we will see a negative effect, this being a result of the speculation that Turner would be dumped as Liberal leader in early days of the campaign, and the Conservatives' ultimately successful effort to counter the Liberal challenge on the free trade issue.

The free trade issue should have had other consequences as well. Although public attitudes towards the agreement were divided both before and during the 1988 election campaign, attitudes toward it varied across the country. In Ontario, Canada's industrial heartland, the free trade agreement was of particular concern because its possible adverse impact on industry, manufacturing, and jobs (Nelles, 1990:80–81, 86–88). Accordingly, in this region the agreement should have permanently diminished support for the Conservatives while boosting that for the Liberals, with these effects starting when the pact was signed in October, 1987.

The Meech Lake Accord of June 1987 also should have affected party support. The Accord, which was designed to secure Quebec's ratification of the new constitution in exchange for recognition of its status as a "distinct society," was strongly championed by Prime Minister Mulroney and the governing Conservatives. Although Liberal leader Turner also favored the agreement, some of the most influential members of his party, notably former prime minister Pierre Trudeau and long-time cabinet minister Jean Chretien, passionately argued that Meech Lake would destroy Canadian federalism and balkanize the country. Their resistance not only publicized a critical policy disagreement within the party, but also again highlighted the question of Turner's leadership and fueled speculations about Chretien's aspirations to replace him. Although the Accord and the debates which surrounded it did not initially prompt strong public reactions in most parts of the country, it was considerably more popular in Quebec than elsewhere.[3] We thus hypothesize that it should have permanently increased support for the Conservatives but reduced that for the Liberals in that province.

Other government initiatives may have had region-specific effects as well. For example, after considerable intraparty debate, the Conservatives had decided to award a lucrative Air Canada/CF-18 maintenance contract to Canadair in Montreal rather than to Bristol Aerospace in Winnipeg (Gratton, 1988:ch. 21). This decision was announced in October 1986 and interpreted in Manitoba and the other Prairie provinces as a blatant display of favoritism to the prime minister's native province of Quebec. As a result, we expect that the decision should have temporarily reduced

Conservative popularity and bolstered that of the opposition parties in the Prairies.

Finally, "region" needs to be incorporated in models of party support in Canada for substantive and, as we shall see below, methodological reasons. Substantively, region reflects long-term sources of party strength (Thorburn, 1985), as well as short-term regionally related forces on party popularity not captured by other variables included in our models. With respect to long-term forces, since the Diefenbaker era in the late 1950s and early 1960s Conservative strength has been centered in the Prairie provinces, and thus "Prairie effects" on Tory support should be positive. The Liberals have been strong in Ontario and particularly Quebec, and so positive Quebec and Ontario effects on Liberal support are predicted. The NDP and its forerunner, the CCF, long has been a strong force in national and provincial politics in all of the provinces west of Ontario except Alberta, but it never has established a viable base in the Atlantic provinces or Quebec. Accordingly, there should be positive Prairie and British Columbia effects, but negative Atlantic and Quebec ones, on NDP support.

## Measures and Methods

The economic variables in the party support models include the inflation rate measured as the monthly percentage increase in the consumer price index on an annual basis, and the unemployment rate measured as the seasonally adjusted percentage of the labor force in a given month without jobs and seeking work.[4] As foreshadowed by the data presented earlier in Figure 5.4, preliminary diagnostics conducted for each region separately indicate that the national and regional unemployment series are nonstationary in their means and, hence, these series are (first) differenced. The inflation series is a simple first-order autoregressive process and, thus, is used in undifferenced form.

As noted in Chapter 1, the timing of the effects of inflation and unemployment on party support is debatable. Although we believe contemporaneous or short-lagged effects for unemployment are most plausible, theory and previous research are insufficient to indicate exactly which lag is preferable *a priori*. We therefore proceed empirically and investigate possible unemployment effects at zero, one- and two-month lags. In keeping with the assumption that the market provides the electorate with continuous information on prices, inflation is treated as a contemporaneous effect.

Regarding the several political variables in the model, the four scandals (Tunagate, the Blais-Grenier affair, the Speaker's resignation, the Oerlikon affair) are hypothesized to exert permanent step effects. Accordingly, each is coded as 0 in each region prior to the date of occurrence and 1 afterwards. Two other interventions, the Liberal caucus revolt and the 1988 election campaign are treated in a similar fashion. Two of the three regionally specific interventions, the Meech Lake Accord and the free trade agreement, also are expected to have permanent effects, but ones that operate only in Quebec and Ontario, respectively. The Shamrock Summit and the government's abortive attempt to de-index pensions for senior citizens are modeled as nationwide temporary interventions, a one-month "pulse" effect in the former case, and a three-month one in the latter. Finally, the government's decision to place the new Air Canada maintenance facility in Montreal rather than in Winnipeg is treated as a one-month pulse operating in the Prairie region only.

Pooled cross-sectional time series analysis (Stimson, 1985) is employed to estimate the effects of the several economic and political variables.[5] Since we are investigating the possible impact of national and regional unemployment at zero, one and two lags on support for three parties, 18 such analyses are performed.[6] In each case the model estimated is as follows:

$$PS_t = \beta_0 + \beta_1 INF_t + \beta_2 UNEMP_{t-i} + \Sigma\beta_{3-14} INT_t + \Sigma\beta_{15-18} REGION + 1/\phi_1(B^1)a_t$$

where:

$PS_t$ = Progressive Conservative, Liberal or NDP support at time t

$INF_t$ = inflation rate at time t

$UNEMP_{t-i}$ = unemployment rate (national or regional) at time t-i

$INT_t$ = political interventions at time t

REGION = Atlantic, Quebec, Prairies, British Columbia regional dummy variables (Ontario is the reference category)

$\beta_0$ = constant

$\beta_i$ = regression coefficient

$\phi_1$ = autoregressive parameter

$B^1$ = backshift operator

$\tilde{a}_t$ = error term at time t

### The Determinants of Party Support

We begin by considering support for the governing Progressive Conservatives. Although the estimated impact of inflation is consistently negative in all six PC models, none of the effects are statistically significant (see, e.g., Table 5.1). The effects of unemployment are smaller in five of six cases, and likewise insignificant in all of them. Such results are consistent with our earlier observations that Canadians are much more prone to blame a government for bad or deteriorating economic conditions than to praise it for good or improving ones, and that after 1984 the national issue agenda changed as the economy improved. In the new economic climate the salience of inflation and unemployment, the "twin evils" which had bedeviled the Canadian economy since the early 1970s, receded, as did related issues concerning which areas of the country would bear the costs and reap the benefits of the escalation in world prices for oil and other natural resources that had occurred during that decade. In particular, the new PC government's decision to scrap the Liberals' contentious National Energy Programme both reflected and contributed to the changed focus of elite and public attention.

An improving economy thus created a vacuum in the issue agenda. This was filled by various noneconomic events and conditions including the several scandals and political embroglios that beset the new Conservative government. Our analyses reflect the changed focus of attention. Each of the four scandals considered (Tunagate, Blais-Grenier, Oerlikon, the resignation of the Speaker of the House of Commons), had large, permanent negative effects on PC popularity. Depending upon which specific model is analyzed, these four interventions are estimated to have jointly cost the Conservatives from slightly over 18% to in excess of 21% in public support (Table 5.1).

The effects of the government's policy initiatives were mixed, both in direction and significance. Most consistent was the Meech Lake Accord—in every model it had the anticipated permanent positive impact on PC support in Quebec and, in each case, the impact was large (between 7 and 8%). The proposal to de-index old-age pensions had the anticipated temporary negative effect in each model, but in only two instances did the estimate achieve statistical significance. Similarly, the free trade coefficient, although correctly signed, was small and insignificant.

Other political intervention variables in the PC models behaved as expected. Thus, the Liberal caucus revolt against party leader John Turner

Table 5.1. Pooled Cross-Sectional Time Series Analysis of Progressive Conservative, Liberal and NDP Support, February 1985 - November 1988

| Predictor Variables | PC Unemployment National | PC Unemployment Regional | Liberal Unemployment National | Liberal Unemployment Regional | NDP Unemployment National | NDP Unemployment Regional |
|---|---|---|---|---|---|---|
|  | b | b | b | b | b | b |
| Inflation rate | -1.08 | -1.32 | -2.81c | -3.09c | 3.90b | 4.49a |
| Unemployment rate (t-1) | 0.40 | -0.29 | 0.93 | -0.20 | -1.71 | 0.45 |
| Scandals: Tunagate | -5.19a | -5.02b | 3.03c | 3.07c | -2.77c | 2.59 |
| Blais-Grenier affair | -3.24a | -3.23a | 5.79a | 5.76a | -0.39 | -0.42 |
| Speaker resignation | -3.61a | -3.71a | 0.99 | 0.96 | 2.22c | 2.42c |
| Oerlikon affair | -6.26a | -6.15a | -0.02 | 0.05 | 5.79a | 5.51a |
| Pension de-indexation | -1.83 | -1.86 | -0.09 | -0.30 | 1.70 | 1.98 |
| Shamrock summit | 10.91a | 11.09a | -10.96a | -10.86a | -0.56 | -0.88 |
| Air Canada-West | -6.10c | -5.87 | -0.47 | -0.29 | 4.84 | 4.30 |
| Free Trade-Ontario | -0.95 | -0.92 | 1.41 | 1.36 | 0.95 | 0.86 |
| Meech Lake-Quebec | 7.65a | 7.66a | -7.74a | -7.81a | 2.92c | 2.93c |
| Liberal caucus revolt | 3.75a | 3.64a | -3.30a | -3.30a | -3.51a | -3.34a |
| 1988 election campaign | 2.55b | 2.57b | -3.85a | -3.80a | -0.39 | -0.45 |
| Region: Atlantic | 5.22a | 5.24a | -0.48 | -0.49 | -3.84a | -3.88a |
| Quebec | -4.96a | -4.92a | 8.91a | 8.94a | -6.26a | -6.33a |
| Prairies | 16.48a | 16.49a | -19.73a | -19.74a | 1.38 | 1.32 |
| British Columbia | -0.56 | -0.56 | -16.97a | -16.99a | 14.03a | 14.01a |
| Constant | 46.71a | 47.53a | 48.34a | 49.44 | 2.66 | 0.51 |
| Adjusted $R^2$ | .65 | .63 | .81 | .81 | .51 | .50 |

a $p \leq .01$
b $p \leq .05$
c $p \leq .10$; one-tailed tests

permanently bolstered PC fortunes by over three points in every model, and the 1988 election campaign kickoff increased Tory support by a slightly smaller amount. As for the government's decision to place the Air Canada maintenance shop in Montreal rather than Winnipeg, it temporarily decreased PC popularity in the Prairies by approximately 6%, this effect being significant in five of six models.

The regional dummy variables also had large effects in the Conservative models. In keeping with their historically high levels of support in the Prairie provinces, the dummy variable for this region carried an estimated coefficient of over 16 points. The effects of the other regional variables also were in accord with expectations, i.e., the Atlantic dummy was significant and positive, whereas that for Quebec was significant and negative.[7]

The analyses of support for the two opposition parties, the Liberals and the NDP, reveal that inflation consistently had a significant negative impact on Liberal support, whereas unemployment manifested a mixture of weak and oppositely signed effects (Table 5.1). In the one case where significance extended beyond the .10 level, the coefficient indicated that a 1% increase in unemployment was associated with a 2% increase in Liberal popularity. The NDP analyses are different—in all six models inflation had a significant positive impact, with the estimates indicating that a 1% rise in the consumer price index was associated with a 4% to 5% increase in NDP support. Although this might seem like a large effect, it should be recalled that inflation varied by only 1% across the 1985–88 period. As for unemployment, its impact was insignificant in every model but one, where a 1% increase in unemployment was associated with a 1.4% decrease in NDP support.

Political interventions were very much in evidence in the Liberal and NDP analyses, and, overall, the two opposition parties divided the popularity gains attendant upon government embarrassments. In the NDP case, the resignation of the speaker and the Oerlikon affair had significant positive effects ranging in magnitude from slightly over two to slightly under six points. Depending upon which specific model is being considered, these scandals provided the NDP with a boost in support ranging from 9.3% to 10.4%. The Liberals benefitted from the other two, with Tunagate raising party support by from 3% to 6%, and the Blais-Grenier affair doing so by approximately 6%. Overall, the two scandals provided the Liberals with popularity gains of between 9.8% and 13.7%.

The effects of other political interventions varied. The Liberals suffered predictable losses as a result of the revolt against leader John Turner and the Meech Lake Accord. The former cost the Liberals about three points across the country; the latter, seven to eight points in Quebec. Also as anticipated, Liberal support eroded when the 1988 election was called (by about 4%), and did so temporarily after the widely publicized Shamrock summit (by 6% to 11%). In contrast, the party did not benefit significantly from the free trade deal or the Air Canada announcement, and the expected positive influence of pension de-indexation was significant in only two instances, with the size of the impact being slightly over 3%.

The NDP generally was not much affected by most of these interventions, but the two cases in which effects were apparent deserve comment. First, the party gained about 3% in Quebec because of the Meech Lake Accord. Although one might anticipate that Meech Lake would hurt both opposition parties in Quebec, one of its most salient immediate results was to create conflict within the Liberal Party. Leader John Turner endorsed the pact but, as noted, other prominent Liberals sharply criticized it, arguing that the accord represented an explicit repudiation of the party's longstanding and hard-fought position on Quebec's place in confederation. The result was to erode Liberal support in that province, with a cohort of erstwhile Liberals moving to the NDP rather than the governing Tories.

The other intervention of note is the Liberal caucus revolt which had a negative impact on NDP popularity. As argued above, historically the NDP has been very much a "third force" in Canadian federal politics and, as such, it has not been considered a serious alternative to an incumbent government. NDP claims of a solid and progressively expanding partisan base are unfounded,[8] and it appears that much of the party's support in the interim between elections has come from those who wish to voice a protest against the status quo. When the public is reminded that an election is forthcoming, the party has tended to suffer a third-party squeeze, with at least some supporters moving to either the PCs or the Liberals, the two parties seen as having a realistic chance to form a government (Clarke, Stewart and Zuk, 1987). The timing of the Liberals' revolt against their leader and the rationale for it (he had to go because he could not lead the party to victory in the next election) served to remind NDP supporters that a federal election probably would be held within the next year and that hard choices soon would have to be made.

The hypothesis that the NDP suffered a squeeze in the period preceding the 1988 election may be tested directly by modeling the effect. Although the precise timing of the onset of the squeeze is uncertain, Canadian general elections typically are held at four-year intervals. Thus, when a parliament enters its fourth year, party activists typically begin to make preparations for the contest, and media speculation regarding it begins to build. Accordingly, we model the start of the NDP squeeze in September 1987—three years after the 1984 election. Consonant with the idea that the squeeze has a gradual, permanent impact on NDP support, the effect is modeled with a dynamic $\delta$ parameter. Other variables in the model are

Table 5.2. Pooled Cross-Sectional Time Series Analysis of Third-Party Squeeze Effect on NDP Support, February 1985-November 1988

| Predictor Variables | b |
|---|---|
| Inflation rate | 5.20a |
| Regional unemployment rate (t-1) | 0.42 |
| Scandals: Tunagate | 2.58 |
|     Blais-Grenier affair | -0.41 |
|     Speaker resignation | 2.35c |
|     Oerlikon affair | 5.30a |
| Pension de-indexation | 2.11 |
| Shamrock Summit | -0.63 |
| Air Canada - West | 4.08 |
| Free Trade - Ontario | 0.50 |
| Meech Lake - Quebec | 2.79c |
| Third-Party squeeze: impact | -2.36b |
|     dynamic effect ($\delta$) | 0.89b |
| Region: Atlantic | -3.99a |
|     Quebec | -6.38a |
|     Prairies | 1.21 |
|     British Columbia | 13.88a |
| Constant | -2.34 |
| Adjusted $R^2$ = | .48 |

a $p \leq .01$
b $p \leq .05$
c $p \leq .10$; one-tailed tests

the same as those described above, except that the Liberal caucus revolt and the 1988 campaign interventions are omitted, these being conceptualized as contributing to the more general squeeze effect. As previously, national and regional unemployment are modeled at 0, 1 and 2 lags.

The analyses are consistent with expectations. For example, a model using regional unemployment at a lag of one month shows that in September 1987, when the squeeze is hypothesized to have begun, NDP support dropped by over 2% (Table 5.2). The large and significant $\delta$ parameter (.89) associated with the effect indicates that it gradually increased in size as the election approached, and that over the next 14 months, the total impact exceeded 17%.[9] Other models yield very similar results. In the year preceding the election, then, the squeeze cost the NDP nearly half of the public support that it had enjoyed in August 1987.

Finally, as in the PC case, general regional differences in support are evident in the Liberal and NDP analyses. All of these regional effects accord well in magnitude and direction with the historic strengths and weaknesses of the two parties in the several regions. Thus, the Quebec coefficient in the Liberal models is consistently large (over 8%) and positive, whereas those for the Prairies and British Columbia are larger still (16 to 20%) and negative. The Atlantic and Quebec coefficients are negative (3-4% and 6-7%, respectively) in the NDP models, and that for British Columbia, large (13-14%) and positive.

### Region, Economy, Politics

The overall explanatory power of the party support models is impressive—the variance explained ranges from 58% to 63% for the PCs, from 81% to 83% for the Liberals, and from 46% to 52% for the NDP. However, the similarity in variance explained in the six models for each party, as well as the detailed results presented above, indicate that using regional rather than national unemployment rates does not improve our ability to account for party support. Moreover, the finding that the estimated effects of the economic variables frequently were insignificant and typically small, strongly suggests that politics rather than economics was the key to understanding the fortunes of Canada's three national parties between 1985 and 1988.

This inference is bolstered by results of analyses in which the independent variables in the models were entered in a stepwise fashion. In the first step, we entered the regional variables that proxy long-term forces on party support as well as regionally specific short-term forces not explicitly incorporated in our models. In the second step we entered the measures of inflation and unemployment, and in the third step, the several political interventions. The increment in variance explained at the second step clearly reveals the weakness of the economic variables. For example, in the PC analysis where regional unemployment is modeled with a two-month lag, the regional dummies accounted for 13% of the variance in Tory support. The explained variance increased marginally (to 17%) when the measures of inflation and unemployment were added but, when the political interventions were included, it climbed to fully 58% (Figure 5.5). The NDP pattern is very similar, with the percentages climbing from 20% to 24% to 46% as the regional, economic and political variables entered the analysis.

The Liberal results are different—regional effects are very large, accounting for 63% of the variance in party support in the case where regional unemployment is lagged two months. Entering the economic indicators increased the explanation by less than 1%, and including the political variables boosted it to 81% (Figure 5.5). Weak economic effects also are evident in the other Liberal analyses. The failure of the economy to aid Liberal fortunes between 1985 and 1988 is consistent with the proposition that the party was still suffering from the criticism that it had

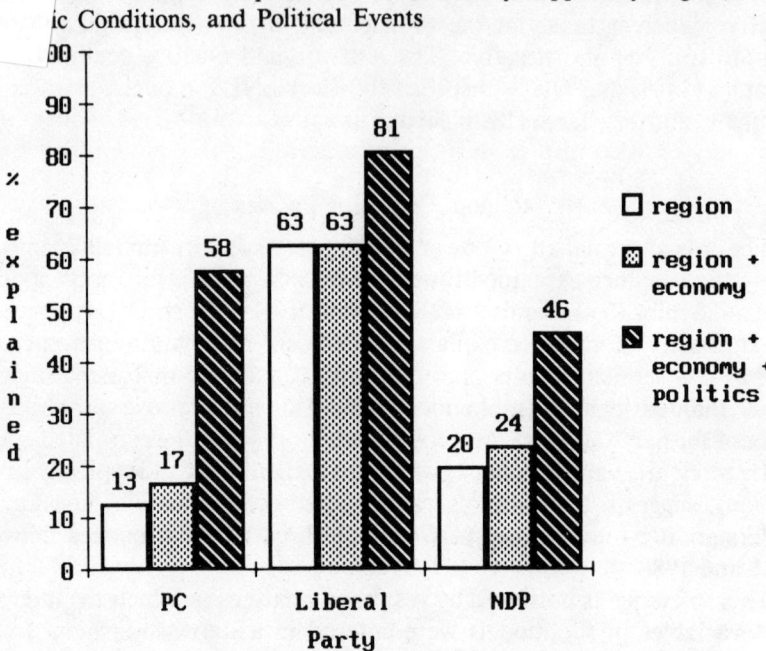

5.5 Variance Explained in Federal Party Support by Region, Economic Conditions, and Political Events

badly mismanaged the country's economic affairs during its long stint in power in the "stagflated" 1970s and early 1980s. This period had culminated in extraordinarily high rates of unemployment, which, in turn, had made jobs a key issue in the party's disastrous 1984 election campaign (Kornberg and Clarke, 1988). Undoubtedly, the party's managerial credibility regarding the economy and other aspects of national affairs was eroded further by the widely publicized intraparty divisions and policy disarray that characterized it in the aftermath of its 1984 electoral rout.

## Conclusion: The Politics (and Economics?) of Party Support

This chapter has investigated economic and political determinants of party support in Canada. Previous analyses of the impact of the economy on public feelings about Canadian parties have suggested that economic effects are weak and inconsistent over time (e.g., Clarke, Stewart and Zuk, 1987; Monroe and Erickson, 1986). However, Canada is a country in which there are important regional differences in macroeconomic conditions, and economic effects on political support may be stronger in models that utilize regional rather than national economic variables. The argument is plausible, but there is precious little empirical support for it. Pooled cross-sectional time series analyses for the 1985–88 period using regional measures of unemployment show that they had small effects on the popularity of the governing Progressive Conservatives and the opposition Liberals and New Democrats. The weakness of economic effects is not confined to *regional* unemployment; national-level measures of unemployment and inflation also fail to explain much variance in support for any of the parties.

The inability of the economic variables to account for party support stands in sharp contrast to the power of political interventions. Between 1984 and 1988 several scandals progressively and profoundly eroded the popularity of the new Tory government while bolstering the popularity of one or both of the opposition parties by large amounts. Other political interventions associated with Conservative policy initiatives also were influential—some of these operated across the country as a whole, whereas others did so within particular regions.

There also is evidence that a party's competitive position in an ongoing party system conditions its support. As in the run-up to the 1984 election, NDP popularity eroded sharply as the 1988 election approached. Like its minor-party counterparts in other countries, the New Democrats appear to suffer from a "legitimacy gap" that leads many potential supporters to conclude that a NDP ballot is essentially a wasted vote. Although disgruntled voters may "park their vote" with the NDP in the interims between elections, many of them are unwilling to actually cast a ballot for it. When reminded that an election is in the offing, these persons move on to the serious business of choosing between the two parties, the Liberals and the PCs, that are seen as having realistic chances of forming the next national government.

More generally, the present analyses of party support in mid- and late-1980s Canada testify to the importance of the *politics* rather than the *economics* of party support. It is possible, however, that national or regional economic effects might be greater in other periods. The plausibility of this conjecture is heightened when one recalls that in the period under consideration the Canadian economy was finally on an upswing after a "stagflated" decade characterized by bouts of high inflation, skyrocketing unemployment and sluggish growth. Between 1985 and 1988 things took a turn for the better—unemployment declined, albeit unevenly, in every region, and inflation, which had decreased during the recession of the early 1980s, remained modest. If the forces governing party support are shaped by the prevailing context of political debate, it is sensible that economic effects will be weak when renewed prosperity takes the economy "off the front page."

More general political cultural forces also are at work. Surveys show that an overwhelming majority of Canadians expect that government should play an active role in managing the country's economic affairs. Importantly, however, although Canadians readily attribute responsibility to government for economic conditions, the process is highly asymmetric—they are quick to blame governments when the national economy turns sour but slow to praise them when times are good. Similarly, they readily attribute responsibility to government when their personal economic circumstances are judged to be in decline, but are reluctant to do so when they think their lot is improving. Such lopsided responsibility attributions minimize the ability of good or improving economic conditions to influence party support.

There is mounting evidence that the Canadian case is not unique. The literature (see Chapter 1) is replete with diverse and conflicting findings concerning how the economy affects party support in various countries during different time periods. Although some have argued that these spatial and temporal discrepancies are a result of the methods and measures used, we believe that they have important substantive causes as well. Although many political events and conditions are theoretically intractable and unpredictable "one off" occurrences, this does not mean that their impact is inconsequential. On the contrary, their effects are readily discernible and often profound. Such results make good sense if one adopts a political debate model of party support which recognizes the extreme mutability of public attention to economic versus other issue concerns and the important roles parties and the mass media play in setting the agenda of political discourse.

Adoption of a political debate model is helpful, but by itself, inadequate. *Context* and *choice* are the other and, hitherto, often unrecognized pieces of the puzzle. Political debate shapes the set of short-term forces affecting party support, but it occurs in a context in which long-term political cultural forces affect public reactions to such forces. Also important are the choice sets provided to the electorate by varying party systems. Such contexts and choices vary between political systems and within them over time. These considerations suggest that the search for *stable* economic effects on party support will prove unsuccessful, and that context-sensitive models of the political economy of party support are inherently complex.

## Notes

1. These data were collected by Canadian Facts, Ltd. of Toronto, Ontario in a project commissioned by the authors. We wish to thank Mary Auvinen, Senior Project Director, Canadian Facts for her generous assistance with this project. Canadian Facts' monthly national "Monitor" survey (average N = approximately 1800) includes the questions, "Now, I would like to ask you a couple of political questions. If a federal election were held today, which party's candidate do you

think you would favor?" [If undecided or refused] "Well, are you leaning in any special direction? Which party do you favor right now?"

2. Subnational data on inflation is available for major cities only. The regional figures cited here are the averages for such cities in each region.

3. A national survey conducted prior to the 1988 election as part of the Political Support in Canada project (Kornberg and Clarke, 1992) revealed that 65% had heard of the Accord. Of those who had heard of it, 75% of Quebecers were in favor, as compared to 59% in the Atlantic region, 45% in Ontario, 43% in the Prairies, and 45% in British Columbia.

4. National data on the consumer price index and national and provincial unemployment data are published by Statistics Canada (various bulletins). For the Atlantic region regional unemployment rates are averages for the provinces of Newfoundland, Prince Edward Island, Nova Scotia and New Brunswick. For the Prairie region, these rates are averages for the provinces of Manitoba, Saskatchewan and Alberta. The unemployment figures for Quebec, Ontario and British Columbia are available directly from the Statistics Canada bulletins.

5. Combining cross-sectional and time series data into a pool typically creates situations where the assumptions of OLS regression are violated. Since the data set is created by "stacking" time series for two or more units (here regions), the equal variance (homoscedasticity) assumption is problematic. Also, because time series data for each unit are used, the assumption of uncorrelated disturbances is questionable. Depending upon the nature of the pooled data set, various estimation procedures may be employed. Here, GLS-ARMA is selected. As Stimson (1985:927) notes: "GLS-ARMA becomes relatively desirable when design is time dominant and when explanatory variables are dynamic. . . . Where there are significant between-unit effects, error will be nonstationary and GLS-ARMA inappropriate unless modified by the addition of dummy variables." Our data clearly are time dominant (with 46 time points for each of five regions), and GLS-ARMA procedures enable us to control for time series dependencies that otherwise would bedevil attempts to estimate the effects of inflation and unemployment on party support.

6. GLS-ARMA is an iterative model building, estimation and diagnosis technique. Preliminary OLS regressions of PC, Liberal and NDP support confirmed the anticipated unit heterogeneity. Models using regional unemployment lagged two months are illustrative. The variance of the residuals for PC support ranged from a low of 4.14 for Ontario to a high of 31.4 for the Prairies, and those for the Liberal and NDP support models from 8.50 to 36.51, and from 3.09 to 32.91, respectively. These diagnostics provide empirical evidence that regional dummies are required to control for heteroscedasticity. Inclusion of these terms in a second round of OLS regressions yielded regional ACFs as well as pooled ACFS and Durbin-Watson D's that indicated the need to control for serial correlation in the residuals. This was done on a unit-by-unit basis and, in all cases, the serial correlation was modeled as a first-order autoregressive process with the values of $\phi$ estimated using the residual ACFs for the regions.

7. This finding underscores the extent to which PC successes in Quebec in the 1984 and 1988 elections were products of short-term forces rather than partisan

realignment. On party identification in Quebec see Kornberg and Clarke (1992:ch. 5).

8. As noted, partisan instability is widespread in Canada. The Political Support in Canada panel surveys show that NDP party identifiers generally are somewhat more likely to switch their partisan attachments than are persons who identify with other parties. For example, surveys conducted immediately after the 1984 and 1988 federal elections show that 67% of those who identified with the NDP continued to do so in 1988. The comparable percentages for the Liberals and PCs are 73% and 75%, respectively. Also, the size of the cohort of NDP partisans in the electorate has grown only very slightly and irregularly—in 1965, 12% identified with the party; in 1988, 16% did so.

9. The total effect after n months is: $\Sigma_{i=0}^{n} b\delta^{i}$. An analysis of NDP support for the 1980–84 period produces similar estimates of the size of the squeeze effect. For that period the initial impact was slightly over 3% and the $\delta$ parameter was .79. See Clarke, Stewart and Zuk (1987:333).

# 6

# Campaign Context, Economic Evaluations, and Electoral Choice: The 1988 American Presidential Election

*The Bush organization simply seemed to realize something that Dukakis and his people never did: presidential campaigns are about choices. Candidates had to give voters reasons either to vote for them or against their opponents. The Dukakis campaign strategy had no plan to do either; Bush intended at least to give them something to vote against.*
—Abramson, Aldrich and Rohde (1990:44)

During the past two decades a growing emphasis on public evaluations of economic conditions as major determinants of electoral choice has transformed V.O. Key's once "perverse" argument that "voters are not fools" (Key, 1968:7) into prevailing scholarly wisdom. Many studies, however, have neglected to investigate how contextual factors condition the impact of national and personal economic circumstances on party support (see Chapter 5). This chapter considers the effects of economic evaluations on voting behavior in the 1988 American presidential election. It first develops a model of the structure of these evaluations that challenges standard conceptualizations of their dimensionality. It next argues that the influence of economic judgments on electoral choice reflects the mix of forces at work in specific campaign contexts. The 1988 campaign provides an important opportunity to assess this argument. Its failure to inform the electorate about alternative economic policy options or to stimulate public thinking about other important issues created a context which influenced how economic evaluations and various other short-and long-term factors affected voting decisions. The causal model we develop in this chapter illustrates this argument by unravelling the skein of forces that shaped presidential voting decisions in 1988.

## Contemporary Approaches to Economic Evaluations

Although studies of party support have stressed the effects of objective conditions, i.e., inflation rates and unemployment levels, the transmission of these effects through subjective evaluations means that the latter play important mediating roles in the political economy of electoral choice (see Chapter 3). Economic evaluations are typically conceptualized in multi-dimensional terms (for reviews, see Asher, 1983; Lewis-Beck, 1988a; for an emotional component, see Conover and Feldman, 1986). *Temporal* evaluations are retrospective, i.e., judgments about past conditions, or prospective, i.e., assessments of future developments in the economy (Conover, Feldman and Knight, 1986, 1987; Fiorina, 1978, 1981). Retrospective judgments involve processing of known "facts," whereas prospective assessments require possibly complex searches for uncertain information. Many individuals presumably avoid the demands of these searches by converting retrospective judgments into forecasts about the future. The process by which such forecasts is made is subject to debate (see Begg, 1982; Conover, Feldman and Knight, 1986, 1987; Mitchell, 1988; Sheffrin, 1983). Rational expectations theorists argue that people possess economic models that contain information which is regularly adjusted, error free, and reliably projected, at least in the aggregate. Two "backward-looking" processes (Begg, 1982:25) are extrapolation, i.e., straightforward projections from retrospective information to future developments, and adaption, i.e., the adjustment of projections for predictive errors reflecting unanticipated events. Recent evidence suggests that people's economic forecasts involve a quasi-adaptive process that discounts current information and relies on prior projections, personal conditions, and "politicized guesses" (Conover, Feldman and Knight, 1987). *Subject-referent* evaluations are egocentric, i.e., assessments of personal economic circumstances, or sociotropic, i.e., judgments of collective economic well-being (Kiewiet, 1983; Kinder and Kiewiet, 1979, 1981; Sears et al., 1980; for group-related evaluations and personal experiences, see Kinder, Adams and Gronke, 1989). Egocentric assessments rely on facts about one's personal economic condition, whereas sociotropic judgments rest more heavily on uncorroborated information that often is presented selectively by political strategists and the mass media (Chapter 3; see also Entman, 1989; Iyengar and Kinder, 1987; Weatherford, 1983c). Although some analysts have argued that the links between these two types of subject-referent evaluations are quite tenuous (Kinder, Adams and Gronke, 1989; Schlozman and Verba, 1979; Sniderman and Brody, 1977), some studies of information processing maintain that there is a substantial relationship between them. For example, economic information conveyed via interpersonal communication or media coverage can heighten individuals' awareness of sociotropic circumstances which, in turn, validates their assessments of personal conditions (Conover, Feldman and Knight, 1986; Kinder and Mebane, 1983; Mebane, 1988; Weatherford, 1983c).

## The Model of Economic Evaluations

To ascertain how voters actually think about national and personal economic circumstances, we initially analyze a baseline model which posits an undifferentiated structure of economic evaluations. We then consider two models which correspond to the prevailing conceptualizations of their dimensionality outlined above. The temporal model proposes two latent factors, i.e., retrospective and prospective judgments. The subject-referent alternative also has two latent factors, i.e., egocentric and sociotropic assessments. Most previous studies have explicitly or implicitly assumed that the indicators of these factors are weighted equally and are "parallel," i.e., they have equal true score and (zero) error variances (Joreskog and Sorbom, 1988:79). We believe that these assumptions are highly problematic and require rigorous testing. Moreover, we challenge these bidimensional conceptualizations of economic thinking and argue that the structure of economic evaluations consists of three dimensions. *Egocentric* evaluations contain relatively reliable information and consist of judgments about past, present and, possibly, future individual well-being. *Sociotropic retrospective* evaluations incorporate generally available information about the prior performance of the national economy. *Prospective* evaluations involve hypothetical information and considerable projection between expectations for the household economy and forecasts of the state of the national economy. This three-factor model is not developed *ab nihilo*. Rather, these dimensions of economic evaluation have been detected in earlier analyses of data from the 1980 and 1984 American national election surveys (Elliott and Zuk, 1989), as well as in analyses of data gathered in the 1983, 1988, and 1990 Canadian support studies (see Chapter 7; Clarke and Kornberg, 1989; Kornberg and Clarke, 1992).

The alternative models of the structure of economic evaluations are analyzed using the following questions from the 1988 American NES (N = 2,040):[1]

1. Would you say that you (and your family living here) are better off or worse off financially than you were a year ago? Is that much better off or somewhat better off [much worse off or somewhat worse off]?
2. Now looking ahead, do you think that a year from now you (and your family living here) will be better off financially, or worse off, or

just about the same as now? Is that much better off or somewhat better off [much worse off or somewhat worse off]?
3. Do you think that over the past year (your/your family's) income has gone up by more than the cost of living, has it fallen behind, or has it stayed about even with the cost of living? Has it gone up a lot more or a little more [fallen behind a lot or a little]?
4. Would you say that over the past year, the level of unemployment in the country has gotten better, stayed about the same, or gotten worse? Would you say much better or somewhat better [much worse or somewhat worse]?
5. Would you say that over the past year, inflation has gotten better, stayed about the same, or gotten worse? Would you say much better or somewhat better [much worse or somewhat worse]?
6. How about the economy, would you say that over the past year the nation's economy has gotten better, stayed about the same, or gotten worse? Would you say much better or somewhat better [much worse or somewhat worse]?
7. What about the next 12 months? Do you expect the national economy to get better, get worse, or stay about the same?

Regarding our three-factor model, we hypothesize that items 1–3, items 4–6, and items 2 and 7 load on the egocentric retrospective, sociotropic retrospective, and future factors, respectively (see Figure 6.1).

The dimensionality of economic evaluations is investigated using confirmatory factor analysis (CFA) as implemented by LISREL 7 (Joreskog and Sorbom, 1988). This technique provides goodness-of-fit tests for theoretically-specified models, estimates loadings of observed indicators on hypothesized factors, and computes interfactor correlations which are population parameter estimates (rather than arbitrary values as in obliquely rotated exploratory factor analysis). CFA also estimates measurement error variances in the indicators and correlations among these error variances (Bollen, 1989). The ability to model the error components in the indicators is useful for addressing arguments (e.g., Kramer, 1983) that substantial amounts of measurement error in individual-level survey data, such as the NES indicators, can generate problematic estimates of the effects of economic evaluations on party support. LISREL 7 offers a variety of estimation procedures, including weighted least-squares (WLS). WLS, unlike maximum likelihood and other methods, relaxes the unrealistic assumptions of interval-level measurement and multivariate normality, and therefore, is appropriate for survey data that involve dichotomous or ordinal measures and skewed distributions (Browne, 1984; Joreskog and Sorbom, 1988).

FIGURE 6.1  Measurement Model of Economic Evaluations, 1988

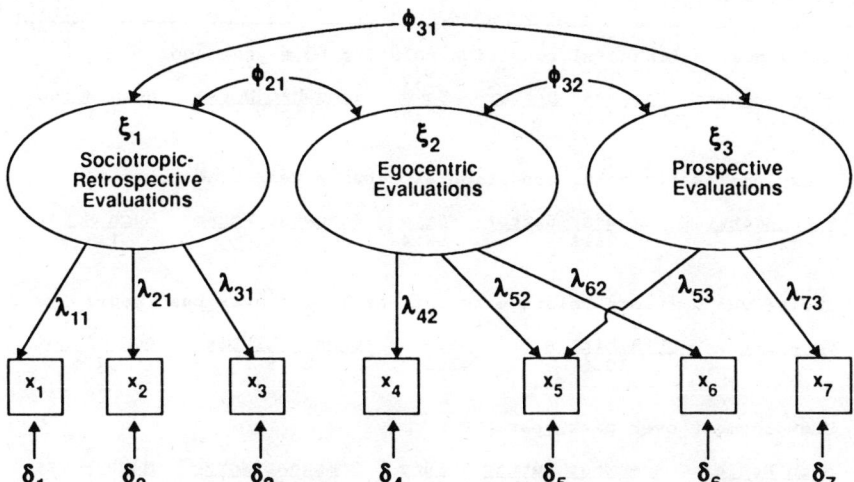

Note: $X_1$-unemployment over past year; $X_2$-inflation over past year; $X_3$-national economy over past year; $X_4$-personal financial condition relative to a year ago; $X_5$-personal financial condition expected a year from now; $X_6$-personal income relative to cost of living over past year; $X_7$-national economy over next 12 months

## The Distribution and Structure of Economic Evaluations

Table 6.1 shows that in 1988 many Americans believed that the national economy and their personal circumstances had remained the same in the year prior to the election and would do so for another year. Sizable numbers, however, thought that their financial condition had improved during the previous year (42.4% said much or somewhat better) and would continue to do so (37.9% stated their situations would get much or somewhat better in the year ahead). Evaluations of personal income in cost-of-living terms over the past year were less sanguine (37.3% said their income would go down a little or a lot). Regarding the national economy, although slightly over 40% reported that unemployment had gotten much or somewhat better, large minorities also believed that inflation and the national economy as a whole had become somewhat or much worse over the past year. More generally, approximately one-quarter expected an improvement, whereas 22% forecast a downturn in the national economy during the upcoming year. Thus, the overall pattern of economic evaluations in the run-up to the 1988 election was quite diverse—many voters saw little or no change in economic circumstances, whereas others judged that there had been an improvement or a decline in either personal situations or national conditions, or both.

Table 6.1. Responses to Economic Evaluation Questions, 1988 (in percent)

---

**Individual's financial condition relative to a year ago:**

| Much Better | Somewhat Better | Same | Somewhat Worse | Much Worse |
|---|---|---|---|---|
| 11.7 | 30.7 | 32.8 | 17.7 | 7.1 |

**Individual's financial condition expected a year from now:**

| Much Better | Somewhat Better | Same | Somewhat Worse | Much Worse |
|---|---|---|---|---|
| 12.1 | 25.8 | 53.4 | 6.8 | 1.9 |

**Individual's income relative to cost of living over past year:**

| Up A Lot | Up A Little | Same | Down A Little | Down A Lot |
|---|---|---|---|---|
| 6.8 | 10.6 | 45.3 | 22.5 | 14.8 |

**Unemployment over past year:**

| Much Better | Somewhat Better | Same | Somewhat Worse | Much Worse |
|---|---|---|---|---|
| 9.1 | 32.0 | 32.6 | 17.0 | 9.2 |

**Inflation over past year:**

| Much Better | Somewhat Better | Same | Somewhat Worse | Much Worse |
|---|---|---|---|---|
| 2.1 | 8.9 | 44.7 | 31.9 | 12.4 |

**National economy over past year:**

| Much Better | Somewhat Better | Same | Somewhat Worse | Much Worse |
|---|---|---|---|---|
| 2.5 | 16.4 | 50.0 | 21.9 | 9.3 |

**National Economy Over Next 12 Months:**

| Get Better | Stay Same | Get Worse |
|---|---|---|
| 23.2 | 54.8 | 22.0 |

---

Note: horizontal percentages; N's for response distributions vary from 1883 to 2022, missing data removed.

An initial CFA analysis using data from a random half-sample of the 1988 NES respondents shows that the model postulating that all items load on one factor has a poor fit ($\chi^2_{14} = 169.20$, $p = .000$).[2] Analyses of the two-factor models reveal that the retrospective-prospective model also performs poorly ($\chi^2_{13} = 155.62$, $p = .000$), but the egocentric-sociotropic alternative does considerably better ($\chi^2_{13} = 36.87$, $p = .000$). LISREL modification indices (Joreskog and Sorbom, 1988:44–46) for the latter model suggest that further improvements in fit could be achieved by stipulating a more complex model of economic evaluations and correlating error terms for selected indicators. The former approach accords with our

Table 6.2. Confirmatory Factor Analysis of Economic Performance Evaluations, Entire Sample, 1988

| | Factor Matrix ($\lambda$) | | |
|---|---|---|---|
| | Sociotropic-Retrospective | Egocentric | Prospective |
| Unemployment over past year | .65 | .00 | .00 |
| Inflation over past year | .67 | .00 | .00 |
| National economy over past year | .70 | .00 | .00 |
| Individual's financial condition relative to a year ago | .00 | .78 | .00 |
| Individual's financial condition expected a year from now | .00 | .29 | .24 |
| Individual's income relative to cost of living over past year | .00 | .72 | .00 |
| National economy over next 12 months | .00 | .00 | .83 |

$\chi^2_{10}$ = 12.07, p = .281, AGFI = .996, N = 1729

| | Inter-Factor Correlations ($\phi$) | | |
|---|---|---|---|
| | Sociotropic-Retrospective | Egocentric | Prospective |
| Sociotropic-Retrospective | 1.00 | | |
| Egocentric | .53 | 1.00 | |
| Prospective | .36 | .13 | 1.00 |

Note: Coefficients are WLS estimates; all estimates p $\leq$ .05, one-tailed test, except error variance of "national economy over next 12 months" item.

theoretical expectations concerning the dimensionality of economic evaluations.

We therefore proceed to test our three-factor model. The analysis demonstrates that it fits the data for the first random half-sample extremely well ($\chi^2_{10}$ = 7.13, p = .713). An additional test using data from the second random half-sample further illustrates its applicability ($\chi^2_{10}$ = 11.28, p = .336). Given these results, parameter estimates are obtained using data for the entire sample (see Table 6.2). The three-factor model again has an excellent fit ($\chi^2_{10}$ = 12.07, p = .281). Moreover, all indicators have expected loadings on the three factors and, with one minor exception, all factor loadings ($\lambda$'s), error terms ($\delta$'s) and interfactor correlations ($\phi$'s) are statistically significant (p < .05). Moreover, the three-factor model explains substantial amounts of the variance in all indicators (except individual's financial condition a year from now), and various diagnostic statistics have acceptable values.[3] Accordingly, the multivariate model of presidential voting incorporates this tridimensional structure of economic evaluations.

## Recent Controversies over Economic Voting

Many previous studies have suggested that costly searches for unreliable information depreciate the role of prospective assessments, whereas known facts about past economic performance enhance the use of retrospective judgments in electoral choice (e.g., Fiorina, 1978, 1981; Kiewiet and Rivers, 1984). As noted in Chapter 1, such retrospective voting accords well with the dominant "Keysian" reward-punishment model which posits that an incumbent, regardless of his/her partisanship or other political attributes, is rewarded for a good economic performance and punished for a bad one (Butler and Stokes, 1976; Downs, 1957; Key, 1968; Monroe, 1979a, 1984; Page, 1978). Other analysts, however, have argued that voters are not as naive as the reward-punishment model assumes. Rather, they have knowledge about economic processes which leads them to discount past performance and emphasize future expectations about the state of the economy should incumbent or opposition candidates be elected (e.g., Alt, 1991; Chappell and Keech, 1985; Kuklinski and West, 1981; Lewis-Beck, 1988a). These prospective influences are consistent with policy-voting and issue-priority models of how the economy affects voting decisions. These models hypothesize that voters believe that the economy will perform differently depending upon which party holds office (Budge and Farlie, 1983:ch. 2; Kiewiet, 1983:ch. 2). Thus, for example, individuals who believe that the Republicans are better equipped to deal with inflation would choose this party, whereas Democratic support would come from those who think that this party is more inclined to remedy unemployment. A further possibility, that voters focus on the past performance of the incumbent and the future-oriented policies of a challenger (e.g., Miller and Wattenberg, 1985), suggests that both the reward-punishment and policy voting/issue priority models may capture some aspects of the reality of how economic evaluations affect electoral choice.

Empirically, studies of American voting behavior have reported that sociotropic economic evaluations have much stronger effects on party support than do egocentric evaluations (e.g., Kiewiet, 1983; Kinder, Adams and Gronke, 1989; Kinder and Kiewiet, 1979, 1981). One explanation for the prevalence of "sociotropic voting" is that American culture promotes the belief that personal initiatives and idiosyncratic life chances largely determine the condition of one's pocketbook, whereas government actions influence economic circumstances in the country as a whole (Abramowitz, Lanoue and Ramesh, 1988; Feldman, 1982; Feldman and Conley, 1991; McClosky and Zaller, 1984; Schlozman and Verba, 1979). Three challenges to the phenomenon of sociotropic voting, however, have emerged. First, as argued in Chapter 1, such voting subordinates self-interest to collective concerns and, thus, is "irrational." Second, some studies have found that prospective egocentric evaluations do influence voting decisions (e.g., Lewis-Beck, 1985; Whiteley, 1991). Third, from a methodological viewpoint, some analysts (e.g., Kramer, 1983) have argued that cross-sectional survey data are inappropriate for analyzing how economic conditions affect political choice since they cannot fathom the relationship between changing personal circumstances and varying macroeconomic conditions attributable to the government's policies.

A fourth consideration is also relevant. This is that assumptions about government's responsibility for the economy and observable differences in parties' concerns with various economic issues interact to determine how economic conditions affect party support by creating *mediated* perceptions of a government's economic performance (e.g., Alt, 1979, 1991; Miller, 1989, Peffley, 1984; Stigler, 1973). Moreover, since mediated perceptions contain politically relevant information, they should have stronger and more proximate influences on electoral decisions than do simple, unmediated perceptions involving straightforward judgments about the economy (Abramowitz, Lanoue and Ramesh, 1988; Alt, 1991; Butler and Stokes, 1976; Fiorina, 1981).

## A Contextual Model of Presidential Voting

Proper estimates of the determinants of presidential voting require a model of information processing that specifies economic evaluations and other forces operating in varying electoral contexts. Recent theoretical work suggests that decision-making processes begin with individuals' rules that determine their search for the attributes of competing options. This search is followed by an evaluation that compares positive and negative aspects of these attributes. The evaluation is adjusted to compensate for other qualities and then leads to the choice of one option. A suboptimal choice, however, results from a context that generates uncertain information about some attributes (for a review, see Plott, 1990:179-82). An example of such a context is an election campaign in which political debate does little to inform people's thinking about viable alternatives on economic issues or other concerns, and thereby exacerbates the difficulty involved in making decisions about party choices (see Alt, 1979; Miller, 1989).

*The 1988 Campaign:* Public opinion polls conducted during the 1988 presidential campaign revealed considerable volatility in candidate preferences. Although Governor Dukakis ran well very early in the campaign, Vice-President Bush soon overtook his Democratic rival, and Bush's lead in the polls grew after the candidates' debate on October 13. The race remained in some doubt, however, because a sizable number of voters remained undecided until the campaign was in its final stages (Abramson,

Aldrich and Rohde, 1990:ch. 2; Farah and Klein, 1989). Such volatility and ambivalence in candidate preferences suggest the importance of short-term, campaign-specific forces on presidential voting.

The Republican candidate launched a campaign which emphasized the economic achievements of the previous (Reagan) administration. Although Reagan's second term had been marred by the October 1987 stock-market crash, there had been good economic news as well. Unemployment had been on a modest downward curve for much of the period, while inflation hovered at 3–4% throughout 1985 before falling modestly in 1986, increasing slightly in early 1987 (to 4.5%), and then decreasing again to just over 4%. The Bush campaign reinforced its economic message by inviting the electorate to "read the vice president's lips" when he pledged "no new taxes." His campaign had noneconomic aspects as well. To provoke ideological reactions, Bush characterized his Democratic rival, Michael Dukakis, as another Northeastern liberal whose patriotism was problematic (the Pledge of Allegiance controversy) and soft on crime (i.e., the "Willie Horton" affair). The Democratic candidate also was portrayed as lacking governmental experience, particularly in the area of foreign affairs.

Dukakis attempted to counter the Republican offensive by seizing on lingering uneasiness about the stock-market crash and the mounting budget deficit. He also tried to tarnish Bush's image by raising questions about the Republican's involvement in wrong-headed policies such as the Iran-Contra scandal, and his removal from Reagan's inner circle. Bush's judgment also was called into question for selecting the inexperienced Dan Quayle as his running-mate. At the same time, however, the Democratic campaign was marked by considerable uncertainty about how best to portray the party's candidate in a positive light. For example, Dukakis' positions on government assistance to disadvantaged Americans did little to offset his image as being simultaneously a liberal Democrat and an indifferent person. Similarly, his attempts to show he was not "soft" on national defense were less than convincing and, in one case, (the "photo opportunity" showing a grinning Dukakis piloting an Abrams tank), they verged on the bizarre.

Overall, the campaign was characterized by little genuine discussion of pressing economic issues and, as it wore on, the parties subjected the electorate to a mounting barrage of negative advertising concerning the qualities of the rival candidate. The general absence of informed debate and the pervasive negativism led many observers to conclude that the 1988 contest represented a new "low" in presidential campaigns (Abramson, Aldrich and Rohde, 1990:ch. 2).

***Campaign-Related Effects:*** The context of the campaign, then, was one that should have had significant effects on how economic evaluations, mediated perceptions of economic issues,[4] and other factors involving party identification[5] and candidate feelings[6] affected voting decisions.[7] More specifically, the vacuous nature of the campaign should have encouraged voters to employ decision rules which obviate the necessity of making costly searches for scarce and possibly ambiguous information. In this regard, the campaign's lack of much concrete future-oriented discussion should have generated uncertainty and thereby compelled reliance on retrospective judgments and mediated perceptions of candidate/party performance. Thus, people who held positive views of the evolution of personal and national economic conditions, and those who judged that the Republicans had demonstrated that they were best able to remedy economic problems, should have been disposed to vote for Bush rather than Dukakis.

Relatedly, since the campaign generated little light on important issues and more heat over candidates' characteristics, we expect that many voters relied on "preexisting" attitudes involving partisan cues or generalized perceptions of the candidates. Regarding the former, party identification traditionally has been conceptualized as a long-term affective orientation with two components—direction and strength (e.g., Campbell et al., 1960:121–28). Alternative rational-choice perspectives have described party identification as an evaluative attitude, i.e., a "running tally" of parties' past performances (Fiorina, 1981:89–91), that is susceptible to short-term change as information updating occurs. The empirical evidence of much greater variation in the strength rather than the direction of party identification, and the often demonstrated influence of partisan attachments on other political attitudes and electoral choice (Campbell et al., 1960; Lewis-Beck, 1988a:119–20; Markus and Converse, 1979; Whiteley, 1988b), lead us to specify a model of the vote in which the directional component of party identification is an exogenous variable that exerts a direct effect on electoral choice and other factors that influence that choice.

Conventional wisdom also has portrayed candidate images as inchoate attitudes and short-term bases of party support (see the review in Asher, 1983). Contrariwise, however, some analysts contend that people's evaluations of the (in)adequacy of particular candidates for public office may be based on general standards that are relatively enduring and evoked by political beliefs, the longevity of some politicians, and campaign-related factors (Conover and Feldman, 1989; Marcus, 1988; Miller, Wattenberg and Malanchuk, 1986). Such factors, in conjunction with media coverage and party strategies, prompt voters to see candidates as personal embodiments of issues and parties. Thus, our model specifies people's feelings about the candidates are proximate influences on vote choice (Asher, 1983:360–63, 375; Markus and Converse, 1979; Page and Jones, 1979).

In addition to direct effects, the model posits a stream of indirect influences among the independent variables. We hypothesize a linkage between party identification and egocentric evaluations such that Republican identifiers should have more positive judgments of their economic circumstances than non-Republicans. Party identification also should affect sociotropic-retrospective evaluations, mediated perceptions of economic issues, and feelings about the candidates. Thus, Republican identifiers should express more favorable views of the past performance of the national economy, the party's ability to handle important economic problems, and the party's candidate than do non-Republicans.

We further expect that retrospective-egocentric evaluations affect other factors in the model and thereby have indirect effects on presidential voting (see Markus, 1988). Our argument is that since many people have better access to reliable information about personal circumstances than national or future ones, retrospective-egocentric evaluations guide sociotropic and prospective judgments (see Abramowitz, Lanoue and Ramesh, 1988; Conover, Feldman and Knight, 1986, 1987; Weatherford, 1983c). In turn, since there is more information about the prior performance of the economy rather than future economic developments, sociotropic-retrospective evaluations should shape future expectations. All three types of evaluations, albeit prospective ones to a lesser extent, should inform perceptions of the parties' abilities to address salient economic problems. Finally, economic evaluations, coupled with mediated perceptions, should influence feelings about the candidates. Thus, individuals who make positive judgments about their economic circumstances or the past performance of the national economy, or who perceive that the Republicans are better able to deal with economic problems, should hold Bush in higher regard than do those who do not share such sanguine views of economic conditions and doubt the Republicans' ability to address important economic issues.

## Economic Evaluations and Presidential Voting in 1988

Our model of the determinants of presidential voting in 1988 is assessed using covariance structure analysis (Joreskog and Sorbom, 1988). The analysis yields simultaneous estimates of both measurement and structural parameters in the model, goodness-of-fit tests for the model as a whole, and significance tests for various parameters (Bollen, 1989:ch. 8; Hayduk, 1987; Long, 1983b). An initial analysis reveals that the model has an excellent fit ($\chi^2_{27} = 36.75$, $p = .100$),[8] and the several estimated effects are consistent with expectations (data not shown in tabular form). In particular, party identification affected sociotropic retrospective evaluations, mediated perceptions of economic issues, and relative feelings about the

FIGURE 6.2  Structural Model of Presidential Vote, 1988

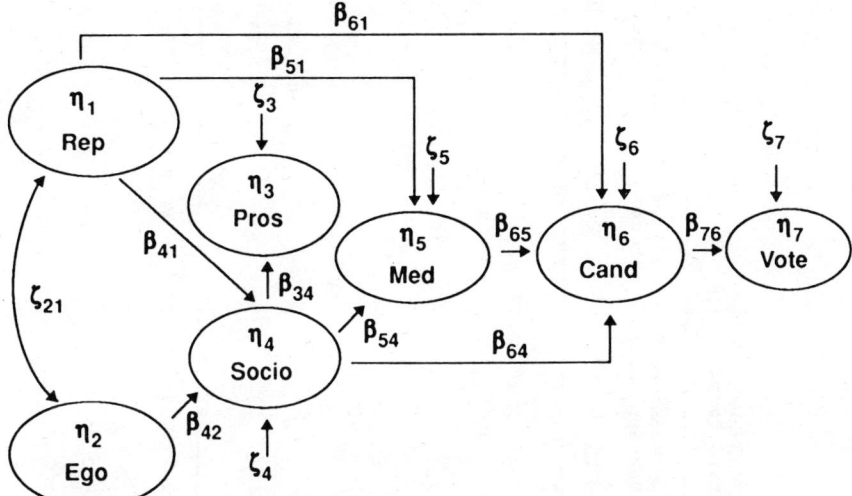

Note: Rep-Republican party identification; Ego-egocentric economic evaluations; Socio-sociotropic-retrospective evaluations; Med-mediated economic issue perceptions; Cand-relative candidate affect; Vote-presidential vote

candidates. Egocentric evaluations shaped sociotropic retrospective ones. People's judgments of the past performance of the national economy influenced prospective economic assessments, mediated perceptions, and candidate feelings. As expected, future expectations did not influence mediated perceptions or feelings about the candidates. Also as anticipated, mediated perceptions influenced voters' feelings about the candidates. However, partisanship and all types of economic judgments had insignificant direct effects on presidential voting, whereas the impact of candidate affect was strong and significant. This is not to say that the effects of partisan attachments were trivial; rather they were large, but indirect. Egocentric evaluations, sociotropic-retrospective judgments, and mediated perceptions also had significant indirect impacts on voting decisions.

We next reestimate the model using only the significant predictors. In keeping with the results described above, this model posits that party identification, egocentric evaluations, sociotropic-retrospective assessments, and mediated perceptions all had indirect influences on the vote, whereas candidate affect had the only direct effect (see Figure 6.2). The analysis shows that the revised model fits the data very well ($\chi^2_{37} = 41.66$, $p = .275$) and accounts for 82% and 96% of the variance in candidate affect and presidential choice, respectively (see Table 6.3). As expected, Republican identifiers had more positive sociotropic retrospective evalu-

Table 6.3. Covariance Structure Analysis of Presidential Vote, Entire Sample, 1988

| Predictors | Sociotropic-Retrospective | | | Prospective | | | Mediated Economic Issue Perceptions | | | Candidate Affect | | | Presidential Vote | | |
|---|---|---|---|---|---|---|---|---|---|---|---|---|---|---|---|
| | UD | SD | IND | UD | SD | IND | UD | SD | IND | UD | SD | IND | UD | SD | IND |
| Republican party identification | .32 | .49 | | | | .13 | .44 | .44 | .10 | .55 | .56 | .25 | | | .81 |
| Egocentric | .29 | .38 | | | | .12 | | | .09 | | | .10 | | | .10 |
| Sociotropic-retrospective | | | .41 | .40 | | | .31 | .20 | | .24 | .16 | .10 | | | .34 |
| Prospective | | | | | | | | | | | | | | | |
| Mediated economic issue perceptions | | | | | | | | | | .33 | .33 | | | | .33 |
| Candidate affect | | | | | | | | .35 | | | .82 | | 1.00 | .98 | .96 |

$R^2$ = .49 .16
$\chi^2_{37}$ = 41.66, $p$ = .275, AGFI = .997, N = 1035

Note: UD is unstandardized direct effect; SD is standardized effect; IND is indirect effect; coefficients are WLS estimates; all estimates $p \leq .05$, one-tailed test.

ations, were more inclined to see the Republicans as capable of addressing important economic issues, and felt more positively about Bush than did non-Republicans. Partisanship had indirect effects on prospective evaluations, mediated perceptions, candidate affect, and presidential voting, and assessments of personal economic circumstances influenced judgments regarding the past performance of the national economy. Personal economic assessments were relevant in other ways as well—they had indirect effects on future expectations, issue perceptions, candidate feelings, and vote choice. Judgments about the past performance of the national economy grounded evaluations of future circumstances, parties' ability to remedy economic problems, and relative feelings about presidential candidates. Thus, persons who made positive judgments about past national conditions were likely to be more favorable about the future and to believe that the Republicans were best able to address important problems. Sociotropic retrospective judgments also had positive indirect effects on candidate affect and presidential voting, and prospective evaluations again failed to exert either direct or indirect effects. Mediated perceptions had a direct impact on candidate feelings and an indirect one on voting decisions. Overall, the largest influences on the presidential vote were the direct impact of candidate affect and the several indirect effects associated with party identification.

## Conclusion

This chapter has developed a model of economic evaluations based on general assumptions about the availability and the processing of economic information. Many individuals should possess adequate knowledge of personal circumstances and, accordingly, these egocentric judgments should constitute a distinct dimension of economic evaluation. The relative lack of access to reliable national-level economic information should focus people's assessments on prior developments in the national economy, thus giving rise to a retrospective sociotropic economic evaluation factor. Ambiguous and imprecise information about the future of personal and national economic conditions should encourage the formation of global prospective assessments as a third dimension of economic evaluations. Confirmatory factor analyses reveal that, in fact, these three dimensions did define the structure of economic thinking in the American electorate in 1988. This structure is very similar to that identified in studies of American voters conducted during the 1980 and 1984 presidential elections. It also is similar to that manifested by Canadian voters in studies carried out at various times over the past decade.

Recent analyses of decision-making processes and political debates in campaign contexts have important implications for understanding how economic evaluations affect electoral choice. The failure of the 1988 presidential candidates to address public concerns, notably the future of the economy, and their propensity to engage in destructive criticisms of each other during the campaign, should have discouraged prospective thinking, and encouraged reliance on egocentric and sociotropic retrospective evaluations as well as preexisting attitudes, most notably, party identification, and generalized perceptions of the candidates, when making their voting decisions.

A covariance structure analysis of a model based on these expectations reveals that people's feelings about the candidates had the only direct impact on presidential voting. Party identification, egocentric and sociotropic retrospective evaluations, and perceptions of parties' abilities to remedy economic problems had indirect effects. In keeping with the nature of the 1988 campaign, prospective judgments had no influence on electoral choice.

Our emphasis on the importance of the campaign context for conditioning the impact of economic (and other) factors on voting behavior is consistent with the results of other recent research. Particularly relevant are analyses of voting in the 1988 Canadian national election and support for the governing Conservatives since that time (Chapter 7; see also Clarke and Kornberg, 1992). Unlike the 1988 American contest, the 1988 Canadian campaign witnessed future-oriented debates between party leaders over the merits of a proposed free trade agreement between Canada and the United States. John Turner, the leader of the opposition Liberal Party, forecast that the free trade pact would adversely affect the economy and important social welfare programs, and argued that the agreement posed a grave threat to Canada's culture and political sovereignty. Conservative Prime Minister, Brian Mulroney, in sharp contrast, dismissed charges about the agreement's social and political consequences, and predicted that it would produce major benefits for Canadian businesses and consumers in the years ahead. Voters' evaluations of personal and national economic conditions influenced their judgments about free trade, and both evaluations, coupled with prospective economic assessments and attitudes toward the agreement, had significant effects on their electoral decisions. Future-oriented economic evaluations have continued to influence party support in Canada in the post-1988 period, as voters and parties have renewed debate concerning how free trade and other clearly articulated and highly salient government economic policy initiatives will affect the country.

Taken together, the U.S. and Canadian analyses have several implications for comprehending how campaigns affect voters' use of information when making political support decisions. Citizens' response to candidates' failure to provide useful information about issues during a campaign fosters reliance on a variety of cues that compensate for this failure. Such cues may consist of previously established attitudes such as party identification that may be grounded in both "rational-action" elements and social-psychological referents. This combination challenges the credibility of theoretical arguments that present simple "either-or" explanations of the nature of voting decisions. From a methodological perspective, the dynamic properties of election campaigns recommend that future research should employ survey designs capable of capturing individual-level changes in various determinants of electoral choice.

Ultimately, election campaigns are important because they affect the quality of voters' choices and the quality of information that those choices impart to elected officials. A vacuous campaign such as that which occurred in the United States in 1988 provides voters with little real opportunity for either the exercise of informed reward-punishment decisions or policy voting. Such campaigns thereby inhibit the ability of both the electorate and the government to act responsibly. The electorate is hindered because information needed to make rational choices based on the past and likely future performance of rival candidates and their parties is in short supply. For its part, a newly elected government is given precious little information about voters' policy preferences and, as a result, policy mandates cannot be enacted because they are necessarily absent. In sharp contrast, a campaign of sophisticated dialogue, rather than sophist debate, provides a context that enhances the role of elections as institutions of governance in a representative democracy.

## Notes

1. The data from the 1988 American National Election Study (NES) (preelection and postelection waves) were collected by Warren Miller and associates and provided by the Inter-University Consortium for Political and Social Research. The principal investigators and the ICPSR are not responsible for the analyses and the interpretations of the data presented here.

2. In such goodness-of-fit tests, large $\chi^2$ values indicate a bad fit and small $\chi^2$ values, a good fit (Joreskog and Sorbom, 1988:42).

3. The 1988 NES included other questions about economic attitudes. Additional analyses show that the fit of our model employing nine (excluding mediated) indicators is somewhat worse ($\chi^2_{19} = 36.75$, p= .009) and its fit using fourteen (including mediated) items is substantially worse ($\chi^2_{64} = 279.33$, p = .000) than the results of the analysis with seven measures. LISREL diagnostics suggest that further improvements would require unacceptable item loadings and multiple correlated errors in both additional analyses. The nine indicators include the seven measures used in our original analysis and two unmediated variables, i.e., unemployment and inflation relative to 1980. The fourteen items include the above nine and five mediated variables. The latter include four items measuring percep-

tions of the impact of the federal government's economic policies and the Reagan administration's economic program on one's personal financial situation and the national economy, and a fifth item regarding Reagan's handling of the economy.

4. These perceptions are based on responses to two questions: (a) "Of those [most important problems] you've mentioned, what would you say is the single most important problem the country faces?" (b) "Which political party do you think would be most likely to get the government to do a better job in dealing with this problem—the Republicans, the Democrats, or wouldn't there be much difference between them?" The response categories are scored: mentioned an economic issue as most important and stated that the Republicans are best able to handle it = +1; cited an economic problem and stated the Democrats are best able to handle it = -1; stated other or no problems, or perceived no party differences in the ability to handle the problem = 0.

5. Partisan direction is based on the summary party identification measure, with strong or weak Republicans coded 1 and independents, Democrats, and others scored 0.

6. Candidate affect involves respondents' feelings about Bush and Dukakis on 0–100 thermometers. Greater-than-50 scores, a 50 score, and less-than-50 scores indicate, respectively, increasing warmth, neutrality, and increasing coolness towards a candidate. The response categories are: Bush ranked higher than Dukakis = +1; Dukakis rated higher than Bush = -1; and both candidates ranked the same = 0.

7. Presidential vote is scored: Bush voters = 1, and Dukakis voters = 0. Nonvoters are excluded from the analysis.

8. To avoid scale indeterminacy (Long, 1983a:49–52), the loading ($\lambda$) of one indicator of each economic evaluation factor is fixed at 1.0 (egocentric: individual's financial condition relative to a year ago; sociotropic retrospective: national economy over past year; prospective: national economy over next 12 months). Party identification, mediated perceptions, candidate affect and presidential voting are measured using single indicators. In these cases, factor loadings ($\lambda$) are set at 1.0 and error variances ($\varepsilon$) are fixed at non-zero values since each indicator presumably contains some error (see Hayduk, 1987:119–20). Specifically, the error variances specified are: (.202–3% estimate) for Republican partisanship; .0081 (.162–5%) for mediated perceptions; .0246 (.820–3%) for candidate affect, and .00249 (.249–1%) for presidential voting. The 1% estimate for the latter reflects the 1% difference between reported vote shares in the NES and actual vote totals (Bush: 53%–54%; Dukakis: 47%–46%).

# 7

## "It's Their Fault!" The Economics and Politics of Governing Party Support in Canada Since 1988

*If popularity it is, I can guarantee you that I will have my government in first place in the public opinion polls on the first of July: guarantee an income for every fishing village in Canada, cancel the GST, scrap the Meech Lake accord, restore all the subsidies for everything from CBC to Via Rail.*
—Prime Minister Brian Mulroney, *Newscan,* March 9, 1990, p. 2

*The Conservatives have adopted an agenda that the public does not like, that it can't understand, for which it has seen no payoff and against which it rails every day.*
—Jeffrey Simpson, *The Globe and Mail,* November 6, 1990

In democracies, party governments come and go. At least democratic theory holds that they are supposed to come and go, with free, competitive elections the mechanism for achieving peaceful transfers of power. In Canada, party governments at both the federal and provincial level often have had a history of delaying their departure—so much so that, in some cases, whole generations have grown up knowing only one party government as "their government." Research on Canadian voting behavior tells us, however, that the seeming stability of party fortunes is often more apparent than real. As noted in Chapter 5, many Canadians lack durable partisan attachments, and governing parties must work to rebuild their coalitions in successive elections. When they are unsuccessful in doing so, it is usually the result of a combination of short-term forces such as public disaffection from the leader of a governing party, the presence of an attractive opposition party leader, or widespread feelings that the govern-

---

This chapter is coauthored by Allan Kornberg, Department of Political Science, Duke University.

ment has failed to deal adequately with one or more highly salient issues associated with pressing economic or social problems (Clarke et al., 1979; 1991).

These forces certainly seem to be operative currently in Canadian politics. How else can one explain the rapid and precipitous decline in the fortunes of Prime Minister Mulroney and his government since their victory in the dramatic November 1988 election? CIPO (Gallup) poll data show that one month after the contest 49% of the Canadian electorate supported the PCs, but a year later only 26% did so. By the spring of 1990 the party's popularity had deteriorated to 16%, and some cynical commentators noted that if the free fall was not arrested, Tory support would soon be exceeded by the prime interest rate! National survey data from the Political Support in Canada project tell the same story—interviews conducted immediately after the 1988 election showed that Canadians gave Mr. Mulroney an average score of 50, and his party 54, on a 100-point thermometer scale. Moreover, 39% of the electorate identified themselves as Progressive Conservatives, only 1% less than immediately after the "Tory tide" had swept the PCs into power in September 1984. By December 1990, however, Mulroney's thermometer score had declined to 28 and his party's to 35, and the percentage of Canadians willing to accept a Conservative party label had declined to 24%—8% less than that for the Liberals and only 1% more than that for the New Democrats.

Observers have attributed the massive erosion in Conservative support to the failure of the Meech Lake Accord and the constitutional crisis this precipitated, the government's insistence on pushing forward with a policy that was demonstratively unpopular, the General Goods and Services Tax (GST), and the decline in public support for the free trade agreement (FTA), *the* issue in the 1988 election. In this chapter we will argue that although these explanations have merit, a more important factor is that after 1988 many Canadians came to believe that the economy was in poor health, that it was not being managed properly by government, and that both their own and the nation's current and future prospects left much to be desired. In turn, these evaluations had major negative effects on support for the governing Conservatives, net of public attitudes toward free trade and the GST. Indeed, the latter attitudes, in part, were products of the public's changed economic evaluations. In sum, we will argue that one of the principal reasons Canadians were so negative toward the GST and became increasingly so toward free trade was their skepticism about the economy and the government's ability to manage it effectively. Our analyses are based on data gathered in national cross-sectional and panel surveys conducted in 1983, 1987, immediately before and after the 1988 federal election, and in 1990.[1]

Table 7.1. Evaluations of the National Economy and Government Impact, 1983-1990 (in percent)

|  |  | 1983 | 1987 | 1988 | 1990 |
|---|---|---|---|---|---|
| Economy's performance relative to four years* ago: | | | | | |
| | better | 23 | 32 | 49 | 4 |
| | same | 29 | 45 | 38 | 17 |
| | worse | 48 | 23 | 13 | 79 |
| | N | 2103 | 1799 | 2182 | 1948 |
| Present performance of economy: | | | | | |
| | very well | 2 | 6 | 13 | 1 |
| | fairly well | 42 | 55 | 68 | 15 |
| | not very well | 54 | 33 | 16 | 83 |
| | pro/con | 2 | 7 | 3 | 1 |
| | N | 2162 | 1802 | 2192 | 1956 |
| Anticipated performance of economy over next three or four years: | | | | | |
| | better | 38 | 22 | 23 | 10 |
| | same | 52 | 63 | 63 | 32 |
| | worse | 10 | 15 | 14 | 57 |
| | N | 2036 | 1760 | 1961 | 1917 |
| Evaluation of federal government's handling of economy: | | | | | |
| | very good | 3 | 3 | 7 | 1 |
| | good | 38 | 40 | 64 | 19 |
| | poor | 36 | 30 | 19 | 44 |
| | very poor | 15 | 7 | 3 | 33 |
| | pro/con | 8 | 20 | 7 | 4 |
| | N | 2068 | 1773 | 2158 | 1942 |
| Government impact on anticipated performance of economy: | | | | | |
| | great deal | 38 | 34 | 44 | 57 |
| | something | 43 | 45 | 41 | 30 |
| | not much | 20 | 21 | 15 | 14 |
| | N | 2080 | 1711 | 1930 | 1982 |

Note: vertical percentages for each evaluation

* - "five years" in 1983 survey

## Changing Economic Evaluations

Canadians' economic evaluations testify to the truth of the late V. O. Key's (1968:7) famous dictum that "voters are not fools." In 1983, after the country had endured nearly a decade of stagflation and was suffering from an unemployment rate approaching 12%, only 2% of the public said the economy was doing "very well," as opposed to 54% who said the opposite (Table 7.1).[2] As economic conditions subsequently improved significantly, if unevenly, in many parts of the country, so too did public attitudes. Thus, the percentage stating that the economy was doing at least "fairly well" reached 61% in 1987, and fully 81% in 1988. However, by

FIGURE 7.1  Evaluations of Federal Government's Handling of the Economy, 1983–1990

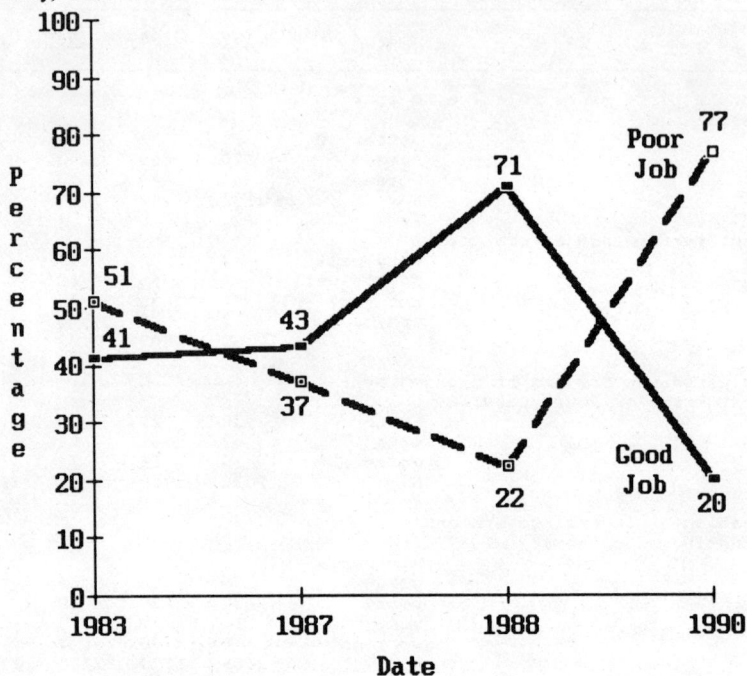

late 1990, the country was in the throes of a recession, and there was a dramatic shift in opinion. The percentage saying the economy was in at least fairly good shape declined markedly (to 16%), whereas those making negative judgments skyrocketed to 84%. As Table 7.1 shows, similar dynamics characterized public judgments about the past performance of the economy and its future prospects.

As judgments about the economy became increasingly negative between 1988 and 1990, those concerning its stewardship by government did so as well. Thus, although only a minuscule number ever reported that the government was doing a "very good" job managing the economy (the maximum being 7% in 1988), between 1983 and 1988 there was a monotonic increase in those stating that the government was doing at least a "good" job and a corresponding decrease in the percent who said it was doing a "poor" or "very poor" job (Figure 7.1). In 1990, however, this trend was sharply reversed. Persons judging the government was doing either a "very good" or "good" job declined from 71% to 20%, whereas those believing the opposite increased from 22% to 77%. Also, the number of people who felt government would have a "great deal" of influence on the economy's future performance increased as the condition of the economy worsened—from 44% in 1988 to 57% in 1990.

Canadians' feelings about their own lives and their assessment of the extent of the government's influence on their material well-being also shifted between 1988 and 1990 but, overall, the changes were not as marked as judgments about national conditions. The largest difference concerned the future, with the percentage believing that their standard of living would be "better" in three or four years decreasing from 34% to 21% (Table 7.2). There was a more modest decline (from 41% to 32%) in the percentage of people who believed they were better off than they had been in the past, and an even smaller one in the number who said they were "very satisfied" with their current economic circumstances (from 25% to 22%). Similarly, there was an increase in the number who felt that the government would have a great deal of influence on their standard of living in the future, but judgments about the government's effect on their current and past material condition were the same in 1990 as they had been in 1988. More generally, and not surprisingly in a country with a liberal democratic political culture and a mixed economy, many Canadians believed government had less of an impact on their personal financial condition than on the economy as a whole.

***Asymmetric Responsibility Attributions:*** Unfortunately for any Canadian government, when judgments about material well-being are considered in conjunction with beliefs about the extent to which one's personal condition is affected by government, it is apparent that the greater people's level of satisfaction with their lives, the less likely they are to credit government for it. In 1988, for example, only 25% of those who said they were "very satisfied" with their standard of living also gave government credit for it, in that they stated that government had a "great deal" to do with their condition. In contrast, the percentage who held government similarly responsible increased from 38% among those who said they were a "little dissatisfied" and to 62% among those who were "very dissatisfied." Response patterns in the 1983 and 1987 surveys were similar, as were those characterizing changes in people's perceived financial condition relative to what it had been in the past and what they anticipated it would be in the future.

Not only were these patterns repeated in 1990, if anything, they were stronger than in previous years. For example, of those who thought the national economy would improve in the future, 34% stated that government would have a great deal of responsibility for the anticipated improvement (Table 7.3). Among those who believed conditions would remain the same the percentage increased to 40%, and it rose to fully 70% among those thinking the economy would deteriorate. For personal economic prospects, the comparable increases were even greater—from 12% to 23%

Table 7.2. Evaluations of Personal Economic Condition and Government Impact, 1983-1990 (in percent)

|  | 1983 | 1987 | 1988 | 1990 |
|---|---|---|---|---|
| **Present financial condition relative to four years* ago:** | | | | |
| better | 40 | NA | 41 | 32 |
| same | 39 | NA | 46 | 49 |
| worse | 21 | NA | 14 | 19 |
| N | 2098 |  | 2189 | 1952 |
| **Satisfaction with present material standard of living:** | | | | |
| very satisfied | 29 | 30 | 25 | 22 |
| fairly satisfied | 53 | 53 | 59 | 58 |
| little dissatisfied | 13 | 12 | 14 | 15 |
| very dissatisfied | 4 | 4 | 3 | 5 |
| N | 2107 | 1853 | 2212 | 1958 |
| **Anticipated personal material standard of living in three or four years:** | | | | |
| better | 35 | 41 | 34 | 21 |
| same | 50 | 49 | 55 | 48 |
| worse | 15 | 11 | 12 | 31 |
| N | 2044 | 1085 | 2098 | 1917 |
| **Government impact on financial condition over last four years*:** | | | | |
| great deal | 23 | NA | 18 | 19 |
| something | 30 | NA | 30 | 25 |
| not much | 47 | NA | 52 | 56 |
| N | 2078 |  | 2174 | 1942 |
| **Government impact on present material standard of living:** | | | | |
| great deal | 28 | 26 | 25 | 24 |
| something | 31 | 35 | 36 | 31 |
| not much | 42 | 40 | 39 | 45 |
| N | 2096 | 1805 | 2173 | 1934 |
| **Government impact on anticipated material standard of living:** | | | | |
| great deal | 31 | 22 | 29 | 37 |
| something | 33 | 33 | 34 | 29 |
| not much | 37 | 45 | 38 | 34 |
| N | 2003 | 1747 | 2063 | 1889 |

Note: vertical percentages for each evaluation

NA question not asked

* "five years" in 1983 survey

Table 7.3. Government Impact on Personal Financial Condition and National Economy by Economic Evaluations, 1990 (in percent)

Present financial condition relative to four years ago:

| Government Impact | better | same | worse |
|---|---|---|---|
| great deal | 6 | 16 | 51 |
| something | 20 | 26 | 31 |
| not much | 74 | 59 | 18 |
| N | 627 | 944 | 371 |

$\chi^2_4 = 402.33$, $p \leq .001$, $\gamma = -.57$

Satisfaction with present material standard of living:

| Government Impact | very satisfied | fairly satisfied | little dissatisfied | very dissatisfied |
|---|---|---|---|---|
| great deal | 14 | 16 | 52 | 75 |
| something | 25 | 34 | 34 | 17 |
| not much | 61 | 51 | 14 | 8 |
| N | 417 | 1123 | 295 | 100 |

$\chi^2_6 = 394.42$, $p \leq .001$, $\gamma = -.51$

Anticipated personal material standard of living in three or four years:

| Government Impact | better | same | worse |
|---|---|---|---|
| great deal | 12 | 23 | 74 |
| something | 24 | 36 | 21 |
| not much | 64 | 41 | 4 |
| N | 393 | 902 | 594 |

$\chi^2_4 = 627.07$, $p \leq .001$, $\gamma = -.71$

Anticipated performance of the national economy:

| Government Impact | better | same | worse |
|---|---|---|---|
| great deal | 34 | 40 | 70 |
| something | 41 | 37 | 24 |
| not much | 25 | 23 | 6 |
| N | 196 | 622 | 1074 |

$\chi^2_4 = 207.91$, $p \leq .001$, $\gamma = -.49$

Note: vertical percentages

to 74%, and similarly strong relationships obtained for government responsibility attributions and evaluations of past and present economic circumstances (Table 7.3). Overall, then, there is consistent evidence of strongly asymmetric attributions of government responsibility for both personal and national economic conditions.

**The Structure of Economic Evaluations:** Studies of public economic evaluations and their impact on party support typically have distinguished between national (sociotropic) and personal (egocentric) judgments, as well as among retrospective, contemporaneous and prospective time ho-

Table 7.4. Confirmatory Factor Analysis of Economic Performance Evaluations, 1990

| Economic Evaluations | Factor Matrix ($\lambda$) | | |
|---|---|---|---|
| | Sociotropic | Egocentric | Future |
| Personal economic condition: | | | |
| past | .00 | .64 | .00 |
| present | .00 | .52 | .00 |
| future | .00 | .00 | .65 |
| National economic condition: | | | |
| past | .80 | .00 | .00 |
| present | .59 | .00 | .00 |
| future | .00 | .00 | .62 |

$\chi^2_5 = 10.69$, p = .058, AGFI = .994, N = 1967

| | Inter-Factor Correlations ($\phi$) | | |
|---|---|---|---|
| | Sociotropic | Egocentric | Future |
| Sociotropic | 1.00 | | |
| Egocentric | .54 | 1.00 | |
| Future | .69 | .50 | 1.00 |

Note: Coefficients are WLS estimates; all estimates p < .05, one-tailed tests.

rizons. Taken together, these distinctions yield six possible types of evaluations. Our survey data enable us to determine if these analytic distinctions correspond to the way in which Canadians actually structure their economic evaluations. Confirmatory factor analyses[3] of variables corresponding to the six types of evaluation[4] show that public economic evaluations are neither inchoate nor unidimensional. Rather, previous analyses of the 1983 and 1988 data have established that a three-factor model fits the data very well (Kornberg and Clarke, 1992:ch. 2). Retrospective and contemporaneous judgments about the national economy load on the first factor. Similar judgments about one's personal economic circumstances load on the second factor, and forecasts about future national and personal conditions load on the third factor. Testing this model with the 1990 data also produces an excellent fit ($\chi^2_{25} = 10.69$, p =.058) (Table 7.4) and, as in the earlier analyses, all of the hypothesized factor loadings are strong and statistically significant (p < .05), and various LISREL diagnostics have acceptable values.[5] In sum, data collected at three different points in time over the past decade reveal that Canadians distinguish between national and personal economic conditions, but that the distinction collapses when they forecast future economic conditions. We therefore label the three factors, "sociotropic," "egocentric," and "future," respectively. Although the three factors have substantial intercorrelations (ranging from +.50 to +.69 in 1990), they clearly are not coterminous. Canadians' economic evaluations are tri-dimensional and, accordingly, we will employ variables based on the three factors in subsequent analyses.

## Economic Issues

### *Free Trade*

1988 undoubtedly will be remembered as the year of the free trade election. The Liberal Party's decision to oppose the agreement, to use their majority in the Senate to thwart its passage, and the prime minister's decision, in turn, to use this action as a pretext for calling an election, meant that it was very likely that the free trade agreement would be a salient campaign issue. However, it was not obvious initially that the FTA would completely dominate the issue agenda. The Conservatives had planned to run a "land is strong" campaign, to claim credit for a reinvigorated economy and, more generally, to argue that they were competent administrators who could "manage change" (Frizzell, Pammett and Westell, 1989; LeDuc, 1989).

The dynamics of the campaign quickly overturned this strategy, largely because Liberal leader John Turner, under heavy fire from his own party, cast about for an issue that could at once mobilize electoral support and salvage his own career. For a variety of reasons free trade was an attractive choice. For one thing, it was a classic "pro-con" issue and, as such, it had the potential to turn the contest into a two-party fight, thereby marginalizing the NDP which had failed to take the lead in opposing the agreement. For another, it could be represented to the electorate as a "national salvation" issue, with the Conservatives portrayed as the party in league with and subservient to the colossus to the south and the Liberals cast as the country's saviors. The nationally televised debates between the party leaders provided Mr. Turner with the opportunity to structure the issue in these terms and to accuse the prime minister of selling out the country for the proverbial mess of pottage. Afterwards, several polls revealed a sharp increase in Liberal support and some showed that they had moved ahead of the Conservatives (Frizzell, Pammett and Westell, 1989:95). Although the surge in Liberal support proved temporary, the remainder of the campaign was dominated by vituperative exchanges between the

Liberals and PCs over the issue, with the NDP and their issue agenda becoming increasingly irrelevant.

The manner in which the voters evaluated free trade and its consequences for the country in our 1988 preelection and postelection studies is shown in Table 7.5.[6] With the exception of a strong consensus that the agreement would hurt some sectors of the economy, opinion was divided but moved in a positive (i.e., pro-free trade) direction.[7] In the preelection survey 31% believed that the FTA would benefit all regions and provinces and 36% thought it would ensure the country's future prosperity. After the election 37% and 46%, respectively, took these positions. Opinions regarding the noneconomic consequences of free trade also revealed deep divisions in the public and similarly modest movements in favor of the agreement. Before the election, 37% believed the pact would threaten culture and the arts and 44% had similar concerns about the country's independence and, afterwards, these percentages declined by 4% and 5% respectively. Overall, support for the pact increased from 39% to 50% immediately after the election, whereas the number of opponents and undecideds declined by 5% and 6% respectively.

By 1990, pronounced changes in public attitudes toward the FTA had occurred. There was an 18% decline in the number of people agreeing that the agreement would ensure future prosperity, a 14% decline in the number agreeing that it would benefit the entire country, and a virtually unanimous belief that even though it might help certain industries, it would hurt others. Growing reservations about the noneconomic consequences of the FTA also were apparent. Majorities (54% and 57% respectively) now agreed that the pact was a threat to the country's independence and cherished social programs, and over 40% agreed that it posed a threat to culture and the arts. Finally, overall opposition to the agreement increased by 17% (to 57%), whereas support declined by almost as much (to 35%).[8]

## *The GST*

At the time of the 1988 election, the goods and services tax was but a gleam in the eye of Conservative Finance Minister, Michael Wilson. However, once the Tories had been returned to office, the GST quickly became a major item on new government's policy agenda, and a highly salient and emotionally charged issue in the country at large. Numerous public opinion polls revealed massive public opposition to the tax, and our 1990 survey is no different—Table 7.6 shows that 70% were opposed to the GST and only 23% were in favor of it. Moreover, many believed that the GST would have a variety of negative consequences.[9] Thus, fully three-quarters believed it would fuel a new round of inflation; two-thirds

Table 7.5. Attitudes Toward Free Trade Agreement, 1988 and 1990 (in percent)

| Statement | 1988 Pre* | 1988 Post** | 1990 |
|---|---|---|---|
| The free trade agreement ensures Canada's future prosperty | | | |
| agree | 36 | 46 | 28 |
| disagree | 48 | 42 | 65 |
| don't know | 16 | 13 | 8 |
| The free trade agreement threatens Canada's political independence | | | |
| agree | 44 | 39 | 54 |
| disagree | 44 | 52 | 41 |
| don't know | 11 | 9 | 5 |
| Economically, the free trade agreement helps some industries but it hurts others | | | |
| agree | 87 | 91 | 93 |
| disagree | 6 | 5 | 5 |
| don't know | 7 | 5 | 2 |
| The free trade agreement threatens Canadian culture and the arts | | | |
| agree | 37 | 33 | 42 |
| disagree | 48 | 55 | 48 |
| don't know | 15 | 13 | 11 |
| The free trade agreement benefits all of Canada, not just certain regions or provinces | | | |
| agree | 31 | 37 | 23 |
| disagree | 57 | 54 | 70 |
| don't know | 12 | 9 | 7 |
| The free trade agreement could threaten important social programs such as unemployment insurance and medical care | | | |
| agree | NA | 41 | 57 |
| disagree | NA | 48 | 33 |
| don't know | NA | 11 | 10 |
| Overall, are you in favor of the free trade agreement or opposed to it? | | | |
| favor | 39 | 50 | 35 |
| opposed | 45 | 40 | 57 |
| don't know | 16 | 10 | 8 |

Note: vertical percentages for each statement

NA question not asked

* 1988 pre-election survey

** 1988 post-election survey

N = 2215, 1988 pre-election survey; N = 2010, 1988 post-election survey; N = 1967, 1990 survey

Table 7.6. Attitudes Toward the Goods & Services Tax (GST), 1990 (in percent)

| Statement | Agree | Disagree | Don't Know |
|---|---|---|---|
| The GST will reduce the size of the federal deficit | 40 | 52 | 8 |
| The GST will start a new round of inflation | 73 | 19 | 8 |
| The GST will help pay for important social programs like medical care and unemployment insurance | 26 | 62 | 12 |
| The GST is unfair because poor people will pay the same rate as the rich | 65 | 31 | 4 |
| | Favor | Opposed | Don't Know |
| Overall, are you in favor of the GST or opposed to it? | 23 | 70 | 7 |

Note: horizontal percentages

N = 1967

said it was unfair because of its regressive character; almost as many were skeptical about the claim that tax revenues would fund social programs; and half felt the tax would not help to reduce the federal deficit. Opposition to the GST was widespread in all regions. It received its greatest support from Francophone Quebecers, who were more likely than other Canadians to believe that the tax would reduce the deficit, that it was fair, and that it would not fuel inflation. Even among in this group, however, only 39% favored the tax.

## Modeling Attitudes Toward Free Trade and the GST

We argued above that Canadians' attitudes toward free trade and the GST in part are a function of their evaluations of national and personal economic conditions and their attributions of responsibility to the federal government for these conditions. To test this hypothesis we specified multivariate models in which attitudes toward free trade and the GST were the dependent variables and sociotropic and egocentric judgments were two of the independent variables.[10] We did not include judgments about future economic conditions in the models since, logically, such judgments might reflect people's assessments of the consequences of free trade and the GST. Other predictor variables included party identification and, since previous studies have shown that political attitudes and behavior at one level of government are influenced by party identifications at the other level (e.g., Clarke and Stewart, 1987; Martinez, 1990), we included measures of both federal and provincial party identification. Given the endogenous character of party identification in Canada (Archer, 1987; Kornberg and Clarke, 1988), and hence the possibility that current party identifications are influenced by attitudes toward free trade and GST, we employed our 1988-90 national panel data and used 1988 measures of party identification at the two levels of government.[11] The models also included several sociodemographic variables (age, education, gender, income, region/ethnicity)[12] as controls for other forces that might affect attitudes toward the two economic issues. The models are:

$$\text{ISSUE} = \beta_0 + \beta_1 \text{EGO} + \beta_2 \text{SOCIO} + \beta_3 \text{EGO} + \Sigma\beta_{4\text{-}5}\text{PID88} + \Sigma\beta_{6\text{-}14}\text{DEMO} + e$$

where:

ISSUE = attitudes toward the FTA or GST

$\beta_0$ = constant

EGO = retrospective-contemporaneous egocentric economic evaluations

SOCIO = retrospective-contemporaneous sociotropic economic evaluations

PID88 = federal and provincial party identifications, 1988

DEMO = sociodemographic characteristics

e = error term

Since the dependent variables (favor-oppose the FTA, GST) are dichotomies,[13] probit was chosen as the estimation technique.

The model estimates indicate that both personal and national economic judgments had statistically significant, positive effects on attitudes toward both the FTA and GST (Table 7.7). So, also, did regional residence. Quebec Francophones were more supportive of both policies and Prairie residents more supportive of free trade than were Ontarians (Ontario is the reference category). In addition, younger Canadians, the better educated, males, higher income earners, and federal and provincial Conser-

Table 7.7. Probit Analyses of Attitudes Toward Free Trade and the GST, 1988 Post-Election-1990 National Panel Survey

| Predictor Variables | Free Trade b | GST b |
|---|---|---|
| Region/Ethnicity: Atlantic | .11 | .06 |
| Quebec-French | .59a | .71a |
| Quebec-Non-French | .24 | -.26 |
| Prairies | .23b | .14 |
| British Columbia | .25c | -.11 |
| Age | -.01b | .01a |
| Education | .12a | .14a |
| Gender | -.43a | -.49a |
| Income | .12a | .07a |
| Federal party identification, 1988 | .17a | .13a |
| Provincial party identification, 1988 | .09a | .02 |
| Economic evaluations: egocentric | .10b | .14a |
| sociotropic | .30a | .26a |
| Constant | -.48b | -1.32a |
| McKelvey $R^2$ = | .39 | .31 |
| N = | 1010 | 1031 |

a $p \leq .01$
b $p \leq .05$
c $p \leq .10$; one-tailed tests

vative party identifiers were significantly more in favor of free trade. Older Canadians, the better educated, males, higher income earners and federal PC identifiers were the most favorably disposed toward the GST. Together, these variables explained sizable proportions of the variance: 39% for free trade and 31% for the GST.

Our next concern was to assess the magnitude of the effects of sociotropic and egocentric economic judgments on attitudes toward the FTA and GST. Unlike OLS regression coefficients, probit estimates do not have straightforward interpretations. However, one can assess the effect of changes in economic judgments on the probability of favoring free trade and the GST by manipulating their values, while fixing other variables in the models at empirically plausible or theoretically interesting values (Aldrich and Nelson, 1984:43). There are, of course, many possibilities. Here, we calculated the probability of supporting the FTA and GST as judgments about the economy change by assuming these judgments are being made by someone who, *ceteris paribus,* might be expected to be predisposed to support a Conservative policy initiative. Specifically, we considered a 46-year-old woman who lives in Ontario, has a university

FIGURE 7.2 Probability of Favoring Free Trade and GST by National and Personal Economic Evaluations

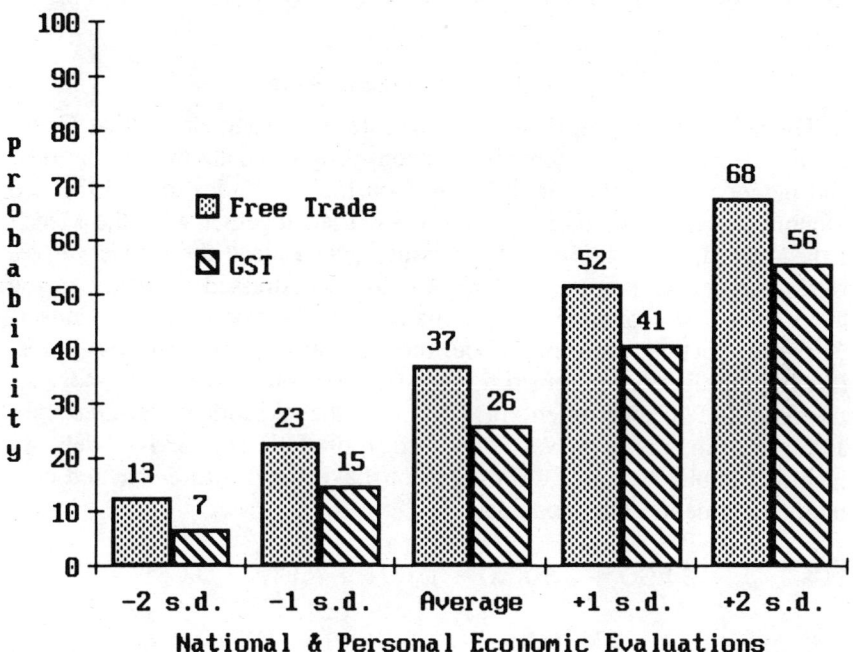

education, enjoys a moderately high income, and identifies (weakly) with the PCs at both the federal and provincial levels in 1988. Such a person had a 37% probability of supporting free trade in 1990 and a 26% probability of supporting the GST if she had made average national and personal economic judgments about the economy and government's impact thereon (Figure 7.2). Changes in the probability of her favoring the FTA and GST as she became more or less positive in her judgments were substantial. If her economic judgments were one or two standard deviations above average, the probability of supporting free trade increased to 52% and 68%, respectively. Conversely, if economic judgments become negative to the same degree, the probability of supporting the agreement declined to 23% and then to 13%.

As for the GST, it was so widely opposed that all of the probabilities were shifted in a negative direction. However, changes in economic evaluations still had large effects. Thus, if the person described above had economic evaluations that were a standard deviation more positive than average the likelihood of supporting the tax increased to 41% (Figure 7.2). If they were two standard deviations more positive, the probability of being pro-GST increased to 56%. If they were negative to the same degrees, the probabilities declined to 15% and 7%, respectively.

## Progressive Conservative Support

The scenarios presented above illustrate the strong effects that Canadians' retrospective and contemporaneous judgments about their national and personal economic conditions had on their attitudes toward the two economic issues, free trade and the GST, that, together with the Meech Lake Accord, have dominated the issue agenda since the Conservatives were returned to power in 1988. Still to be addressed, however, is the hypothesis that economic evaluations have had major effects on Conservative support net of feelings about these issues and other factors. To test this hypothesis we performed a regression analysis in which support for the federal PC government in 1990 was the dependent variable.[14] In addition to the predictor variables used in the FTA and GST models, we included public attitudes toward Meech Lake[15] and future-oriented economic judgments. The model is:

$$PCS = \beta_0 + \beta_1 EGO + \beta_2 SOCIO + \beta_3 FUT + \beta_4 FTA + \beta_5 GST$$
$$+ \beta_6 MEECH + \Sigma\beta_{7\text{-}8} PID + \Sigma\beta_{9\text{-}17} DEMO + e$$

where:

PCS = Progressive Conservative support

$\beta_0$ = constant

EGO = retrospective/contemporaneous egocentric evaluations

SOCIO = retrospective/contemporaneous sociotropic evaluations

FUT = future economic evaluations

FTA = attitude toward free trade agreement

GST = attitude toward GST

MEECH = attitude toward Meech Lake agreement

PID = federal and provincial party identifications, 1988

DEMO = sociodemographic characteristics

e = error term

The estimates revealed that all three economic evaluation factors had statistically significant positive effects on the Conservative government's support over and above those associated with demographic variables, prior party identifications, attitudes toward Meech Lake, free trade and the GST (Table 7.8). This finding is interesting because, as noted in Chapter 1, individual-level analyses of economic evaluations and political support conducted in non-Canadian settings have tended to emphasize the importance of retrospective sociotropic judgments and most have reported that retrospective and prospective egocentric evaluations do not have significant effects. In the Canadian case, in contrast, although retrospective and contemporaneous sociotropic assessments had the strongest effect of any of the independent variables (B = .33), future-oriented judgments, which have an egocentric as well as a sociotropic component, had the second strongest impact (B = .22) (Table 7.8). Additionally, while

Table 7.8. Multiple Regression Analysis of Support for Federal Progressive Conservative Government, 1988 Post-Election-1990 National Panel Survey

| Predictor Variables | | b | B |
|---|---|---|---|
| Region/Ethnicity: | Atlantic | -.41 | -.01 |
| | Quebec-French | 7.60a | .15 |
| | Quebec-Non-French | 1.57 | .01 |
| | Prairies | 1.21 | .02 |
| | British Columbia | .41 | .01 |
| Age | | .02 | .02 |
| Education | | -1.06b | -.06 |
| Gender | | 1.65b | .04 |
| Income | | -.23 | -.02 |
| Economic evaluations: | egocentric | 3.52a | .15 |
| | sociotropic | 7.53a | .33 |
| | future | 5.03a | .22 |
| Free trade | | 2.46a | .10 |
| GST | | 3.32a | .13 |
| Meech Lake | | 1.85b | .07 |
| Federal party identification, 1988 | | 1.80a | .16 |
| Provincial party identification, 1988 | | .89a | .08 |
| Constant | | 27.18a | |
| | Adjusted $R^2$ = | | .46 |
| | N = | | 1120 |

a p ≤.01
b p ≤.05
c p ≤.10; one-tailed tests

FIGURE 7.3 Variance Explained in Support for Federal Progressive Conservative Government

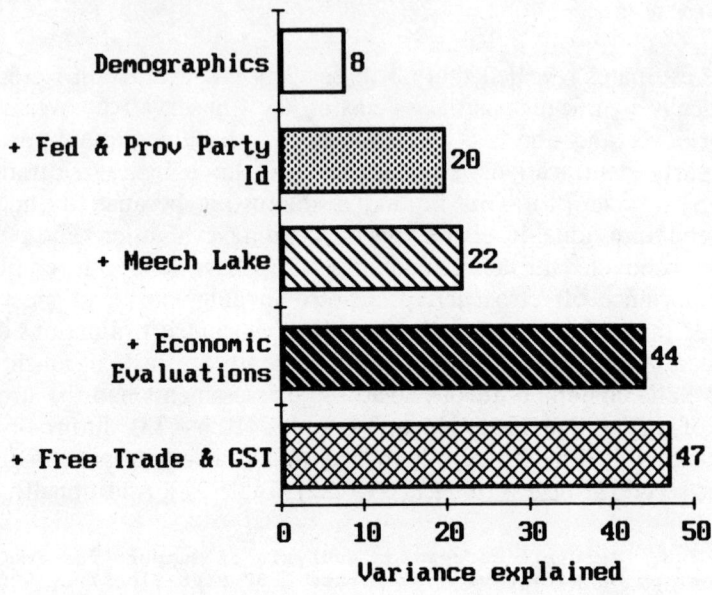

the impact of retrospective and contemporaneous egocentric evaluations was somewhat weaker (B = .15), it was highly significant (t = 6.88), net of controls for the two other types of economic evaluations and all other predictors.

The analysis also revealed that issue variables had significant effects and, as anticipated, people who were positively disposed to the FTA, the GST and the Meech Lake Accord were stronger supporters of the government. As for the other variables in the model, federal and provincial party identifications had the expected effects (federal and provincial PC identifiers were more supportive), but most of the sociodemographic variables were not significant. The two exceptions show that Quebec-Francophones and those with lower levels of formal education manifested higher levels of PC support. Together, the several predictors explained 46% of the variance in support for the Tory government and its leader.

To comprehend the relative explanatory power of economic evaluations and economic issues (the FTA and GST), we conducted two stepwise regression analyses is which we reversed the order of entry of the three types of economic evaluations and the two economic issues, respectively. The results revealed that economic evaluations had stronger explanatory power. Specifically, all of the demographic variables, entered first, explained only 8% of the variance (Figure 7.3). Federal and provincial PC party identifications (measured in 1988) explained an additional 12%, and favorable attitudes toward Meech Lake added 2% to this total, bringing it to 22%. The entry of the economic evaluations then doubled the proportion of explained variance to 44% and people's attitudes to both free trade and the GST increased it to 47%. Thus, free trade and GST attitudes together uniquely explained only 3% of the variance in 1990 Conservative support. Reversing the order of entry of the economic evaluation and economic issue variables showed that the former uniquely explained 15% of the variance in PC support, with 7% of the variance being shared between the two sets of variables.

## Conclusion: From Disaster to Dismissal?

In the September 1984 federal election the Mulroney-led Conservatives won a smashing victory—gaining 50% of the popular vote and 75% (211 of 282) of the seats in what was to be Canada's 33rd parliament. One of the principal reasons for the magnitude of the PC victory was the public's unhappiness with the former Liberal government's stewardship of the economy and their feeling that the Conservatives might do better.[16] The analyses presented above strongly suggest that in the next federal election the current PC government may share the fate of its Liberal predecessor—and for the same reasons. Since the 1988 election there has been a rapid and sharp decline in the electorate's support for the Tories and their leader, and massive increases in negative evaluations of national and personal economic conditions and the government's capacity to manage the economy effectively. Unhappiness with national and personal economic conditions have had large adverse effects on PC support, over and above attitudes toward the free trade agreement, the GST, and the Meech Lake Accord. Moreover, negative economic evaluations have had indirect effects as well, influencing attitudes toward free trade and the GST, both of which have significant influences on Conservative support. Attitudes toward free trade have moved strongly in a negative direction since immediately after the 1988 election, and the GST is massively unpopular. In the face of widespread dissatisfaction with the state of the economy, the Conservatives have been unable to convince Canadians of the wisdom of either of these highly salient economic policy initiatives.

Adding to the Mulroney government's woes is the tendency of Canadians to make asymmetric judgments about government's responsibility for national and personal economic conditions. Many people tend not to credit government when they perceive economic good times and satisfactory personal living standards, whereas they do tend to blame government when they believe conditions are worsening. The implication is that a government cannot expect to gain as much from an improving economy as it loses from deteriorating one.

Can we conclude from the above that all is lost for the Conservatives—that the public will punish them by dismissing them from office in favor of the opposition Liberals, or even the New Democrats? Probably, but recent history and the more general volatility of Canadian political attitudes and behavior suggest a note of caution. Recall that in the wake of their 1984 victory support for the Conservatives eroded rapidly and precipitously. So much so, in fact, that the party's cohort of identifiers, which had increased from 28% to 40% between 1980 and 1984, decreased to 30% within a year after the election and subsequently fell to 25% in 1986 and to 24% in 1987.[17] However, it rebounded to 37% in the run-up to the 1988 election and to 39% immediately afterwards, before beginning another steep decline and returning to its 1987 level. Also, and similar to the case after 1984, a sharp erosion in public feelings about the prime minister has paralleled the negative trends in PC support that have occurred since the 1988 election.

These data strongly indicate that, except for a relatively brief period before the 1984 election, neither the prime minister, nor his party, nor their policies when in office, have inspired any great affection and enthusiasm among Canadians. In the run-up to the 1988 election feelings about the Tories and their leader were at best lukewarm, attitudes towards the party's major issue, free trade, were decidedly mixed, and PC support was very soft. Given this, one might argue that rather than Mr. Mulroney and the PCs winning the 1988 election, the Liberals and the NDP, albeit for different reasons, lost it. However, one also can make a very different argument. To wit, although the prime minister may inspire no great affection or trust in the electorate, he has demonstrated that he is an able political tactician who can skillfully employ the resources at his command to build a winning coalition when it is most needed, on election day. Particularly noteworthy have been his efforts to build support in his native province of Quebec. Recall that in preparation for the 1988 election he made excellent use of the patronage at his disposal to woo the Quebec electorate. Further, the abortive Meech Lake Accord was, and remains, far more popular in Quebec than in other parts of the country, as does free trade. Even the widely disliked GST has more support among Quebec Francophones than other Canadians. As a consequence, a significant source of potential electoral support for the Conservative government is Francophone Quebec—a group and a region that have done much to decide the outcome of virtually every national election since Confederation.

This is not to say that Mr. Mulroney can pull another rabbit out of his hat in the next election or, *a fortiori,* that he is a political magician who

*"It's Their Fault!"* 161

can conjure an era of Conservative hegemony in national politics. It is to say that if Quebec remains a part of Canada, and if the economy improves markedly—two very large "ifs"—the outcome of the next election may be more problematic than midterm levels of party support would indicate.[18] The mutability of Canadians' partisan attachments and the strong impact of highly volatile short-term leader and issue forces on party support always make forecasts of federal election outcomes a very risky enterprise.

## Notes

1. The surveys, conducted as parts of the Political Support in Canada project (Kornberg and Clarke, 1992), involved telephone interviews of national probability samples of the Canadian electorate. Fieldwork was conducted by Canadian Facts, Ltd., Toronto. The weighted national sample sizes for the cross-sectional surveys are: 1983, N = 2117; 1987, N = 1877; 1988 preelection, N = 2215; 1988 postelection, N = 2010; 1990, N = 1967. The 1983, 1988 and 1990 surveys contain interlocking panel components; the 1987 survey is a cross-section only. The weighted sample size for the 1988 postelection–1990 national panel employed below is N = 1120. Details concerning the sampling design and other technical aspects of the surveys are available upon request.

2. For the wording of the several economic evaluation and government responsibility questions see note 4 below.

3. Unlike exploratory factor analysis (EFA), confirmatory factor analysis (CFA) provides goodness-of-fit tests of theoretically specified models, correlations between factors which are parameter estimates (rather than arbitrary values as in an obliquely rotated EFA), and correlations among error variances may be specified. See Bollen (1989:chs. 6, 7). Here, CFA is implemented using LISREL 7's weighted least squares (WLS) estimation procedure (Joreskog and Sorbom, 1988). WLS relaxes the assumptions of interval-level measurement and multivariate normality and, therefore, suits attitudinal data that involve dichotomous or ordinal measures and skewed distributions.

4. The six economic evaluation indices were constructed as follows: (I) Past, Self: Respondents were asked (a) "Do you think that you are financially better off now than you were five years ago, worse off, or are things about the same?" (b) "Do you think that government has had a great deal, something, or not much at all to do with this?" Responses were scored "better off" = +1, "same" = 0, and "worse off" = -1; "great deal" = +2 "something" = +1, "not much" = 0. Scores for (a) and (b) were multiplied to yield an index ranging from +2 to -2. (II) Present, Self: An index ranging from +4 to -4 was constructed by multiplying responses to (a) "Now let's think about the things you can buy or do, all the things which make up your material standard of living. Would you say that you are very satisfied (+2), fairly satisfied (+1), a little dissatisfied (-1), or very dissatisfied (-2) with the material side of your life right now?" (b) "Do you think government has a great deal (+2), something (+1), or not much at all (0) to do with this?" (III) Future, Self: An index ranging from +2 to -2 was constructed by multiplying

responses to: (a) "Still thinking about the material side of things and looking ahead over the next three or four years, do you think that you will be better off (+1) or worse off (-1) or will things stay about the same (0)?" (b)) "Will government have a great deal (+2), something (+1), or not much at all (0) to do with this?" (IV) Past, National: "Would you say that the federal government has done a very good job (+2), a good job (+1), a poor job (-1), or a very poor job (-2) in handling the economy?" Qualified answers, e.g., "depends" were scored 0. (V) Present, National: Unlike the other categories no question referring explicitly to the federal government is available. The following is used as a proxy: "Thinking generally about how the Canadian economy is doing these days, would you say it is doing very well (+2), fairly well (+1), or not very well (0)?" Qualified answers were scored +1. (VI) Future, National: An index ranging from +2 to -2 was constructed by multiplying responses to: (a) "Do you think the Canadian economy will get better (+1), worse (-1), or stay about the same (0) over the next year or so?" (b) "Will the government have a great deal (+2), something (+1), or not much at all (0) to do with this?" For all six indices "don't know" responses were scored 0.

5. When testing the goodness-of-fit of a CFA model, "large $\chi^2$ values correspond to bad fit and small $\chi^2$ values to good fit. The degrees of freedom serve as a standard by which to judge whether $\chi^2$ is large or small" (Joreskog and Sorbom, 1988:42). In this regard, note that a simple one-factor model for the 1983, 1988 and 1990 data has a markedly worse fit than the three-factor alternative. In 1990, for example, testing a one-factor model yields $\chi^2_{29} = 116.69$, $p < .001$.

6. In addition to asking if they were in favor or opposed to the free trade agreement, respondents were asked if they "agreed" or "disagreed" with the following statements: (a) "the free trade agreement ensures Canada's future prosperity;" (b) "the free trade agreement threatens Canada's political independence;" (c) "economically the free trade agreement helps some industries but it hurts others;" (d) "the free trade agreement threatens Canadian culture and the arts;" (e) "the free trade agreement benefits all of Canada economically, not just certain regions or provinces;" (f) "the free trade agreement could threaten important programs such as unemployment insurance and medical care." Items (a)–(e) were asked in the 1988 preelection and postelection surveys and in the 1990 survey; (f) was asked in the latter two surveys only.

7. The electorate's reaction to the party leaders heated discussion of the issue in the television debates strongly suggests that trends in opinion during the campaign were not linear. Analyses of the 1988 preelection data by date of interview reveals that opinion regarding the pact was almost evenly divided at 41% before the debates, that opposition increased to 50% immediately afterwards, with support declining to 35%. Although the balance of opinion fluctuated thereafter, a pro-free trade movement was evident among those interviewed in the closing week of the campaign. See also Johnston (1990:5).

8. Although opposition to the FTA increased in every region of the country after 1988, unhappiness with it was strongest in the Atlantic provinces and Ontario. For example, eight of every 10 Ontario residents and almost as many of those in Atlantic Canada disagreed with the proposition about future economic prosperity and some three quarters disagreed with the statement that it would help all regions

of the country. About 60% of the residents of both areas felt the agreement posed a threat to the country's sovereignty and 70% were similarly worried about its impact on social programs.

9. To assess public opinion on the consequences of the GST, respondents were asked if they "agreed" or "disagreed" with the following statements: (a) "the GST will reduce the size of the federal deficit;" (b) "the GST will start a new round of inflation;" (c) "the GST will help pay for important social programmes like medical care and unemployment insurance;" (d) "the GST is unfair because poor people will pay the same rate as the rich."

10. Factor scores provided by a three-factor principal components analysis model are used to build indices measuring sociotropic, egocentric and future-oriented economic evaluations.

11. The federal and provincial party identification measures are scored: very strong Conservative = +3, fairly strong Conservative = +2, not very strong or leaning Conservative = +1, nonidentifier = 0, not very strong or leaning other party identifier = -1, fairly strong other party identifier = -2, very strong other party identifier = -3.

12. Age is measured in years; annual family income has nine categories ranging from under $10,000 per year =1 to $80,000 a year or more = 9; gender is women = 1, men = 0; formal education is elementary or less = 1, some secondary = 2, completed secondary or technical, community college = 3, some university = 4, completed university (B.A., B.Sc. or more) = 5. Region/ethnicity is a set of dummy variables with Ontario as the reference category.

13. Persons in favor of the FTA are scored 1; those opposed are scored 0. "Don't knows" and "no opinions" are removed from the analysis. Opinions about the GST are scored the same way.

14. PC support is measured by averaging the thermometer scores accorded to the party and its leader, i.e., (PC thermometer + Mulroney thermometer)/2. Respondents with missing values are assigned mean scores on the thermometer variables.

15. Respondents were asked "Overall, were you in favor of the Meech Lake Accord or opposed to it?" Those stating they were in favor are scored +2, those opposed are scored 0, and "don't knows" are scored +1.

16. In our 1984 postelection survey 60% stated that some aspect of the economy was the most important issue in the election. Unemployment was the largest single category (31%), 22% made general references to the "state of the economy," and the remaining 7% referred to various economic problems such as inflation, the deficit or the value of the dollar. Of those mentioning an economic issue, fully 53% stated that they favored the PCs on the issue, 21% and 14% favored the NDP and the Liberals, respectively, and 12% said "no party" or "don't know." On the importance of economic issues for the Conservative victory in 1984, see Archer and Johnson (1988:580–84) and Clarke et al. (1991:143–45).

17. The 1985 and 1986 party identification data are from national cross-sectional surveys (weighted N's = 1852 and 2000, respectively) conducted by Canadian Facts Ltd. as parts of the Political Support in Canada project. Details are available upon request.

18. Of course, other factors will play a role as well, perhaps one of the most important being the impact of the new Reform Party on PC support in Western Canada. The 1990 survey shows that although less than 4% of the entire electorate were Reform identifiers, 16% in the Prairies identified with the party. The largest cohort of Reform identifiers was in Alberta (20%), with the 11% doing so in both Manitoba and Saskatchewan. Again, the instability in Canadian party identification suggests that these figures could change substantially by the time of the next election.

# 8

# Macroeconomic Theories and Political Interests: The Political Business Cycle

*The Lady's not for turning.*
—Prime Minister Thatcher, Brighton, October 10, 1980

*... within an incumbent's term in office there is a predictable pattern of policy, starting with relative austerity in early years and ending with the potlatch right before elections.*
—William Nordhaus (1975:187)

Much of this book has been concerned with the influence of economic performance on political support, a relationship which is of central concern to the political scientist. To understand the interaction between the economy and politics fully, however, we also should consider the reaction of governments to the political consequences of economic performance, i.e., the strategies that they pursue in order to improve their popularity and their chances of reelection. This has two aspects; first there are *reaction* functions, which model the responses of governments to changes in the economy. Second, there are *outcome* functions which model the relationship between policy instruments, such as public expenditure and the money supply, and policy outcomes such as inflation and unemployment. The latter are of course a central concern to the economist. This "closes the circle" of reasoning about relationships between the economy and politics, since policy outcomes are independent variables in the popularity functions discussed earlier.

We shall consider those aspects of the theoretical and empirical literature on reaction and outcome functions which are of direct relevance to the models of political-economic interaction examined in this book. The work on reaction functions is fairly compact and can be easily reviewed within the present context. However, the work on outcome functions is much larger, effectively taking in the whole of macroeconomic theory, and this is increasingly difficult to summarize, since it is both vast and fragmented.

For many years after publication of *The General Theory* (1936), Keynes' pathbreaking book which initiated modern macroeconomics, the Keynesian model dominated discussions in this area. But since the 1970s the field has become more and more fragmented, prompting one leading macroeconomist to write: "There is currently little agreement among macroeconomists about the structure of the economy" (Fair, 1984:1). Rather than attempt to discuss all aspects of modern macroeconomics, we will examine those debates which are particularly important to the question of economic manipulation for political profit.

This chapter is divided into four parts: first, to place the literature in context we examine the most fundamental debate in modern macroeconomics—that between neo-classical and neo-Keynesian theories of the macroeconomy. This is important because contemporary theories of the political business cycle (PBC) reflect these debates, and can only be understood in the light of them. This is followed by a review of the theoretical work on reaction and outcome functions from Kalecki's early insightful analysis of the political consequences of Keynesianism, to the most recent work which incorporates rational expectations into models of political-economic interaction. Next, we discuss the empirical evidence relating to the different theories; and, finally, we examine a case study, namely estimates of reaction and outcome functions for Great Britain from 1983 to 1987, a period particularly favorable for observing political manipulation of the economy. These estimates will in turn throw light on the earlier debates in macroeconomic theory about the circumstances under which the political business cycle will occur.

## The Macroeconomic Foundations

It is beyond the scope of this chapter to review the whole of macroeconomics, which is the theoretical basis of the political business cycle. But, in order to place the literature in context, we will consider the two most prominent schools of thought in contemporary macroeconomics—the neo-classical and neo-Keynesian schools—in order to assess their implications for the political business cycle literature.

There are a number of differences between neo-classical and neo-Keynesian theories in macroeconomics. The first and most important is that neo-classical writers assume that the economy is characterized by high levels of competition and rational utility-maximizing behavior on the part of individuals and firms. This means that economic activity adjusts readily to exogenous disturbances to the system, such as the oil price shocks of the 1970s. In contrast, neo-Keynesians think that the economy is characterized by a number of important rigidities which prevent it from adjusting easily. At the root of these rigidities is the failure of different actors to coordinate their decisions and expectations, a condition which leads to suboptimal outcomes (Gordon, 1990).

Neo-classical analysis is rooted in general equilibrium theory which dates back to the work of Swedish economist Walras (Blaug, 1968:574–614). According to the theory there exists one point of general equilibrium in the economy where welfare is maximized and all resources are used most efficiently. In contrast, in a neo-Keynesian world there are multiple equilibria, many of them involving high levels of unemployment and accompanying reductions in economic welfare. The neo-Keynesians believe that the economy can become stuck in a situation of high unemployment, from which it will not escape in any reasonable period of time unless government takes action. Neo-classicists argue that, although recessions can occur, if the economy is left alone it will tend to right itself in due course, thereby achieving full employment for all those who want to work.

The second major difference between the schools concerns their beliefs about the causes of recession and business cycles. Neo-classicists tend to locate causes of recessions on the supply side of the economy, i.e., in terms of shocks to aggregate supply which produce irregular cyclical behavior in economic growth, employment and productivity. Neo-Keynesians locate the causes of depression primarily on the demand side. In their view, the major causal factor in explaining recession is a deficiency of aggregate demand. By the same token, the major cause of inflation is excess aggregate demand.

A third major difference concerns the role of monetary and fiscal policies in influencing economic outcomes in the short run. In the 1970s, theoretical differences between monetarists and Keynesians prompted sharp controversies concerning the potency of monetary policy and fiscal policy. Monetarists, who generally adhere to the neo-classical school, argued that monetary policy is powerful in influencing the economy, and can be used to control inflation. At the same time they regarded fiscal policy as having very little influence over the economy even in the short run. Keynesians held the opposite view; they regarded monetary policy as a weak influence on the economy in comparison with fiscal policy. More recently, distinctions between neo-classicists and neo-Keynesians have diminished, since many of the former are concerned about the huge budget deficit in the United States, and many of the latter accept the importance of monetary policy. But it is still broadly true that neo-Keynesians attach more importance to fiscal policy and less to monetary policy than do neo-classical theorists, who accord considerably more importance to money.

It can readily be seen that both theories carry implications about the role of government in managing the economy. For a neo-classical economist, government intervention is either unnecessary or even perverse—it can make things worse. For neo-Keynesians, government intervention, particularly to maintain aggregate demand, is essential. Thus, neo-Keynesians are broadly in favor of stabilization policy, i.e., a policy of running budget deficits in a recession in order to sustain aggregate demand, and one of running budget surpluses in booms in order to control inflation. Neo-classicists oppose such policies because they argue that stabilization policies cannot influence productivity and employment. Some neo-classicists go further and argue that such policies can destabilize the economy because they interfere with the natural rate of growth. In this view stabilization policies might stimulate the economy in time of boom, and deflate it in time of slump.

In the debates between these different schools of thought, one criticism of neo-Keynesian theories which has resonated within the economic profession is that the rigidities cited by neo-Keynesians are incompatible with rational utility-maximizing behavior, because agents could improve their welfare by removing these rigidities. For example, one key rigidity in the Keynesian model is the downward "stickiness" of money wages. In time of recession workers resist taking cuts in money wages and managers are reluctant to impose them, and this has obvious implications for an economy attempting to adjust to changes in the economic environment. One prominent neo-classical theorist, Robert Lucas (1972), rejects this rigidity because he points out that the firms can increase profits by cutting money wages in a recession, and this will produce less unemployment in the long run than occurs when workers resist such cuts. Thus, it is rational for both managers and workers to adjust money wages in line with the demand for labor. In other words, Keynesian macroeconomic theories appeared to be inconsistent with macroeconomic theory where agents act to maximize profits and incomes.

The rational expectations "revolution" which swept macroeconomics in the late 1970s and early 1980s accentuated the emphasis on optimization by rational actors in neo-classical theory. The central idea of rational expectations is that agents possess an accurate model of the macroeconomy which enables them to forecast its future behavior with minimum error, and thereby maximize utility in their transactions with other agents (Felderer and Homburg, 1987). This assumption implies that they will make no systematic errors about the behavior of the economy over time; if they are wrong it is because some unforeseen "surprise" occurred which no one could have forecast beforehand, not because of a delay in adjusting to new economic conditions, or because they ignore opportunities to make gains in their transactions with other actors. It is assumed that agents adjust instantly as soon as new information becomes available. The emphasis on rational expectations in modern macroeconomics seems puzzling to many political scientists, particularly when the empirical evidence does not support such an assumption (Lovell, 1986). However, these ideas play a key role in recent work on the political business cycle, a point developed more fully below.

Recent neo-Keynesian work has accepted the idea of rational expectations, and so has sought to explain rigidities in the economy in terms of factors other than imperfections in the ability of actors to adjust to changes in the economy over time. One line of argument is to show that there are problems of collective action when aggregating from the microeconomic to the macroeconomic levels. Apparently small rigidities in behavior at the microeconomic level can have large macroeconomic effects. For example, firms can accept prices for their products which do not quite maximize profits, but get trivially close to doing so; this means they lose a small amount of profit by not adjusting prices to changing conditions of demand. Such behavior can be justified because there are important costs associated with adjusting prices, known as "menu costs," which make it rational to avoid such changes providing the costs of avoidance are small. However, a small deviation from profit maximization by each individual firm will spill over to affect other actors who in turn will magnify the initial effects. Thus, large aggregate rigidities can result from small deviations from profit maximizing behavior. In this situation an increase in nominal money in the economy when nominal prices are fixed because of this rigidity will increase real output and stimulate employment (Ball, Mankiw and Romer, 1988).

A second approach to the controversy has been to examine the extent to which the economy actually adjusts to a new equilibrium in the face of exogenous shocks. Neo-Keynesians have pointed to the fact that in the pre–World War II period large transitory cycles existed in most economic time series, which implies that the economy failed to adjust quickly when in disequilibrium (DeLong and Summers, 1988). It is argued that these cycles do not appear in post-war data because governments intervened to maintain full employment and growth. The success of Keynesian stabilization policies, which were a major feature of post-war economic policies in most advanced industrial societies, is responsible for this difference.

The most obvious example of a long-lasting deviation from equilibrium was the Great Depression of the 1930s. Between 1929 and 1932 output in the United States fell by 30%, and there is nothing in neo-classical theory which would explain this. Neo-Keynesians, in contrast, explain the depression as being the product of a vicious circle of shrinking effective demand and increasing unemployment.

Neo-Keynesians make a number of other criticisms of neo-classical theories, two of which are particularly telling. One concerns theoretical explanations of business cycles; for neo-classical theorists cycles are a product of the statistical properties of technological innovation over time. Since innovation occurs at random intervals, and since technological progress is cumulative, real growth in the economy can be represented by a random walk. It is well known that a random walk is characterized by irregular cycles (e.g., McCleary and Hay, 1980:36–45), which neo-classicists argue is the observed business cycle.

Given this, fluctuations in macroeconomic series should be similar in different countries, since there is no reason to believe that innovations have a bigger impact in the short run in one country than in others. However, there are significant differences in the relative amplitude of fluctuations in output and investment in different countries. For example, between 1967 and 1986 fluctuations in investment in comparison with output were about 60% greater in the United States than in Japan (Greenwald and Stiglitz, 1988). There is no theoretical explanation of such differences within the neo-classical model.

Finally, another important difference between the theories concerns the existence of the natural rate of unemployment in the Phillips curve (Phillips, 1958). The original Phillips curve, which models the tradeoff between unemployment and wage inflation, appeared to break down in most western economies in the 1970s, and unlike the Keynesians, neo-classical writers of a monetarist persuasion provided a theoretical explanation. The Phillips curve was central to the Keynesian view of the world in the 1960s, since it suggested that policy-makers could "fine-tune" the economy to avoid recessions, on the one hand, or serious inflation, on the other (Rees, 1970).

Neo-classical theorists suggested that the Phillips curve was vertical in the long-run at the "natural rate of unemployment," because employment was determined by technological processes impervious to fiscal or monetary policy. This implied that attempts by governments to stimulate the economy by fiscal or monetary means to reduce unemployment below the natural rate would produce accelerating inflation. The neo-classicists differ among themselves about the existence of a short-run Phillips curve. Most monetarists would accept that there is a short-run relationship between unemployment and inflation which implies that unemployment can be reduced by monetary policy for a short period (Friedman, 1968). In contrast, rational expectation theorists deny this, arguing that the natural rate operates in the short run as well as in the long run (Lucas and Sargent, 1980).

The problem with all this however, is that no one has been able to satisfactorily identify the natural rate of unemployment. By means of a variety of ingenious assumptions some writers have tried to construct a time series measure of the natural rate (e.g., Gordon, 1978), but it appears to track actual unemployment fairly closely, which raises doubts about the validity of such a measure. Skepticism about the natural rate is further reinforced by the high levels of unemployment experienced in the west, particularly in western Europe in the 1980s. The so-called "hysteresis" hypothesis suggests that there may be no relationship at all between the level of unemployment and inflation (Cross, 1988). If so, then the economy could experience very high levels of both unemployment *and* inflation indefinitely, (or alternatively low levels of both) which, of course, is inconsistent with a natural rate hypothesis. The hysteresis hypothesis is consistent with the argument in neo-Keynesian analysis which stresses that economic adjustments are inhibited by pervasive rigidities of various kinds.

At present, it appears that neo-Keynesian theories do a better job of explaining the behavior of the macroeconomy than neo-classical theories, though the controversies still continue. In this chapter our primary concern is with the implications of these different theories for the political business cycle, rather than the wider question of which approach does the better job of modeling the economy. We address this issue next.

## Reaction Functions: Theoretical Perspectives

The dependent variables in reaction functions are the policy instruments which governments have available for influencing economic outcomes. These instruments are monetary policy, which is largely concerned with the level of interest rates, and fiscal policy, which is concerned with government expenditure and taxation. There are two types of reaction function which appear in the literature (Whiteley, 1986a). First, there are reaction functions which model the influence of policy outcomes such as inflation on policy instruments. These "economic" reaction functions have a fairly well-established pedigree in mainstream economic analysis (Pissarides, 1972). Second, there are "political" reaction functions which model the influence of political variables such as government popularity, as well as economic variables, on policy instruments. These are more controversial and difficult to reconcile with mainstream economic theory.

The first important theoretical work on government reactions to economic performance was done by Kalecki (1943) who introduced the notion of the political business cycle. He was concerned with exploring the political implications of the full employment policies resulting from the Keynesian revolution, and so his work was very much in the Keynesian tradition of analysis. The key point made was that full employment would profoundly change power relationships between employers and workers

FIGURE 8.1 The Political Business Cycle and the Phillips Curve

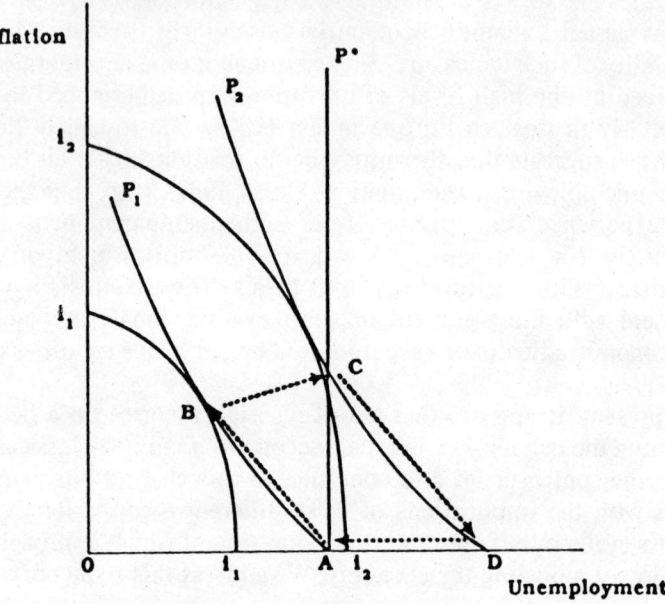

in society, enhancing the bargaining power of the latter compared with the former. Full employment eliminated the "reserve army" of the unemployed, and thus transformed the bargaining power of workers over wages and conditions of service. Kalecki argued that governments would resort to periodic recessions in order to try to restrain the political power of organized labor, but he felt that these recessions would be short-lived and relatively mild.

The link between the Phillips curve and the political business cycle was examined by a number of neo-classical theorists in the 1970s (MacRae, 1977; Nordhaus, 1975; Wagner, 1977). This can be illustrated in conjunction with Figure 8.1, where two short-run Phillips curves $P_1$ and $P_2$, intersect voter indifference curves $i_1$ and $i_2$. Along these latter curves voters are indifferent to the combinations of unemployment and inflation which they represent. Inflation and unemployment are measured on the horizontal and vertical axes, respectively, and, since both are "bads," voters will prefer smaller combinations of both, hence points on indifference curve $i_1$. Each point on $P_1$ and $P_2$ represent a given rate of unemployment which is required to "purchase" a given rate of inflation. The vertical line $P^*$ is the long-run Phillips curve; the assumption here is that a "natural" rate of unemployment exists in the economy (Friedman, 1968) which in the long run cannot be influenced by fiscal or monetary means,

## Macroeconomic Theories and Political Interests

and is determined largely by institutional and technological factors. In the model, the policy instruments only influence the short-run Phillips curves.

The sequence of events which produces the political business cycle can be traced as follows. If, for example, the economy is at point A, with zero inflation and a level of unemployment OA, this is on the long-run curve, and can thus be sustained indefinitely. However, as an election approaches, the government stimulates the economy in order to move it down to a lower voter indifference curve and, thereby, improve its chances of winning the election. This involves a shift to point B, so that the reduction in unemployment is purchased by an increase in inflation to OB. This results from workers bidding up wages, and employers being willing to concede higher wages at a time of buoyant demand. At point B the economy is operating at a lower level of unemployment that can be sustained in the long run.

At this point the government holds the election, since it will enjoy greater popularity when the economy is on the lower voter indifference curve. After the election, however, agents begin to adjust to the new level of inflation, and react accordingly. Managers price their goods up, and wage bargainers seek increases above the rate of inflation in order to increase real wages, and this has the effect of producing unemployment. The changing expectations of inflation shift the Phillips curve to the right, so that the economy experiences higher rates of both inflation and unemployment. This process continues until the economy reaches point C, where it stabilizes at the natural rate of unemployment.

Society is worse off at point C, than it was at point A because it faces a higher level of inflation with the same rate of unemployment, and so postelection economic policy involves deflating the economy down to D, in order to squeeze inflation out of the system. This makes the government very unpopular for a period, until the economy gradually moves back to the natural rate of unemployment at A, and some of the lost popularity is regained. The government is then in a position to start the whole process off once again. The model predicts a clear cycle of popularity with a midterm slump followed by a preelection recovery in both the economy and government popularity. The model tells a plausible story about government reactions to unpopularity, but the authors who developed it produced very little empirical evidence to support it.

A key feature of this model is that voters have short memories—they forget that the incumbent party deflated the economy immediately after the last election, and they only judge economic performance retrospectively over a short period prior to an election. These assumptions fit very badly with rational-expectations theories discussed earlier. In the above model of the political business cycle, expectations of inflation play an important role in moving the economy to a new equilibrium. It is assumed that expectations are essentially adaptive, i.e., they change gradually in response to emerging differences between expectations and outcomes as time goes by.

Recent theories of the political business cycle, again within the neoclassical tradition, incorporate rational expectations. Some of them assume that politicians are merely office seekers, and are not concerned with promoting the interests of particular groups of supporters. This is true of the work of Cukierman and Meltzer (1986), Rogoff (1987) and Rogoff and Siebert (1988). These authors see economic policy making as a game-theoretic exercise between manipulative politicians on the one hand, and voters with rational expectations on the other.

Another theory (Alesina, 1989; Alesina and Rosenthal, 1989) assumes that incumbents pursue both partisan and electoral strategies. A partisan strategy involves adopting policies which are in the interests of the core supporters of a party. Typically, parties on the left will pursue high levels of employment, even if this means high inflation, because this is in the interests of the core constituency of blue collar workers which support these parties (see Hibbs, 1977). Parties of the right will do the opposite for the same reasons. Alesina (1987) explains the origins of the cycle by considering two parties D, and R. D is less inflation averse than R, so if it wins the election it inflates the economy in order to reduce unemployment. Given rational expectations it creates an inflationary "surprise" when it wins, which, in turn, generates a cycle of reflation and enhanced popularity. The model predicts that the effects of the surprise on unemployment will be transitory, but the effects on inflation will be permanent.

The common problem with these theories is that if the full assumptions of rational expectations apply then the political business cycle cannot occur. This is because voters with rational expectations would realize that the government was manipulating the economy for political purposes, and could not be fooled into rewarding this behavior. Moreover, since manipulation of the economy implies a departure from optimal policies which makes the voters worse off, they would have every incentive to punish an incumbent who attempted to create such a cycle. Accordingly, all of these theories have to incorporate arbitrary assumptions of various kinds, which are clearly inconsistent with rational expectations, in order to generate a cycle. Rogoff and Siebert (1988), for example, assume that while voters are rational they are imperfectly informed about the policies pursued by incumbents. Thus, incumbents can increase public expenditure prior to the election, and hide the budgetary consequences of this from the voters until afterwards. Voters reward this behavior because they are assumed to have imperfect information about the true costs of the policy.

It is consistent with rational expectations for voters to have imperfect information and be surprised by unforeseen events. However, it is not consistent with the theory for voters to ignore evidence which is predictable because it is repeated. The Rogoff and Siebert model, for example, requires that voters are unable to observe a repeated pattern of manipulation in circumstances where they have every incentive to do so, since they would gain by preventing it. These models are internally inconsistent.

A smaller point can be made about the Alesina model. In this case the cycle is only possible because it is assumed that bargainers lock themselves into fixed contracts for wages before the election. They cannot change these bargains until the end of a period, during which the incumbent stimulates the economy for electoral benefit. In other words, the model requires the implausible assumption that individuals with rational expectations will agree to wage contracts which they can anticipate will make them worse off in the long run, when they would be better off negotiating contracts after the election result is known.

Another inconsistency in these theories concerns the effectiveness of policy instruments; some neo-classical theorists have argued that traditional policy instruments are ineffective or even perverse in influencing the real economy of productivity and growth (Barro, 1979; Lucas, 1980). Again, this follows from the assumptions of rational expectations where actors react to policy changes in a way which nullifies them. In this view the government should avoid stabilization policy altogether, and simply leave the economy alone to grow at the natural rate. If this is correct voters will not merely punish manipulation, but it appears difficult, if not impossible to achieve that manipulation in the first place.

To summarize, recent work on the political business cycle has been done largely by neo-classical authors, but it appears to be pervaded by inconsistencies with regard to the core assumption of rational expectations, as well as with respect to the analysis of the possibilities for manipulation of the real economy which generates the cycle. The only satisfactory way to avoid these inconsistencies is to accept that the real world is more neo-Keynesian than neo-classical in character, and that while voters may use economic expectations to judge incumbents, these expectations do not meet the unrealistic assumptions of rational expectations. In the light of this discussion we turn next to a review of the empirical evidence on political business cycles.

## Looking for the Political Business Cycle

The empirical evidence on the popularity and vote function side of the cycle is voluminous, and it has been reviewed extensively in earlier chapters. In contrast, the empirical work on reaction functions is more limited. Some of the earliest and best known research on the political business cycle by Tufte (1978) proved ambiguous in its findings. Tufte showed that the cycle appeared to occur in some countries at some periods of time, but it was not a predictable and recurring feature of the economies of these countries. However, he used relatively crude measures of the cycle and very simple methods of analysis.

Much of the empirical work on reaction functions has been done by Frey and Schneider (1978a, 1978b). In their models they make the reaction function dependent on three types of constraints: administrative, economic and electoral. Administrative constraints refer to the problems of bureaucratic inertia characteristic of any political system. Economic constraints refer to the structural characteristics of the economy, or the way in which economic variables respond to fiscal or monetary stimuli. Political constraints refer to the desire of incumbents to be reelected. In the Frey-Schneider model, if an incumbent party perceives a deficit in its current popularity, it will stimulate the economy in order to correct this and improve support and, if current levels of popularity are perceived as satisfactory, it will tend to pursue ideological goals instead. Their estimates appear to demonstrate highly significant relationships between presidential popularity and government expenditure in a reaction function model of the United States.

Alt and Chrystal (1983) challenged these findings, arguing that government expenditure depends on permanent income, or the long-term expectation of national income and, thus, is not subject to short-term manipulation by an incumbent administration. From a different perspective Ahmad (1983) criticized Frey and Schneider for disregarding some of the economic influences on presidential support. In his model presidents always react to changes in economic conditions irrespective of whether they feel their reelection prospects are threatened. More generally, a number of other writers have found empirical support for the existence of politically induced cycles in various macroeconomic variables (Ben-Porath, 1975; Grier, 1987; Keil, 1988; Laney and Willett, 1983; Maloney and Smirlock, 1981). Nevertheless, there also is a good deal of research which suggests the view that there are no such cycles. In their work on fiscal policy Golden and Poterba (1980) and Lowery (1985) found little evidence of a cycle; Beck (1984, 1987), Chappell and Keech (1985), and Elliott and Whiteley (1990) obtained similar results in analyses of monetary policy.

Recently, Alesina and Roubini (1990) have tested their rational-expectations partisan theory for 18 OECD countries over three decades, and found a pattern of cycles in unemployment consistent with their predictions. Their results for inflation are more ambiguous. They argue that incumbents pursue both partisan and opportunistic or election-oriented goals at the same time, which produces a different cycle from the standard version. In contrast, an interesting study by Nordhaus (1989) tested the strong rational-expectations assumptions referred to above. He describes these as "ultrarationality" assumptions, and shows fairly conclusively with a variety of tests that the evidence refutes them. These results cast doubt on the validity of any models which incorporate them.

There are many reasons why these empirical results should be so conflicting and inconclusive. If, as we have suggested, the neo-Keynesian analysis provides a more accurate picture of the macroeconomy than does the neo-classical one, then the economy is a large, complex and relatively inert system which is constantly in the process of adjusting to shocks of various kinds. Policy instruments are hard to control in this environment, and even when they are controlled, they do not always have the same impact on economic outcomes over time. For example, in the 1980s the apparently stable relationship between the money supply and nominal income which is the basis of the advocacy of "fixed-rule" monetarism, has completely broken down (Friedman, 1988). This means that even when actors attempt to manipulate the economy for political purposes, they may be unable to do it.

The political system also is turbulent and uncontrollable, involving a multitude of actors and pervasive uncertainty. It often demonstrates the so-called "law of unintended consequences," whereby outcomes differ radically from the intentions of the policymaker. Thus, even if all incumbents sought to manipulate the economy, it would be difficult if not impossible for them to do it on a continuous basis. At the same time, however, it is possible to point to particular case studies which exhibit strong evidence of manipulation of the economy for political gain; examples include the Nixon election of 1972 (Kettl, 1986), or the period leading up to the British election of 1987 (Miller et al, 1990). But there are many other examples, such as the 1980 U.S. presidential election or the 1974 British general election, where such manipulation looks much less plausible. In some of these cases a political business cycle may have been desired or even attempted, but there is not much evidence of its success. It seems, therefore, that political business cycles are episodic, rather than continuous features of the political economies of advanced industrial democracies.

Given that much of the work on political business cycles has been done by neo-classical theorists, and we have suggested that the neo-Keynesian analysis provides a more realistic picture of the way the world works, it is interesting to consider the implications of neo-Keynesian theories for this literature. Perhaps the most important one is that the Phillips curve is still a very important factor in macroeconomic policy, although most neo-Keynesians would accept that it is influenced by inflationary expectations, which is an argument first put by neo-classical writers. Whether there is a long-run tradeoff, or alternatively a natural rate of unemployment which rules out a long-run tradeoff, is largely irrelevant to the political business cycle, since the short-run Phillips curve is the key concern as far as political actors are concerned. Similarly, the work on the hysteresis hypothesis referred to earlier has not demonstrated that the short-run Phillips curve does not exist, although it has drawn attention to some of the structural and labor market constraints on short-term manipulation.

In the light of these considerations, the key issue for politicians is the size of the inflation-unemployment elasticity coefficient in the Phillips curve, or the price in terms of increasing inflation which they might have to pay in exchange for stimulating the economy and reducing unemployment in an election year. Given voter myopia or informational asymmetries in the system, it will be possible to operate an election cycle providing that the tradeoff between unemployment and inflation is not too severe. It may be that this coefficient is unstable over time, and, for example, differs in the 1980s from what it was in the 1960s. Again, however, this is irrelevant to politicians interested in short-term manipulation of the economy, and if such actors are interested in being reelected only once (e.g., an American president), then postelection costs associated with a successful political business cycle may be very heavily discounted.

Still, short-run costs can be important. For example, one constraint is the balance of payments and the value of the currency. If stimulating a boom is likely to produce short-term balance-of-payments deficits, together with problems for the value of the currency in international markets, then this will inhibit manipulation for political gain among all but the most selfish politicians. This is, of course, more of a problem in countries such as Britain and the United States which have chronic balance-of-payments deficits than it is in countries such as Japan and Germany which have consistent surpluses.

A second implication of neo-Keynesian theories is that the past exercises considerable influence over the present. When the economy does not quickly adjust to changes of various kinds because of rigidities in the system, policies have to be put in place well in advance of election day if they are to come to fruition at the right time. In a neo-classical world merely announcing a change of policy is enough to change the behavior of actors in the system. In a neo-Keynesian world, however, the economy turns around slowly, and the lags before policies take effect are long and variable.

It seems plausible that part of the reason why the evidence for a political business cycle is so mixed is because steering the economy to make its peaks coincide with elections is a very difficult exercise. A large-scale stochastic system subject to frequent random shocks and characterized by considerable inertia is difficult to manipulate in the short run. Given this, it is hardly surprising that the timing of a cycle can go wrong, or that exogenous shocks such as the OPEC oil price hikes of the 1970s will derail even carefully laid plans to manipulate the economy for electoral purposes.

Furthermore, the fact the elections are not coordinated on an international basis is a complication for policymakers in an increasingly interdependent world. Trade and currency relationships have an important influence on economic outcomes. One country may be in the downswing phase of the cycle when its trading partners are in the upswing phase. That interdependence interferes with national policy objectives was amply demonstrated by the policies of the newly elected socialist government in France in 1981. It attempted to reflate the economy in defiance of the conservative deflationary politics of its major trading partners. Difficulties rapidly mounted and the policy was reversed within two years (Petit, 1986).

A third point concerns the natural rate of unemployment. If this exists, then stabilization policies make no difference in the long run. As we have said, in the absence of a long-run Phillips curve it is still possible to operate the political business cycle in the short run, but no long-term differences in policy outcomes would exist between different incumbents. However, if there is a long-run Phillips curve, then stabilization policies can make a permanent difference to outcomes, which means that one party may be able to produce a better long-run performance than another. Some studies have reported such party differences. In the United States, for example, analysts have reported that lengthy periods of Democratic control of the presidency are associated with higher rates of growth (Whiteley, 1986a), reductions in distributional inequalities (Hibbs and Dennis, 1988), and lower unemployment (Hibbs, 1977; 1987:ch. 8). Although the latter finding has been disputed (e.g., Beck, 1982a), such long-run party effects, when they exist, constitute further evidence against the natural rate hypothesis. This means that incumbent parties can pursue policies which favor their supporters in the long run, in addition to operating a short-run political business cycle.

A final point concerns the role of expectations in economic policymaking. We have seen in previous chapters that subjective expectations play a role in influencing support for incumbent parties and their leaders. Clearly, incumbents can try to manipulate subjective expectations directly as an alternative or complement to manipulating the objective economy. Moreover, it is clear that there is scope for governments to influence economic expectations. Recent work on the volatility of the stock market indicates that markets are subject to speculative "bubbles" or fads and fashions which have their origins in human psychology rather than in fundamental economic values (Shiller, 1990). By judiciously controlling the flow of economic information incumbents may be able to generate a short-term bubble of economic optimism which helps their reelection chances.

Overall, a review of key debates among macroeconomic theorists suggests that managing the economy for political profit is possible, but rather difficult to achieve. Part of the manipulation involves attempting to influence economic expectations, which clearly are not characterized by rational expectations. Accordingly, we might expect to see examples of successful political business cycles operating in advanced industrial countries, but it is unlikely that manipulation will be successful in all systems at all times. In light of this, the interesting research question is to identify the circumstances under which successful political business cycles can be implemented. We consider this topic in the next section which examines the British case between 1983 and 1987.

## Manipulating the Economy for Political Profit: Britain, 1983–1987

The background to this case study of manipulation of the economy is a historical experience of "stop-go" economic policies in Britain in the post-war era (Pollard, 1982). This came about because successive governments initially stimulated and subsequently restricted economic activity. They stimulated the economy, primarily by means of fiscal policy, in order to promote economic growth and bring down unemployment, but after a time this produced inflation and balance-of-payments problems, necessitating subsequent deflation.

The 1983–87 period in Britain was chosen in order to estimate reaction and outcome functions because this was a period in which manipulation of the economy was very likely to be observed. In general, the dominance of the executive over parliament in Britain means that there are no significant domestic institutional constraints on government control of economic policy. Thus, the barriers to manipulation are either economic or political. In essence, the government needs political or economic "space" in which to maneuver if it is to create a favorable economic environment for itself in the run-up to a general election.

The major economic constraints relate to the balance of payments and the value of the pound as an international currency. In most of the post-war era balance-of-payments considerations constrained economic policy. However, by the mid-1980s North Sea Oil revenue had considerably reduced the importance of this constraint. By 1984 the direct benefits of North Sea Oil added over £20 billion to the balance-of-payments current account (Walker, 1985:36). This meant that in the run-up to the 1987 election the balance of payments was in surplus, although the surplus was rapidly dwindling as a consumer boom stimulated by government policies got underway.

Second, inflation was running at an annual rate of 3.4% in 1986 (HMSO, 1989), and so it was possible to take risks with reflation at a time when unemployment dominated inflation as the most salient issue in the public mind. We show below that the Phillips curve tradeoff during this period was very favorable, ensuring that a reduction in unemployment in the run-up to the election could be purchased at a low cost in terms of price increases.

Third, although the Conservatives were not doing especially well in public opinion polls, support for the opposition parties was divided and volatile. The former gave the Tories an incentive to attempt to manipulate the economy, whereas the latter gave it considerable political "space" in which to maneuver since neither of the opposition parties appeared to be a credible alternative government. Labour had not recovered from the internecine strife that had led to the 1981 split and formation of the SDP, and its creditability on economic policy remained questionable. The Alliance, for its part, was suffering from internal policy struggles that made it difficult to articulate coherent alternative courses of action to those being pursued by the government. Moreover, high levels of unemployment and public concern with it made it very difficult for the opposition parties to criticize government actions that might have the effect of reducing joblessness.

Here, we focus on the growth of the money supply as a policy instrument that the government might have pursued to achieve this goal. Since the publication of its Medium Term Financial Strategy (HMSO, 1980), the Thatcher government had pursued a monetarist strategy in macroeconomic policy. In essence, the Tory strategy had been one of controlling inflation by monetary methods, and ignoring the consequences of this in terms of rising unemployment. We estimate a money supply reaction function using monthly observations for the June 1983–June 1987 period. The dependent variable in the reaction function is M1, a narrowly defined measure of the money stock.

In the standard economic models the money supply is usually assumed to be exogenously determined by government (Parkin, 1984:257–59). In practice, however, the degree of government control over money is limited (Kaldor, 1982). The level of control partly depends on which definition of the money supply is being used. M1, a restricted definition of money, is subject to greater control than a broader measure such as M3, which include forms of credit difficult to regulate (Bain, 1982). An observation of M1 at any point in time is essentially a combination of money demand and supply factors.

The demand for money depends largely on current levels of economic activity (Goodhart, 1984). Thus, three variables are included in the reaction function model in order to control for these demand-side factors. The variables are inflation, real income and the fiscal policy stance as measured by the Public Sector Borrowing Requirement (the difference between government spending and taxation). Inflation tends to increase the demand for money, as does the growth of real income (Parkin, 1984:258). Theoretically, monetary policy can be quite independent of fiscal policy, but a recurring theme of Conservative economic strategy in this period was the assertion that restraint of government expenditure was required in order to reduce the money supply (Keegan, 1984). Accordingly, the reaction function looks at variations in monetary policy, controlling for the fiscal policy stance, since the government believed that fiscal policy had a direct causal impact on monetary policy.

Several variables are included in the model to test the influence of political factors on the money supply. Perhaps the most obvious political effect relates to the proximity of a general election. We distinguish between "long" and "short" campaigns—the former starting in the third year of incumbency, i.e. 1986, and the latter as soon as the official campaign was announced. Consonant with our earlier arguments, we might expect to see monetary stimulus associated with the long campaign, since monetary policy operates with significant lags. Given this, the first political variable, called the "long campaign" is a dummy variable scoring zero up to the beginning of 1986 and one thereafter. A monetary stimulus to the economy starting in early 1986 would have plenty of time to affect growth by the time of an election planned for mid-1987.

A second political variable is the level of support for the Conservative party in the opinion polls. Since it may be assumed that the government continuously monitored its popularity, one might expect it to stimulate the money supply in response to a loss of support in the polls, particularly as the election approached. A third variable is a control for the miners strike of 1984–85. This year-long strike constituted a great supply shock to the economy and, because of its political significance, the government might have stimulated economic activity in order to offset its effects.

We employ Box-Jenkins (1976) and Box-Tiao (1975) analyses to estimate the impact of the several variables in the monetary policy reaction function (see Appendix A). Considering the effects of the economic control variables only, it appears that inflation and the PSBR are both significant predictors of the money supply, whereas real growth is not (Table 8.1, Model A). Model B, which includes the political variables, shows that Conservative support (lagged one period), the miners strike and the long campaign all had significant impacts on the money supply. The negative coefficient for the effect of Conservative support is consistent with a

Table 8.1. Factors Affecting Growth of the Money Supply (M1), 1983-1987

| Predictor Variables | | | Model A | Model B |
|---|---|---|---|---|
| Inflation | $\omega$ | (B0) | 0.98a | 0.53b |
| Real growth | $\omega$ | (B0) | 0.17 | 0.33a |
| Public sector borrowing requirement | $\omega$ | (B0) | 0.002c | 0.002b |
| Conservative support | $\omega$ | (B0) | + | -0.001c |
| Long campaign | $\omega$ | (B1) | + | 0.016a |
| Miner's strike | $\omega$ | (B0) | + | 0.007b |
| Noise model | $\theta$ | (B1) | -0.27b | + |
| | $\theta$ | (B14) | + | 0.81a |
| Residual mean square (RMS) = | | | 0.000018 | 0.000007 |
| Percent improvement in RMS over univariate noise model = | | | 17.6 | 70.4 |
| Ljung-Box Q (df = 20) = | | | 21.0 | 20.0 |

a  $p \leq .01$
b  $p \leq .05$
c  $p \leq .10$; one-tailed tests

+ Variable not included in model

government strategy of relaxing the money supply in response to a loss of support in the polls. However, the effect is not particularly strong, since a 1% change in support produces only a 0.1% change in the money supply.[1] The miners strike is somewhat more influential, accounting for a 0.7% monthly increase in the money supply during the period of the strike.

The finding of a negative relationship between political support and the money supply is inconsistent with the classical political business cycle, in which a government stimulates the economy prior to the election and deflates it afterwards. According to this scenario the incumbent should not continuously react to a deficit in popularity over time, but only in the run-up to the election. A close look at the record of the Thatcher government over its entire period of office suggests that it did not follow a classical political business cycle strategy. From 1979 to 1982 it drastically deflated the economy in order to squeeze out inflation, and would very likely have lost the 1983 election had it not been for a divided opposition and the massive popularity boost the party and the prime minister enjoyed as a result of the victory in the Falklands war (see Chapters 3 and 4). As a result, the Conservatives were able to embark on the reflationary part of the cycle almost immediately after the 1983 election, since by then inflation had already been substantially reduced. This illustrates the point that a mechanical application of a political business cycle theory can be misleading, and due regard must be given to the political context in which a government operates.

The long campaign variable is highly significant, and the estimates show that form the start of 1986 the government reflated the money supply at a rate of 1.6% per month faster than was warranted by the behavior of the economy. The large reduction in the residual mean square (RMS) statistic in Model B in comparison with Model A is to a considerable extent explained by the long campaign variable. All three economic variables in model B are significant, which means that the behavior of the economy is effectively controlled in the model, and the political effects are independent of economic influences on the money supply. The only plausible explanation of the highly significant effect of the long campaign variable is that from the start of 1986 onwards the government embarked on a conscious policy of rapidly reflating the economy, a policy quite at odds with the declared aims of its original monetarist economic strategy.

In light of these results the next issue is to examine the effects of reflationary policies on inflation and unemployment, the economic outcome variables of interest. We begin by estimating the expectations-augmented Phillips curve for the 1983–87 period to provide an estimate of the tradeoff between unemployment and inflation. To simplify matters we shall take a fairly mainstream position which would be accepted by most neo-Keynesians and many neo-classical theorists, namely, that monetary policy influences the economy via three interrelated channels: interest rate effects on prices and aggregate demand; exchange rate effects on the same variables; and finally, effects of expectations on prices and output (see Fisher, 1987).

We shall examine the relationship between the money supply and outcomes, controlling for the exchange rate and price expectations. This is a partial model of the influence of monetary policy on outcomes, since it focuses on the first of the above channels, controlling for the second and the third. In practice, manipulating interest rates is the only effective policy instrument which the government can use to influence the money supply (Bank of England, 1987); the exchange rate and expectations, in contrast, are not under the control of the government. Thus, we focus on the channel of influence which is subject to effective control, while at the same time holding constant these other important transmission mechanisms.

Model A in Table 8.2 is the expectations-augmented Phillips curve, and this confirms the existence of a statistically significant tradeoff between inflation and unemployment during the 1983–87 period. Since all the economic variables in this table are in log form the coefficients can be interpreted as elasticity coefficients. Thus, a 1% increase in the reciprocal of unemployment (i.e. a decrease in unemployment) increased inflation by

Table 8.2. Factors Affecting Inflation and Unemployment, 1983-1987

| Predictor Variables | Model A: Inflation | | | Model B: Inflation | | | Model C: Unemployment | | |
|---|---|---|---|---|---|---|---|---|---|
| UnemploymentR | $\omega$ | (B0) | 0.06a | | + | | | + | |
| Inflation expectations | $\omega$ | (B0) | 0.0007 | $\omega$ | (B0) | -0.002c | | + | |
| Real growth | | + | | $\omega$ | (B0) | 0.11a | $\omega$ | (B0) | 0.41c |
| Money supply (M1) | | + | | $\omega$ | (B2) | 0.11a | $\omega$ | (B3) | 0.29c |
| Exchange rate: | | + | | $\omega$ | (B3) | -0.02c | $\omega$ | (B5) | -0.18c |
| | | + | | $\delta$ | | 0.49c | | + | |
| Noise model: | $\theta$ | (B1) | -0.31a | $\theta$ | (B1) | -0.22b | | + | |
| | $\theta$ | (B12) | -0.65a | $\theta$ | (B12) | -0.82a | | + | |
| Residual mean square (RMS) = | | 0.0000013 | | | 0.000001 | | | 0.000034 | |
| Percent improvement in RMS over univariate noise model = | | 18.8 | | | 37.5 | | | 5.3 | |
| Ljung-Box Q (df = 20) = | | 20.0 | | | 26.0 | | | 12.0 | |

a  $p \leq .01$
b  $p \leq .05$
c  $p \leq .10$; one-tailed tests

\+ Variable not included in model

R  Reciprocal of unemployment

only 0.06%. This, in turn, indicates that manipulation of the money supply designed to bring down unemployment did not involve a high price in terms of rising inflation. The Conservatives could afford to reflate the economy rapidly without appearing to counter their strongly articulated position that inflation was the chief macroeconomic priority.

Models B and C in Table 8.2 measure the impact of monetary policy, net of the various controls, on inflation and unemployment. Monetary stimulus had a statistically significant impact on both variables—after a lag of two months in the case of inflation, and three months in the case of unemployment. A 1% increase in M1 increased inflation by just over 0.1%, and decreased unemployment (i.e. increased the reciprocal of unemployment) by about 0.3%. The effects are independent of changes in the exchange rate and real growth, and in the case of model B, independent of inflationary expectations.

In fact, the monetary policy reaction function and the outcome function do not tell the whole story of manipulation of the economy prior to the 1987 election, since they say nothing about fiscal policy. In November 1986 the government scrapped its previous targets for public spending and added some £7.5 billion to public spending programs for the 1987-88 financial year. In addition, government deregulation of the financial sector, together with ferocious competition among banks and retailers to promote credit cards, produced a rapid decline in the savings ratio (the ratio of consumer savings to income)—in 1986 it was about half the value it had been in 1980. The result was a veritable explosion in consumer credit and, since the consequences of this in terms of a balance-of-payments deficit were not felt until after the 1987 election, this provided the Conservatives with an additional monetary stimulus to help them in their reelection bid.

Yet another aspect of political manipulation not observed in these results concerns the government's manipulation of the subjective economy. This took several forms including "massaging" the official unemployment statistics, preemptive leaking of selected financial statistics to confuse markets and mitigate possible negative effects, tax reductions in the March 1987 preelection budget, and an ongoing "spin control" to put an optimistic gloss on economic news (Miller et. al. 1990).

## Conclusion: The Future of the Political Business Cycle

When economic and political conditions are auspicious, it is reasonable to expect governments will attempt economic manipulation for political profit. The Conservative government in Britain sought to manipulate the economy by monetary means in order to produce a favorable economic climate in the run-up to the 1987 election. Such manipulation was particularly striking from the start of the long campaign in early 1986. Our analyses show that reflation designed to bring down unemployment could be purchased at relatively low cost in terms of increasing inflation, and that both joblessness and price increases reacted to monetary stimulus within a matter of a few months.

The research agenda in the future should concentrate on examining the variables which promote or constrain such manipulation in different political systems over time. Moreover, if the long-run Phillips curve exists, it is important to link work on the political business cycle with analyses of the effects of partisan incumbency, since under different circumstances cyclical and partisan effects may interact in different ways to influence economic outcomes. Another unresolved question concerns the influence of supply-side policies, such as tax cuts, on political support, since they too may have an important influence on outcomes beyond their effects on fiscal policy. In general, there are many channels of influence linking economic policy and political support, and the research agenda for mapping out these links is large.

In looking to the future, there are reasons for believing that political manipulation of the economy will become more difficult. This is mainly because of the increasing integration of the economies of the western advanced industrial societies, and the resulting increased coordination of macroeconomic policies this creates. Increased coordination is manifest in the growth of multinational currency-swap agreements of the type introduced by the Group of Seven nations (Bryant, 1980). A second and perhaps more significant development is the growth of free trade areas such as the North American Free Trade area of Canada, the US and Mexico and the European Economic Community. In 1992 all internal trade barriers between the twelve EEC countries will be removed and, as a result, individual governments will lose effective power over trade policies.

From the point of view of the political business cycle, however, perhaps a more directly relevant issue is the growing loss of control over monetary policy in these countries. At the present time all the major currencies of the EEC participate in the European Monetary Union which requires them to maintain exchange rates within a fairly narrow range of each other. Britain joined this system at the beginning of 1991. This development constrains monetary policy sufficiently to make it difficult for the individual governments to manipulate interest rates and exchange rates. Most probably, before the end of the century there will be a common "eurocurrency," which for all intents and purposes will replace the individual domestic currencies. Such a eurocurrency will be managed by a "Euro-Fed," or a multinational central bank analogous to the Federal Reserve in Washington. When this is in place the individual nations of the EEC will have completely lost any discretionary control over monetary policy, thereby eliminating one of the key policy instruments in the PBC.

In addition to a loss of control over monetary policy, there is also a loss of control over fiscal policy for countries with large public sector deficits like the United States. Fiscal policy has always been a difficult instrument of American policy makers to use because of the separation of powers between the Executive and Congress and the independent status of the Federal Reserve Board, but any residual discretion is taken away by the budget deficits which grew out of control during the Reagan administration. The same is true for countries like Britain which have a serious balance-of-payments problem, although not a significant domestic budget deficit. In both cases attempts at deficit spending in the run-up to an election can seriously destabilize currency values and stimulate high inflation. Thus, a Phillips-curve tradeoff such as we observed in our 1983–87 British case study is likely to become more adverse in situations of high budget deficits.

Finally, microeconomic developments can serve to constrain macroeconomic policies. The growth of multinational corporations which can effectively negate national macroeconomic policies is the most obvious example. Such corporations can use internal transfer pricing mechanisms in order to bypass government manipulation of currency values. In addition, since their investment policies have significant implications for employment in host countries, multinationals have considerable political clout which has generally been used to promote greater economic integration.

For all of the above reasons we might expect the political business cycle to become an even more episodic phenomenon in comparative political economy in the years ahead. The possibilities for PBCs will be considered further in the next chapter which focuses on international economic constraints on political action.

## Notes

1. With a logged dependent variable the interpretation of the estimates is slightly more complex than in a conventional model. The coefficient measures the relative change in Conservative support, so that multiplying the coefficient by 100 gives the percentage change in money for a 1% change in support.

# 9

# International Developments and Presidential Factors: Political Business Cycles in the United States

*The United States has less control over economic events than in the past, and that will persist. In addition, the economic knowledge required for rational control of the economy has become pathetically thin, overwhelmed by external events and discredited by predictive failures.*
—Edward Tufte (1978:x–xi)

The complexity of political business cycles (PBCs) has stirred several controversies over their incidence and their implications in representative democracies (Haynes and Stone, 1988:276–78; Lewis-Beck, 1988a:137; Weatherford, 1987:925–26; Williams, 1990:767–68). These debates have emphasized domestic conditions of the PBC while its operation in international contexts has received little attention. This chapter suggests that greater recognition of international developments promises better understanding of the interplay between political events and macroeconomic outcomes. Our models posit that major wars, the end of fixed-exchange rates, oil prices, and the shift in trade shares have influenced inflation rates and/or unemployment levels and have generated apparent *episodes* of presidential effects on America's economy from 1947–48 to 1985. Current developments portend tighter constraints on political manipulation of macroeconomic policy and fewer instances of political business cycles.

### The Controversies over Political Business Cycles

The PBC develops when the government expedites a boom (stronger growth, lower unemployment) before, and postpones the downturn (higher inflation) after, an election (see Lewis-Beck, 1988a:138). PBCs are highly controversial among political economists. One debate entails government's role and people's attitudes towards the economy (see ch. 8; Stein, 1984). Older wisdom maintains that political parties are macroeconomic agents and vote-seeking opportunists. Governing parties can exercise Phillips-curve options that create short-term improvements in economic conditions and their popularity among the electorate. Moreover, most voters have shortsighted views and/or incomplete information about the economy (see, relatedly, Asher, 1983:365–67; Backus and Driffill, 1985; Phlips, 1988:ch. 1). Accordingly, the government can swap publicly preferred expansions in the period preceding an election for soon-forgotten contractions after voting day (see ch. 8).[1]

Recent reconsiderations of the PBC identify large-scale obstacles to short-run manipulations. Large modern economies, serious structural problems, and decentralized political institutions impede the government's maneuvering of the preelection economy. Voters' awareness and their expectations of macroeconomic performance also frustrate economic manipulations at election time (Alt, 1991; Lewis-Beck, 1988a:149–51; Stimson, 1989; Williams, 1990). Thus, general elections rarely coincide with a burst in the use of expansionary policies or a boom in macroeconomic performance.[2]

Another dispute involves administration effects versus party influences on economic conditions. One assertion is that American parties are brokerage institutions which articulate pragmatic policies to attract widespread support. This pragmatism has directed *all* presidential administrations towards similar economic outcomes, particularly with regard to unemployment (Beck, 1982a, 1982b; Dinkel, 1981; Golden and Poterba, 1980; Monroe, 1983b; Thompson and Zuk, 1983). Rival claims see American parties as "quasi-principled" organizations whose issue priorities address the concerns of core constituents. These priorities have moved presidential administrations towards different results. Democratic executives have promoted employment, growth, and income opportunities for New Deal–Great Society supporters. Republican presidents have confronted inflation problems that negatively affect business groups and upper-income voters (Alesina and Rosenthal, 1989; Hibbs, 1977, 1983, 1987a:chs. 7–8; Hibbs and Dennis, 1988; Whiteley, 1988a; Woolley, 1988).

Both controversies, in turn, have spurred another argument. One position aligns administration effects with, but decouples party influences from, political business cycles. Administration effects on unemployment conditions represent economic maneuvering by vote-seeking incumbents *before* an election (Lewis-Beck, 1988a:146–47). Party influences on different outcomes reflect the implementation of economic priorities by governing parties *after* an election. These latter influences prevail *until* a party adopts expedient policies as a reaction to economic pressures on its support (Frey and Schneider, 1978a, 1978b; Woolley, 1988:337–39). An alternative position, as discussed below, is that party influences on specific conditions during election periods can be indistinguishable from the PBC.

Finally, each controversy has emphasized the domestic setting and downplayed the international context of the political business cycle. In the case of the United States, this neglect once was credible given America's commanding role and its electoral-economic spinoffs in international political economy. Indeed, several observers have suggested that simultaneous elections in the United States and its major partners have driven global economic activity (Gilpin, 1987:138; Isaak, 1991:187-90; Tufte, 1978:ch. 3). The oversight of international developments, however, now is problematic in the face of substantial growth in economic interdependence (Alt, 1979, 1985, 1987; Cooper, 1986; Garrett and Lange, 1986; Stewart, 1983). Relatedly, America's role in international economics has changed from cooperative leadership after World War II to self-serving behavior starting in the Vietnam War era (Gilpin, 1987:90, 141-44, 343-52). We argue below that various propellants of this change have affected two components of America's economy and created apparent PBCs (Stewart and Zuk, 1989).

## Two Models of the Macroeconomy

Most depictions of political business cycles have been simple specifications of election forces on economic activity. Our models elaborate presidential factors *and* international determinants of inflation rates and unemployment levels in the United States from 1947-48 to 1985. Presidential factors include election forces, administration effects, party influences, and presidential "switches." International developments involve major wars, the collapse of fixed-exchange rates under Bretton Woods, oil-price hikes, and the change in American shares of inter-OECD exports.

***Election Forces:*** These forces are tied to the timing of presidential elections. Three time frames for their operation are possible. The short period expresses the strength of presidential efforts to manipulate the economy, the swiftness of its reactions, and its salience among the electorate as the election campaign and the media's coverage intensify during the final quarter (post-Labor Day) of the president's four-year term. "The last minute," however, may be a political gamble. Accordingly, two longer periods signify that American presidents must intervene earlier since the economy responds slowly and the upturn must arrive before (not after) election day to produce political advantages (Haynes and Stone, 1988; Lewis-Beck, 1988:148-51; Williams, 1990). The intermediate period is the election year (caucus/primary season) whereas the long period is the third year of a presidential term.

***Administration Effects, Party Influences, Presidential Switches:*** As noted, administration effects arise when all presidents use available policies to lower unemployment levels. These effects in election periods synchronize the movements of political business cycles. Party influences occur as the Democrats and the Republicans wield appropriate instruments that reduce joblessness and inflation, respectively. Our argument regarding party influences in election periods recognizes that political parties combine policy priorities with vote-seeking interests. This argument also expands Tufte's (1978:102) "rule of normal times" when placid circumstances free a president to impose the program of his party on the macroeconomy before an election. Accordingly, Democratic executives stimulate preelection employment and thus activate the PBC while Republican presidents dampen not only preelection inflation but also political business cycles.

We further propose that American presidents can *switch* macroeconomic priorities during election periods. This proposal adapts Tufte's (1978:101) "rule of crisis times" when an acute problem compels a president to shift from his party's priority to the opposition's issue as a preelection remedy to this economic problem (see also Woolley, 1988). In election periods, Democratic assaults on inflation (Truman in 1947–48, Carter in 1979–80) mute, while Republican moves against unemployment (Ford in 1975–76, Reagan in 1983–84) augment, the PBC. This argument is consistent with recent studies showing that right-of-center parties in the United States and elsewhere have expanded preelection economies to bolster their popularity, while maintaining long-run commitments or policy reputations (Backus and Driffill, 1985; Williams, 1990).

Finally, American presidents who seek second terms should strengthen macroeconomic responses to administration effects, party influences, and presidential switches in election periods. Most presidents are not content with one term in the White House. Between 1947–48 and 1985, only two presidents decided not to pursue reelection (Truman in March, 1952; Johnson in March, 1968).

***Major Wars:*** Various observers have argued that major wars have manifold implications for macroeconomic performance.[3] Large-scale conflicts boost government spending and military-related employment and, accordingly, are associated with economic expansions. The surge in government spending, however, increases the likelihood of budget deficits. Spending deficits, combined with the pressures on labor markets and the supply of goods and services, tend to raise inflation rates. Higher inflation pervades the international economy in the post-war phase.

The United States was involved in two major wars between 1950 and 1975. The first began abruptly when North Korea invaded South Korea in June, 1950 and ended with the ceasefire in July, 1953. Although some observers have suggested that the Vietnam War started during the Eisenhower Administration and ended with Vietnam's 1975 reunification (Dupuy and Dupuy, 1970; Small and Singer, 1982), its duration has been a matter of some debate. The war, however, escalated sharply as American troops were committed to Vietnam in the wake of the Tonkin Gulf Resolution of August, 1964. Troop withdrawals commenced in 1969 and a ceasefire began in January, 1973, but American involvement continued until Saigon's fall in April, 1975 (Karnow, 1983).

We hypothesize that both wars had temporary effects on unemployment levels. Joblessness decreased with the initiation/escalation of conflict but rose with the diminishing of hostilities. We also propose that the wars influenced inflation rates, but that the effects were much larger for Vietnam than for Korea. Truman's awareness of price increases during World War II and its aftermath prompted his efforts to avert the inflationary pressures of the Korean conflict. These efforts included tax increases and monetary restrictions in 1950, and price ceilings in 1951 (Acheson, 1969:ch. 50; Stein, 1988:119-20). In contrast, the Johnson Administration was indifferent to the inflationary problems of the Vietnam era. Its wage-and-price guidelines were toothless while its military spending was voracious. Intermittent loosening of the money supply (Stein, 1988:120-22), coupled with the obligatory absorption of the dollar glut under the fixed-exchange provision of the Bretton-Woods Agreement (Gilpin, 1987:138), inflicted the war's inflation on America's economic partners and Johnson's successor in the White House.

*Nixon's Policies:* The Nixon Administration devised a "new" policy of controlling inflation rates and suspending the dollar-gold exchange at $35.00 per ounce to facilitate economic maneuvering (Gilpin, 1987:134-42; Keohane, 1985; Odell, 1982:ch. 4; Stein, 1988:164-66, 176-87). We hypothesize that the controls temporarily produced the intended effect (see Russell, 1983), whereas the end of fixed-exchange rates subsequently rekindled inflationary pressures. Nixon's frustration with anti-inflation initiatives under fixed rates prompted the adoption of mandatory controls in 1971, but reelection concerns induced looser spending in 1972 (Willett and Banaian, 1988:51-52). The latter provoked larger deficits, inflationary strains, and the eventual repeal of the controls (Stein, 1988:184-185). In turn, the differences in inflation rates among America's partners eroded global faith in the dollar and fixed exchange and led to floating exchange in March, 1973. This *transition* to floating rates undermined the Bretton-Woods provisions of 1944 and, thus, their deterrence of inflationary activity in the industrial countries (Keohane, 1985:84-88, 96; see also Kegley and Wittkopf, 1985:178-93 and Triffin, 1978). The types of exchange rates, however, have debatable effects on economic conditions. One debate involves whether fixed rates provide international constraints on government's use of monetary policy and, thus, lower inflation, whereas flexible rates boost government's discretion over monetary instruments and, hence, stimulate inflation.[4]

*Oil Prices:* In 1948, Middle-East oil accounted for only 12% of global output and the United States became a net importer for the first time since the 1920s (Frank, 1966:31). Despite the latter development, American-Canadian imports of Middle-East oil averaged only 166,000 barrels per day in 1950 (Leeman, 1962:269). By the early 1970s, however, American imports from the region approached one million barrels per day and Middle-East production reached 40% of global output. Against the background of increasing reliance on foreign oil, the Arab OPEC countries quadrupled per-barrel prices from approximately $3 in September, 1973 to $11 in January, 1974. The "price shock," however, had little apparent effect on America's foreign-oil consumption. By 1978, American imports were 6.4 million barrels per day, 55% of which came from the Middle East, and America's annual consumption of nearly 19 million barrels per day was four million more than the total for other "big seven" countries (*Petroleum Economist,* 1986; U.S. Central Intelligence Agency, 1983). One year later, the Iranian revolution caused another shock in which per-barrel prices more than doubled from $13 in early 1979 to $31 in late 1980.

Our hypothesis that both hikes fueled American stagflation accords with the arguments of other analysts (Alt, 1985; Hibbs, 1985; Rostow, 1978; Schmidt, 1982; Spero, 1981). Inflationary effects of higher prices grew with intense competition over oil supplies that reflected the deficiency of energy programs in oil-importing countries (Keohane, 1985:89–92). Moreover, unemployment problems worsened as American consumers adjusted to inflated prices for petroleum-based products and other commodities. America's economic woes prompted disjointed policies from successive administrations, and defied "jawboning" schemes as well as vacuous slogans, such as Ford's WIN (Whip Inflation Now). During Ford's entire term and Carter's first two years, anti-inflation measures were avoided while monetary policies promised to sustain economic growth and lower oil prices (expressed in dollar terms) by depreciating the dollar. These policies stimulated import costs and inflation problems (Keohane, 1985:97–101; Stein, 1988:213–18). Carter's remaining years and Reagan's first term, however, witnessed anti-inflation battles as Paul Volcker, the Federal Reserve Chairman, tightened monetary policy which raised interest rates, strengthened the dollar, and jeopardized investment, exports, and employment (Gilpin, 1987:352; Isaak, 1991:67–68, 188-89; Kenski, 1989; Keohane, 1985:97–101; Stein, 1988:226–33, chs. 7-8).

*Trade Shares:* A major development in international political economy has been the declining competitiveness of the United States with major export-oriented countries (Gilpin, 1987:194, 368–73). Indeed, America's share of the exports among the countries that became OECD members and most active in international trade (Isaak, 1991:8-9) dropped from 75% in 1948 to 35% in 1985. Falling exports and mounting imports have produced substantial trade deficits. Although American deficits were relatively minor in the quarter century after World War II (Stein, 1988:379) and its surplus was almost $3 billion in 1975, since then trade deficits have ballooned with *monthly* shortfalls reaching double-digit billions of dollars in 1985. We suggest that America's changing portion of the inter-OECD exports has had a deleterious effect on its unemployment. Unprotected workers face possible layoffs when economic production misadjusts to consumer preferences for particular goods or relocates to other countries with competitive advantages, and restrictive policies, *inter alia,* boost export costs (Alt, 1985:1020; Gilpin, 1987:ch. 5, 350-54, 369-73; Zysman, 1985:146-48, 166-67).

## Measures and Methods

Our models of macroeconomic outcomes specify domestic events including presidential elections and Nixon's controls, and international incidents involving both wars and the end of fixed-exchange rates, as dichotomous interventions. These events are scored 1 for each active quarter and 0 for other times. Presidential elections comprise election quarters (the short period), four quarters of election years (the intermediate period), and four quarters of third years of presidential terms (the long period). These variables are designed to capture election-timed maneuvering of all presidents (administration effects), all Democrats or all Republicans (party influences), Truman-Carter with Republicans and Ford-Reagan with Democrats (presidential switches), and (re)election-seeking presidents. The latter were Truman (1948, first quarter of 1952), Eisenhower (1956), Johnson (1964, first quarter of 1968), Nixon (1972), Ford (1976), Carter (1980), and Reagan (1984). The macroeconomic effects of various presidential factors are estimated separately.

The Korean War is specified as influencing inflation and unemployment in all quarters from its beginning in June, 1950 to its conclusion in July, 1953. The Vietnam War affected unemployment in all quarters from initial commitments that required more military-related personnel in the first quarter of 1965, to initial withdrawals that forced various workers to seek other jobs in the third quarter of 1969. Despite this early withdrawal, American spending continued. Accordingly, the Vietnam War is treated as an inflationary event for all quarters from the escalation in the first quarter of 1965 to the ceasefire in the first quarter of 1973. Wage-and-price controls are hypothesized to have affected inflation during all quarters from their introduction in the fourth quarter of 1971 to their suspension in the second quarter of 1973. The end of fixed-exchange rates (Bretton Woods) started in March, 1973 and is modeled as a permanent intervention. The effects of the termination of Bretton Woods and the controls on inflation rates are estimated separately.

International developments involving both rounds of oil-price hikes and American shares of inter-OECD exports are modeled using continuous variables. The posted price of Saudi Arabian light crude oil is a conventional measure reported in Frank (1966), *Petroleum Intelligence Weekly,* and Seymour (1981). These prices are expressed as quarterly averages. The data on American exports to OECD countries and all exports among these countries from 1947 to 1985 were ascertained from the U.S. Bureau of the Census (1949–61) and the OECD (1961–86). The values of American exports to the values of all exports are calculated as quarterly ratios. The dependent variables, inflation rates (1947–85) and unemployment levels (1948–85), are continuous series obtained from U.S. Department of Commerce reports (1976, 1986). Unemployment levels are quarterly averages and inflation rates are quarterly averages of six-month changes in consumer prices (base period is 1967 = 100).

Both macroeconomic models are estimated with Box-Jenkins-Tiao time series methods (see Appendix A). Inflation and unemployment are first differenced to control for mean nonstationarity. Their univariate ARIMA (noise) models include a first-order, moving average parameter ($\theta(B^1)$) to control for within-series correlation. In sum, the models are:

$$(1-B)INF_t = \omega_1(1-B)EINT_t + \omega_2(1-B)CINT_t + \omega_3(1-B)KINT_{t-1}$$

$$+ \omega_4(1-B)VINT_t + \omega_5(1-B)FINT_t + \omega_6/(1-\delta B)(1-B)OIL_{t-1}$$

$$+ (1-\theta_1 B)a_t$$

$$(1-B)UNEMP_t = \omega_1(1-B)EINT_t + \omega_2(1-B)KINT_{t-1} + \omega_3(1-B)VINT_t$$

$$+ \omega_4(1-B)OIL_{t-1} + \omega_5/(1-\delta B)(1-B)EXP_{t-1} + (1-\theta_1 B)a_t$$

where:

$INF_t$ = inflation rate at time t

$UNEMP_t$ = unemployment level at time t

$EINT_t$ = domestic intervention - presidential election at time t

$CINT_t$ = domestic intervention - inflation controls at time t

$KINT_{t-1}$ = international intervention - Korean War at time t-1

$VINT_t$ = international intervention - Vietnam War at time t

$FINT_t$ = international intervention - end of fixed-exchange rates at time t

$OIL_{t-1}$ = international development - oil prices at time t-1

$EXP_{t-1}$ = international development - export shares at time t-1

B = backshift operator

t-i = time lag, i = 0, 1

$\omega$ = impact parameter

$\delta$ = decay parameter

$\theta$ = moving average parameter

$a_t$ = error term at time t

## Presidents, International Developments, and the Economy

Table 9.1 presents the results of several analyses of the effects of presidential factors and international developments on inflation rates. The analyses show that price increases accelerated in election quarters, albeit less so during Republican administrations. Higher inflation also occurred in election years and third years of presidential terms when administration effects are considered.[5] Consumer prices, however, dropped in election years and third years when Republicans or Republicans and two conservative Democrats (Truman, Carter) presided. The largest reductions reflect the influence of Republican presidents in election years ($\omega$ = -.12), reelection-seeking Republicans in third years ($\omega$ = -.16), and the latter with two Democrats (Truman, Carter) who switched to anti-inflation concerns one year before election years ($\omega$ = -.16). Although these results suggest that inflation rates during presidential elections manifested Republican influences and Democratic switches, the larger point is that all presidential factors are statistically insignificant (p > .05). Accordingly, arguments specifying election forces and party differences in inflation outcomes are problematic.

Table 9.1. Effects of Presidential Factors and International Developments on Inflation, 1947-1985

| Predictor Variables | | Coefficients |
|---|---|---|
| **Presidential elections:** | | |
| Election quarter | – All administrations | $\omega$ (B0) .07 |
| | – Republican administrations | $\omega$ (B0) .02 |
| | – Republican with Truman/Carter administrations | $\omega$ (B0) .04 |
| | – All reelection seekers | $\omega$ (B0) -.01 |
| | – Republican reelection seekers | $\omega$ (B0) -.08 |
| | – Republican reelection seekers with Carter | $\omega$ (B0) -.02 |
| Election Year | – All administrations | $\omega$ (B0) -.04 |
| | – Republican administrations | $\omega$ (B0) -.12 |
| | – Republican with Truman/Carter administrations | $\omega$ (B0) -.06 |
| | – All reelection seekers | $\omega$ (B0) -.00 |
| | – Republican reelection seekers | $\omega$ (B0) -.07 |
| | – Republican reelection seekers with Truman/Carter | $\omega$ (B0) -.01 |
| Third Year | – All administrations | $\omega$ (B0) .02 |
| | – Republican administrations | $\omega$ (B0) -.07 |
| | – Republican with Truman/Carter administrations | $\omega$ (B0) -.09 |
| | – All reelection seekers | $\omega$ (B0) -.01 |
| | – Republican reelection seekers | $\omega$ (B0) -.16 |
| | – Republican reelection seekers with Truman/Carter | $\omega$ (B0) -.16 |
| Korean war+ | | $\omega$ (B1) -.35 |
| Vietnam war+* | | $\omega$ (B0) .52b |
| Nixon's wage-and-price controls+ | | $\omega$ (B0) -.92b |
| Fixed exchange rates (Bretton Woods) end+* | | $\omega$ (B0) 2.70b |
| Oil prices+* | | $\omega$ (B1) .27b |
| Noise model | | $\delta$ .78b |
| | | $\theta$ (B1) -.78b |

+ Effects of these events are reported for election quarters. There are minor variations in its coefficients and significance across election periods.

b $p \leq .05$; one-tailed test

\* Permanent effect

Table 9.1 also shows that consumer prices fell by an insignificant quarterly average of .35 points during the three years of the Korean War. Contrariwise, inflation rates rose by a significant quarterly average of .52 points throughout the eight years of the Vietnam War. These effects accord with our expectations that Truman's timely caution partially relieved, while Johnson's persistent indifference strongly intensified, the inflationary pressures associated with their military commitments. The Nixon administration inherited the Vietnam inflation, and the analyses reveal that inflation rates dropped by a significant quarterly average of almost one point during the period of his wage-and-price controls. The move towards looser exchange rates and the demise of the Bretton-Woods system, however, prompted an increase of 2.7 points in the inflation index. This effect, *ceteris paribus*, amounted to an increase of nearly 11 points on an annual basis. Oil-price hikes had both immediate and longer-lasting effects on American inflation. Their initial impact was felt in the following quarter ($\omega = .27$) and, as the dynamic term ($\delta = .78$) indicates, the effect persisted across several subsequent quarters. Each rise of $1 in oil prices eventually produced an increase of 1.23 points in consumer prices.[6]

The relative impact of international developments and presidential factors on inflation rates is further evident in a comparison of their ability to reduce the RMS (residual mean square) statistic. The RMS for the univariate ARIMA model of inflation is 1.48. It decreases by only 1.4% (to 1.46) with the addition of Republican incumbency in the year before an election (a larger presidential factor in Table 9.1) and Nixon's wage-and-price controls. In sharp contrast, the inclusion of international developments reduces the RMS by 51% (from 1.46 to .72). The Vietnam War, the Bretton-Woods failure, and the oil-price hikes clearly overshadowed presidential influences in election periods on American inflation.

Table 9.2 reports the effects of presidential factors and international events on unemployment levels. Administration effects in the short period (election quarter) resulted in slightly higher joblessness. All presidential factors in the third year triggered somewhat bigger increases.[7] Unemployment figures, however, fell during election quarters for Democratic presidents or all Democrats and two Republicans (Ford, Reagan) who switched their priority to unemployment. The largest declines occurred in election years involving administration effects ($\omega = -.11$), Democratic influences ($\omega = -.13$), or these influences combined with Republican shifts ($\omega = -.13$). The bigger story, however, is that all presidential factors are statistically insignificant. This evidence challenges the hypothesis that administration effects, Democratic influences, or Republican switches in election periods have major effects on unemployment levels and, by extension, casts doubt on the operation of political business cycles.

Table 9.2. Effects of Presidential Factors and International Developments on Unemployment, 1947-85

| Predictor Variables | | Coefficients |
|---|---|---|
| **Presidential Elections:** | | |
| Election Quarter – All administrations | 3 (B0) | .02 |
| – Democratic administrations | 3 (B0) | -.09 |
| – Democratic administrations with Ford/Reagan | 3 (B0) | -.07 |
| – All reelection seekers | 3 (B0) | .03 |
| – Democratic reelection seekers | 3 (B0) | -.07 |
| – Democratic reelection seekers with Ford/Reagan | 3 (B0) | -.05 |
| Election Year – All administrations | 3 (B0) | -.11 |
| – Democratic administrations | 3 (B0) | -.13 |
| – Democratic administrations with Ford/Reagan | 3 (B0) | -.13 |
| – All reelection seekers | 3 (B0) | -.07 |
| – Democratic reelection seekers | 3 (B0) | -.07 |
| – Democratic reelection seekers with Ford/Reagan | 3 (B0) | -.08 |
| Third Year – All administrations | 3 (B0) | .09 |
| – Democratic administrations | 3 (B0) | .07 |
| – Democratic administrations with Ford/Reagan | 3 (B0) | .06 |
| – All reelection seekers | 3 (B0) | .07 |
| – Democratic reelection seekers | 3 (B0) | .03 |
| – Democratic reelection seekers with Ford/Reagan | 3 (B0) | .03 |
| Korean war+ | 3 (B1) | -.46b |
| Vietnam war+ | 3 (B0) | -.30c |
| Oil prices+ | 3 (B1) | .13b |
| Export shares+ | 3 (B1) | .03b |
| Noise model | $\delta$ | .71b |
| | $\theta$ (B1) | -.55b |

+ Effects of these events are reported for election quarters. There are minor variations in its coefficients and significance across election periods.

b $p \leq .05$
c $p \leq .10$; one-tailed test

\* Permanent effect

In contrast, unemployment declined by a significant quarterly average of .46% during the three-year Korean War and .30% during the first four years of the Vietnam War. Oil-price increases, however, worsened American joblessness—each $1 hike fuelled a .13% rise. The magnitude of this effect suggests that, *ceteris paribus,* the approximately $30 increase in oil prices between 1973 and 1982 was responsible for a nearly 4% rise in unemployment over this period. Finally, growing trade imbalances between the United States and other OECD countries also have had consequences for unemployment. The impact was immediate ($\omega = .03$) as each 1% decrease in America's share of inter-OECD exports provoked a .03% increase in American joblessness. The significant dynamic parameter in the model ($\delta = .71$) indicates that these effects grew over time such that every 1% fall in America's share eventually triggered a .10% increase in its unemployment.[8] *Ceteris paribus,* the total effect of the 35% decrease in the ratio of American exports to all OECD exports between 1948 and 1985 was 3.5% more joblessness during this period.

A comparison of the ability of international developments and presidential factors to reduce the RMS furthers our understanding of their relative effects on unemployment levels. The RMS for the univariate ARIMA model of unemployment is .14. This statistic declines slightly (to .137) with the addition of Democratic influences in election years (a larger presidential factor in Table 9.2). The RMS, however, falls to only .126 with the inclusion of international events. These results thus belie earlier indications that foreign occurrences, rather than presidential factors, constitute dominant explanations of American unemployment. The similarity of their impact connotes not only the properties of modern economies that involve rigid structures or market operations, but also an overlap in the effects of American presidents and foreign developments. One commonality was the conduct of two wars by two Democrats in the periods prior to presidential elections.

## Conclusion

This chapter has investigated competing claims about the operation of political business cycles. Our analyses detect little evidence of administration effects, Republican influences, or Democratic switches to price issues in election periods on American inflation from 1947–48 to 1985. During this period, unemployment levels also proved unresponsive to election timings of Republican shifts to joblessness problems, Democratic priorities, or administration effects.

In contrast, international developments had larger consequences. Both wars in Southeast Asia reduced domestic unemployment and Vietnam spurred inflation. Nixon's wage-and-price controls had the intended effect, but the end of fixed rates under Bretton Woods reignited inflationary problems in early 1973. Subsequently, the oil-price hikes severely aggravated both macroeconomic conditions. The growing imbalance in the export trade between the United States and other OECD countries, particularly Japan and Canada, also has worsened American unemployment.

These findings suggest that presidential elections and party priorities are relatively insignificant determinants of economic outcomes. The results also dispute the views that administration effects, Democratic influences, or Republican adoption of unemployment concerns in election periods have propelled political business cycles in the United States. It is noteworthy, however, that presidential actions have unleashed international developments which, in turn, have precipitated election-timed boosts and party differences in macroeconomic performance, and several apparent episodes of the PBC. Unemployment fell while both wars escalated pending two elections (1952, 1968) in Democratic terms (Truman, Johnson). Joblessness, however, rose as military demobilization proceeded during the successive tenures of two Republican presidents (Eisenhower, Nixon). The Johnson Administration accorded little attention while Nixon's incoming administration assigned high priority to Vietnam's inflationary consequences. This inflation succumbed temporarily to Nixon's use of wage-and-price controls from the summer of 1971 through the 1972 election (despite expansionary actions at this time) to the spring of 1973. The wars, then, largely account for party differences in economic priorities as well as "surge-decline" episodes in macroeconomic conditions that mimic political business cycles.

Other developments in international relations have restrained presidents' operation of a PBC and party priorities on macroeconomic issues. Events in the Middle East in the 1970s sharply increased oil prices which effected higher inflation *and* higher unemployment. These events prodded Carter's shift from a traditional Democratic preoccupation (unemployment) to a conventional Republican concern (inflation) in the year before the 1980 election, while Gerald Ford and Ronald Reagan switched from "Republican inflation" to "Democratic unemployment" in the 1975–76 and 1983–84 election periods, respectively. Despite possible economic effects of the 1984 election and Reagan's policy change, falling oil prices were the major force behind America's economic upturn.

Finally, two developments have had protracted implications for macroeconomic performance. The end of fixed-exchange rates generated higher inflation while the erosion of America's exports produced more unemployment. The latter, in turn, has contributed to long-term correlations between party control of the presidency and unemployment levels. Between 1948 and 1985, export shares on average were somewhat higher during Democratic administrations (56%) than Republican ones (51%), with the largest differences occurring between the Truman Administration (64%) and Reagan's first term (44%).

In the quarter century after World War II, the United States played an acquiescent role in the international political economy, but exchange-rate concerns and trade deficits have led successive administrations to elevate American interests since that time (see Gilpin, 1987:90, 343–52; Keohane, 1985). The opposition of the United States to a fixed-exchange system hastened the demise of a centripetal force in international political economy. The collapse of Bretton Woods, however, became the impetus to EEC arrangements that would implement stable currencies, but restrict the use of monetary instruments for electoral manipulation in member countries. In the United States, political maneuvering of macroeconomic policy may yield to America's problems of falling exports and rising deficits and its posture towards free trade in North America. These problems should constrain government's ability to employ expansionary policies that implement PBCs because they would devalue the dollar and worsen the debt. Free trade portends structural improvements and mutual benefits that partially depend on presidents' willingness to endorse responsible policies and long-term goals. This willingness would entail a rejection of the self-serving motives that underlie political business cycles.

Over the past forty years, international events have generated apparent episodes of the PBC in the United States. Recent international developments may exert comparably strong influences on the American economy. These influences have contradictory implications for the process of representative government and, more specifically, the attribution of political responsibility for economic outcomes. A negative implication is that elected officials increasingly may blame bad economic conditions on international forces, but assume credit for good ones that are the products of such forces. Such fictitious bombast would attenuate voters' ability to hold incumbents accountable for the performance of America's economy. A positive implication of America's exposure to international events is a further restriction of policy manipulations for vote-getting purposes. Fewer electoral-economic antics, in turn, could facilitate the electorate's scrutiny of incumbents' overall records and competing parties' policy proposals. This process would enrich public discourse about parties' abilities to resolve pressing problems as well as enhance the quality of voters' decisionmaking. International economic developments, then, may help to elevate the cause of representative government over the aspirations of self-serving politicians by further restraining their ability to practice the arts of the political business cycle.

## Notes

1. See also Borooah and van der Ploeg (1983); Grier (1989); Haynes and Stone (1988); Hibbs (1987a); Nordhaus (1975); Tufte (1978); and Williams (1990).

2. Previous studies are Alt and Chrystal (1983:ch. 5); Beck (1984, 1987); Elliott and Whiteley (1990); Golden and Poterba (1980); Lewis-Beck (1988a:ch. 9); Lowery (1985); MacRae (1977); and Woolley (1984).

3. Such observers include Berry (1991:ch. 9); Calleo (1981); Gilpin (1987:100–111); Hamilton (1977); Krell (1981); Nincic and Cusack (1979); Rasler and Thompson (1985); Russett (1982); Thompson and Zuk (1982); Zuk (1985); and Zuk and Woodbury (1986).

4. See Alt (1987); Gilpin (1987:138–51); Odell (1982:ch. 5); Willett and Banaian (1988:45–47, 51–52); and Winer (1986).

5. Additional analyses reveal that inflation rates rose during full terms (16 quarters) of Republican presidents (.48 point, quarterly average = .03 point) and Democratic presidents (1.4 points, quarterly average = .09 point). These effects, however, were statistically insignificant.

6. The effect is calculated as $\omega/(1-\delta)$.

7. Other analyses show that unemployment levels increased during four-year terms of Republican presidents (1.4%, quarterly average = .15%) but fell in equivalent intervals of Democratic presidents (-1.1%, quarterly average = -.07%). These influences again were statistically insignificant.

8. See note 6 above.

# Appendix A: Box-Jenkins-Tiao Time Series Analysis

The Box-Jenkins-Tiao (B-J-T) approach to time series analysis (Box and Jenkins, 1976; Box and Tiao, 1975) provides a powerful and flexible method for analyzing a wide variety of theoretically interesting models of the effects of continuous independent variables and dichotomous (0–1) interventions on a dependent (outcome) variable of interest. The effects of both types of independent variables may be modeled as acting contemporaneously and/or with lags, and their full magnitude may be realized either immediately or over multiple time periods.

An example of a B-J-T model of party support is:

$$POP_t = \omega_1 INF_t + \omega_2 UNEM_{t-1} + \omega_3/(1-\delta_1 B^i)INTER_t + \theta_q(B^i)/\phi_p(B^i)a_t$$

where:

$POP_t$ = party support at time t

$INF_t$ = inflation rate affecting party support at time t, i.e., without a lag

$UNEM_{t-1}$ = unemployment rate affecting party support at time t-1, i.e., with a lag of one period

$INTER_t$ = an intervention (e.g., a scandal, war, policy innovation) affecting party support at time t

$a_t$ = error term

$\omega_{1-3}$ = coefficients measuring the effects of the independent variables

$\delta_1$ = coefficient measuring the rate at which the impact of INTER is realized if INTER has a permanent effect, or the rate at which the impact of INTER decays if the effect is temporary

$\theta_q$ = coefficient measuring a moving average process in the noise model for POP with q designating the order of the process

$\phi_p$ = coefficient measuring an autoregressive process in the noise model for POP with p designating the order of the process

$B^i$ = backshift operator to denote effects operating at a previous point (i) in time

t = time period, i.e., month, quarter, year, etc.

B-J-T procedures analyze models such as the above through an iterative process of model identification, estimation and diagnosis. Major steps in the process are as follows: (a) Identifying and estimating a univariate ARIMA (autoregressive, integrated, moving average) model for the dependent variable: B-J-T procedures require that the dependent variable be stationary in its mean and variance. Various diagnostics such graphic displays of the data and autocorrelation and partial autocorrelation functions (ACFs and PACFS) are used to diagnose nonstationarity. If a series is characterized by processes of trend or drift such that its mean evolves systematically over time, the series is differenced to achieve mean stationarity. Variance nonstationarity is addressed by transforming the series; a natural logarithmic transformation typically is employed for this purpose.

The stationary series is then modeled in terms of its history (i.e., its past values). The ACF and PACF of the stationary series are employed as diagnostic tools to identify autoregressive ($\phi_p$) or moving average ($\theta_q$) processes. If it appears that such processes are operating, appropriate parameters are estimated. The resulting ARIMA or "noise model" is deemed adequate if estimated $\phi$ or $\theta$ parameters are statistically significant and model residuals are "white noise" (uncorrelated). The Ljung-Box Q (Ljung and Box, 1978), which is distributed as $\chi^2$ provides an overall test for correlated residuals at lags 1 through N periods. (b) Identifying and estimating univariate ARIMA models for the continuous independent variables: The procedures described above are applied to each of the independent variables. (c) Specifying the time-lag(s) at which continuous independent variables affect the dependent variable: Lags can be specified theoretically a priori or, lacking "strong theory," by cross-correlating each independent variable with the dependent variable. When computing cross-correlations the dependent variable is first "prewhitened" by filtering it using the univariate ARIMA model for the independent variable in question. The filtered dependent variable is then cross-correlated with the residuals from the noise model for the independent variable to ascertain the lags at which the latter affects the former. Note that cross-correlations are an aid to model identification—hypothesized lagged effects must make sense theoretically, and effects which are not statistically significant in bivariate analyses may become so when a full multivariate model is tested. (d) Specifying the effects of dichotomous independent variables (interventions): Such effects may be hypothesized to be permanent or temporary, and abrupt or gradual. Gradual effects are modeled through the use of "adjustment" ($\delta_i$) parameters. In the case of permanent effects, $\delta$ estimates the rate at which the full impact of the intervention is realized; in the case of a temporary effect, $\delta$ estimates the rate at which the impact of an intervention decays. (e) Specifying the multivariate model and estimating its parameters: Steps (a)-(d) provide the information needed to specify the full multivariate model. Model parameters are then estimated. (f) Model diagnosis: Estimated parameters are tested for statistical significance. Also, model residuals should be white noise and, again, this is ascertained by computing an ACF and Ljung-Box Q for the residuals. If there is significant information in the residuals, a new noise model is specified, and the entire multivariate model is reestimated and rediagnosed. This procedure continues until residuals are white noise and the model is judged to be otherwise satisfactory. (g) Goodness-of-Fit: The goodness-of-fit of fit of a B-J-T model is typically assessed by computing the residual mean square (RMS) statistic: RMS = $1/N(\Sigma r^2_t)^{1/2}$ for a set of N residuals ($r_t$). Unlike $R^2$ in conventional ordinary least squares regression analysis, RMS is not standardized. The explanatory power of a set of continuous and dichotomous independent variables often is assessed by computing the RMS for the univariate ARIMA (noise) model of the dependent variable and then calculating the percentage reduction in RMS when the independent variables are added and the model is reestimated.

Major statistical software packages such as BMDP, RATS, and SAS contain routines for estimating the parameters in B-J-T models and computing diagnostics such as ACF's and PACF's. The analyses presented in this book were performed using BMDP 2T.

A detailed, but relatively nontechnical, discussion of B-J-T modeling procedures may be found in McCleary and Hay (1980). For a useful introduction see Norpoth (1986).

# References

Abramowitz, Alan I., David J. Lanoue, and Subha Ramesh. 1988. "Economic Conditions, Causal Attributions, and Political Evaluations in the 1984 Presidential Election." *Journal of Politics* 50:848–63.

Abramson, Paul R., John H. Aldrich, and David W. Rohde. 1990. *Change and Continuity in the 1988 Elections.* Washington, D.C.: Congressional Quarterly Press.

Abramson, Paul R. and Charles W. Ostrom, Jr. 1991. "Macropartisanship: An Empirical Reassessment." *American Political Science Review* 85:181–92.

Acheson, Dean. 1969. *Present at the Creation: My Years in the State Department.* New York: W. W. Norton.

Ahmed, Kabir V. 1983. "An Empirical Study of Politico-Economic Interaction in the United States: A Comment." *Review of Economics and Statistics* 65:173–77.

Aldrich, John H. and Forrest D. Nelson. 1984. *Linear Probability, Logit, and Probit Models.* Sage University Paper Series on Quantitative Applications in the Social Sciences, series no.07–045. Beverly Hills: Sage Publications.

Alesina, Alberto. 1987. "Macroeconomic Policy in a Two-Party System as a Repeated Game." *Quarterly Journal of Economics* 102:651–78.

———. 1989. "Politics and Business Cycles in Industrial Democracies." *Economic Policy* 8:57–98.

Alesina, Alberto and Howard Rosenthal. 1989. "Partisan Cycles in Congressional Elections and the Macroeconomy." *American Political Science Review* 83:373–98.

Alesina, Alberto and N. Roubini. 1990. "Political Cycles in OECD Economies." Paper given at a conference on Economic Policy in Political Equilibrium, Stockholm, June 1990.

Alesina, Alberto and Jeffrey Sachs. 1988. "Political Parties and the Business Cycle in the United States, 1948–1984." *Journal of Money, Credit and Banking* 20:63–82.

Alt, James E. 1979. *The Politics of Economic Decline: Economic Management and Political Behavior in Britain Since 1964.* Cambridge: Cambridge University Press.

———. 1985. "Political Parties, World Demand and Unemployment: Domestic and International Sources of Economic Activity." *American Political Science Review* 79:1016–40.

———. 1987. "Crude Politics: Oil and the Political Economy of Unemployment in Britain and Norway, 1970–1985." *British Journal of Political Science* 17:149–99.

———. 1991. "Ambiguous Intervention: The Role of Government Action in Public Evaluation of the Economy." In *Economics and Politics: The Calculus of Support*, ed. Helmut Norpoth, Michael S. Lewis-Beck, and Jean-Dominique Lafay. Ann Arbor, MI: University of Michigan Press.

Alt, James E. and K. Alec Chrystal. 1983. *Political Economics*. Berkeley: University of California Press.

American Political Science Association (APSA), Committee on Political Parties. 1950. "Toward a More Responsible Two-Party System." *American Political Science Review* 44:Supplement.

Antunes, George and James A. Stimson. 1988. *User's Guide to Micro-Crunch*. Houston: Softex Micro Systems.

Archer, Keith. 1987. "A Simultaneous Equation Model of Canadian Voting Behavior." *Canadian Journal of Political Science* 20:553–72.

Archer, Keith and Marquis Johnson. 1988. "Inflation, Unemployment and Canadian Federal Voting Behaviour." *Canadian Journal of Political Science* 21:569–85.

Arrow, Kenneth J. 1963. *Social Choice and Individual Values*. Revised Edition. New York: John Wiley and Sons.

Asher, Herbert B. 1983. "Voting Behavior Research in the 1980s: An Examination of Some Old and New Problem Areas." In *Political Science: The State of the Discipline*, ed. Ada W. Finifter. Washington: American Political Science Association.

Backus, David and John Driffill. 1985. "Inflation and Reputation." *American Economic Review* 75:530–38.

Bain, A.D. 1982. *The Control of the Money Supply*. Harmondsworth, Middlesex: Penguin.

Ball, L., N. Gregory Mankiw, and D. Romer. 1988. *The New Keynesian Economics and the Output-Inflation Trade-Off*. Brookings Papers on Economic Activity 1:1–82.

Bank of England. 1987. "The Instrument of Monetary Policy." *Bank of England Quarterly Bulletin* 27:365–70.

Barro, Robert J. 1979. "Second Thoughts on Keynesian Economics." *American Economic Review*. Papers and Proceedings of the Ninety-First Annual Meeting of the American Economic Association. 69:54–59.

Barry, Brian. 1970. *Sociologists, Economists, and Democracy*. London: Collier-Macmillan.

Beck, Nathaniel. 1982a. "Parties, Administrations and Macroeconomic Outcomes." *American Political Science Review* 76:83–93.

———. 1982b. "Presidential Influence on the Federal Reserve in the 1970s." *American Journal of Political Science* 26:415–45.

———. 1984. "Domestic Political Sources of American Monetary Policy 1955-82." *Journal of Politics* 46:786–817.

———. 1987. "Elections and the Fed: Is There a Political Monetary Cycle?" *American Journal of Political Science* 31:194–216.

———. 1991. "The Economy and Presidential Approval: An Information Theoretic Perspective." In *Economics and Politics: The Calculus of Support,* ed. Helmut Norpoth, Michael S. Lewis-Beck and Jean-Dominique Lafay. Ann Arbor, MI: University of Michigan Press.
Beck, Paul Allen. 1986. "Choice, Context, and Consequence: Beaten and Unbeaten Paths Toward a Science of Electoral Behavior." In *Political Science: The Science of Politics,* ed. Herbert F. Weisberg. New York: Agathon Press.
Beer, Samuel. 1965. *British Politics in the Collectivist Age.* New York: Alfred A. Knopf.
———. 1982. *Britain Against Itself: The Political Contradictions of Collectivism.* New York: W. W. Norton.
Begg, David K. H. 1984. *The Rational Expectations Revolution in Macroeconomics.* Baltimore: John Hopkins University Press.
Ben-Porath, Y. 1975. "The Years of Plenty and the Years of Famine—A Political Business Cycle?" *Kyklos* 28:400–03.
Berry, Brian J. L. 1991. *Long-Wave Rhythms in Economic Development and Political Behavior.* Baltimore: Johns Hopkins University Press.
Blaug, Mark. 1968. *Economic Theory in Retrospect.* London: Heinemann.
Bloom, Howard S. and H. Douglas Price. 1975. "Voter Response to Short-Run Economic Conditions: The Asymmetric Effects of Prosperity and Recession." *American Political Science Review* 69:1240–54.
Bogdanor, Vernon, ed. 1983. *Liberal Party Politics.* Oxford: Clarendon.
Bollen, Kenneth. 1989. *Structural Equations With Latent Variables.* New York: Wiley Interscience.
Borooah, Vani K. and Frederick van der Ploeg. 1983. *Political Aspects of the Economy.* Cambridge: Cambridge University Press.
Box, George E. P. and Gwilym Jenkins. 1976. *Time Series Analysis: Forecasting and Control,* 2nd edition. San Francisco: Holden-Day.
Box, George E. P. and G. C. Tiao. 1975. "Intervention Analysis with Applications to Economic and Environmental Problems." *Journal of American Statistical Association* 70:70–79.
Bradley, Ian. 1981. *Breaking the Mould?* Oxford: Martin Robertson.
Braybrooke, David and Charles Lindblom. 1963. *A Strategy of Decision.* New York: The Free Press.
Brittan, Samuel. 1978. "Inflation and Democracy." In *The Political Economy of Inflation,* ed. Frederick Hirsch and John H. Goldthorpe. Cambridge: Harvard University Press.
———. 1983. *The Role and Limits of Government: Essays in Political Economy.* Minneapolis: University of Minnesota Press.
Brodie, Janine and Jane Jenson. 1990. "The Party System." In *Canadian Politics in the 1990s,* 3rd edition, ed. Michael S. Whittington and Glen Williams. Scarborough, Ontario: Nelson Canada.
Browne, M. W. 1984. "Asymptotically Distribution-Free Methods for the Analysis of Covariance Structures." *British Journal of Mathematical and Statistical Psychology* 37:62–83.
Budge, Ian and Dennis J. Farlie, eds. 1976. *Party Identification and Beyond.* London: John Wiley and Sons.

_____. 1983. *Explaining and Predicting Elections: Issue Effects and Party Strategies in Twenty-Three Democracies.* London: George Allen & Unwin.
Butler, David. 1973. "By-elections and Their Interpretation." In *By-elections in British Politics,* ed. Charles Cook and Jorgen Ramsden. London: Macmillan.
Butler, David and Dennis Kavanagh. 1984. *The British General Election of 1983.* London: Macmillan.
_____. 1988. *The British General Election of 1987.* London: Macmillan.
Butler, David and Donald Stokes. 1976. *Political Change in Britain,* 2nd college edition. New York: St. Martin's Press.
Calleo, David P. 1981. "Inflation and American Power." *Foreign Affairs* 70:70–79.
Cameron, David R. 1978. "The Expansion of the Public Economy: A Comparative Analysis." *American Political Science Review* 72:1243–61.
Carmines, Edward G. and James A. Stimson. 1989. *Issue Evolution.* Princeton: Princeton University Press.
Campbell, Angus, Philip E. Converse, Warren E. Miller, and Donald Stokes. 1960. *The American Voter.* New York: John Wiley and Sons.
_____. 1966. *Elections and the Political Order.* New York: John Wiley and Sons.
Campbell, Angus, Gerald Gurin, and Warren E. Miller. 1954. *The Voter Decides.* Evanston, IL: Row, Peterson.
Carlson, John A. and Michael Parkin. 1975. "Inflation Expectation." *Economica* 42:123–38.
Chappell, Henry W. and William Keech. 1985. "A New View of Political Accountability for Economic Performance." *American Political Science Review* 79:10–27.
Chrystal, K. Alec and James E. Alt. 1981. "Some Problems in Formulating and Testing a Politico-Economic Model of the United Kingdom." *Economic Journal* 91:730–36.
Chubb, John. 1985. "The Political Economy of Federalism." *American Political Science Review* 79:994–1015.
Clarke, Harold D. and Euel Elliott. 1990. "New Models of Presidential Approval: Carter, Reagan and their Predecessors." *European Journal of Political Economy* 5:551–69.
Clarke, Harold D., Jane Jenson, Lawrence LeDuc, and Jon Pammett. 1979. *Political Choice in Canada.* Toronto: McGraw-Hill Ryerson.
_____. 1991. *Absent Mandate: Interpreting Change in Canadian Elections,* 2nd edition. Agincourt, Ontario: Gage Publications.
Clarke, Harold D. and Allan Kornberg. 1989. "Public Reactions to Economic Performance and Political Support in Contemporary Liberal Democracies: The Case of Canada." In *Economic Decline and Political Change: Canada, Great Britain, the United States,* ed. Harold D. Clarke, Marianne C. Stewart, and Gary Zuk. Pittsburgh: University of Pittsburgh Press.
_____. 1992. "Risky Business: Partisan Volatility and Electoral Choice in Canada, 1988." *Electoral Studies* 11: forthcoming.
Clarke, Harold D., Allan Kornberg, and Marianne C. Stewart. 1992. "Canada." In *Political Parties of the Americas—1980s to 1990s,* ed. Charles D. Ameringer. Westport, CT: Greenwood Press.

Clarke, Harold D., William Mishler, and Paul Whiteley. 1990. "Recapturing the Falklands: Models of Conservative Popularity, 1979–83." *British Journal of Political Science* 20:63–81.

Clarke, Harold D. and Marianne C. Stewart. 1984. "Dealignment of Degree: Partisan Change in Britain, 1974–1983." *Journal of Politics* 46:689–718.

———. 1987. "Partisan Inconsistency and Partisan Change in Federal States: The Case of Canada." *American Journal of Political Science* 31:383–407.

———. 1988. "Representing Electorates: Parties, Voters and Political Support in Canada and the United States." Unpublished paper presented at the Conference on Representation and the Policy Process in Federal Systems, University of California, Berkeley, Berkeley, California.

———. 1992. "Canada." In *Electoral Change: Responses to Evolving Social and Attitudinal Structures in Western Countries,* ed. Mark N. Franklin, Tom T. Mackie and Henry Valen. Cambridge: Cambridge University Press.

Clarke, Harold D., Marianne C. Stewart, and Gary Zuk. 1986. "Politics, Economics and Party Popularity in Britain, 1979–83." *Electoral Studies* 5:123–41.

———. 1987. "Political Support in Multiparty Canada: 1980–84." In *The Logic of Multiparty Systems,* ed. Manfred J. Holler. Dordrecht, The Netherlands: Martinus Nijhoff Publishers.

———. 1988. "Not For Turning? Beliefs about the Role of Government in Contemporary Britain." *Governance* 1:271–87.

———. 1989. "Three Political Economies in an Era of Economic Decline." In *Economic Decline and Political Change: Canada, Great Britain, the United States,* ed. Harold D. Clarke, Marianne C. Stewart, and Gary Zuk. Pittsburgh: Pittsburgh University Press.

———. eds. 1989. *Economic Decline and Political Change: Canada, Great Britain, the United States.* Pittsburgh: University of Pittsburgh Press.

Clarke, Harold D. and Paul Whiteley. 1990. "Perceptions of Macroeconomic Performance, Government Support and Conservative Party Strategy, 1983–87." *European Journal of Political Research* 18:97–120.

Clarke, Harold D. and Gary Zuk. 1987. "The Politics of Party Popularity: Canada, 1974–79." *Comparative Politics* 19:299–315.

———. 1989. "The Dynamics of Third-Party Support: The British Liberals, 1951–79." *American Journal of Political Science* 33:196–221.

Conover, Pamela Johnston and Stanley Feldman. 1986. "Emotional Reactions to the Economy: I'm Mad as Hell and I'm Not Going to Take It Anymore." *American Journal of Political Science* 30:50–78.

———. 1989. "Candidate Perception in an Ambiguous World: Campaigns, Cues, and Inference Processes." *American Journal of Political Science* 33:912–40.

Conover, Pamela Johnston, Stanley Feldman, and Kathleen Knight. 1986. "Judging Inflation and Unemployment: The Origins of Retrospective Evaluations." *Journal of Politics* 48:565–88.

———. 1987. "The Personal and Political Underpinnings of Economic Forecasts." *American Journal of Political Science* 31:559–83.

Converse, Phillip E., Warren Miller, Jerrold Rusk, and Arthur C. Wolfe. 1969. "Continuity and Change in American Politics: Parties and Issues in the 1968 Election." *American Political Science Review* 63:1083–1105.

Cooper, Barry, Allan Kornberg, and William Mishler, eds. 1988. *The Resurgence of Conservatism in Anglo-American Democracies*. Durham, NC: Duke University Press.

Cooper, Richard N. 1986. *Economic Policy in an Interdependent World: Essays in World Economics*. Cambridge, MA: The MIT Press.

Craig, Fred W. S. 1981. *British Electoral Facts, 1832-1980*. London: Parliamentary Research Services.

Crewe, Ivor. 1985. "How to Win a Landslide Without Really Trying: Why the Conservatives Won in 1983." In *Britain at the Polls, 1983*, ed. Austin Ranney. Durham, NC: American Enterprise Institute and Duke University Press.

Crewe, Ivor and Martin Harrop. 1986. *Political Communications: The General Election Campaign of 1983*. London: Cambridge University Press.

Crewe, Ivor, Bo Sarlvik, and James Alt. 1977. "Partisan Dealignment in Britain 1964-1974." *British Journal of Political Science* 7:129-90.

Crewe, Ivor and Donald D. Searing. 1988. "Ideological Change in the British Conservative Party." *American Political Science Review* 82:361-84.

Cross, R., ed. *Unemployment, Hysteresis and the Natural Rate Hypothesis*. Oxford: Oxford University Press.

Cukierman, Alex and Allan H. Meltzer. 1986. "A Positive Theory of Discretionary Policy, the Cost of a Democratic Government, and the Benefits of a Constitution." *Economic Inquiry* 24:367-88.

Darby, Michael R. 1976. "Rational Expectations under Conditions of Costly Information." *Journal of Finance* 31:889-95.

DeLong, J. B. and L. H. Summers. 1988. "How Does Macroeconomic Policy Affect Output?" *Brookings Papers on Economic Activity* 2:433-94.

Dinkel, Reiner. 1981. "Political Business Cycles in Germany and the United States: Some Theoretical and Empirical Implications." In *Contemporary Political Economy*, ed. Douglas A. Hibbs and Heino Fassbender. Amsterdam: North-Holland Publishing Company.

de Menil, George and Surjit S. Bhalla. 1975. "Direct Measurement of Popular Price Expectations." *The American Economic Review* 65:169-80.

Downs, Anthony. 1957. *An Economic Theory of Democracy*. New York: Harper and Row.

Dunleavy, Patrick and Christopher T. Husbands. 1985. *British Democracy at the Crossroads: Voting and Party Competition in the 1980s*. London: George Allen and Unwin.

Dupuy, R. Ernest and Trevor N. Dupuy. 1970. *The Encyclopedia of Military History*. New York: Harper and Row.

Edwards, George C., III. 1983. *The Public Presidency: The Pursuit of Popular Support*. New York: St. Martin's Press.

Elazar, Daniel J. 1972. *American Federalism: A View from the States*. 2nd edition. New York: Crowell.

Elliott, Euel W. 1989. *Issues and Elections: Presidential Voting in Contemporary America—A Revisionist View*. Boulder: Westview Press.

Elliott, Euel W. and Paul Whiteley. 1990. "Political Influences on Monetary Policy, 1914-84." *Governance* 3:367-93.

Elliott, Euel and Rose-Marie Zuk. 1989. "The Structure of Public Economic Evaluations: The United States 1976-84." In *Economic Decline and Political Change: Canada, Great Britain, the United States,* ed. Harold D. Clarke, Marianne C. Stewart, and Gary Zuk. Pittsburgh: Pittsburgh University Press.

Entman, Robert M. 1989. "How the Media Affect What People Think: An Information Processing Approach." *Journal of Politics* 51:347-70.

Epstein, Leon D. 1964. "A Comparative Study of Canadian Parties." *American Political Science Review* 58:46-60.

_____. 1967. *Political Parties in Western Democracies.* New York: Praeger Publishers.

Eulau, Heinz and Michael S. Lewis-Beck, eds. 1985. *Economic Conditions and Electoral Outcomes: The United States and Western Europe.* New York: Agathon Press.

Farah, Barbara G. and Ethel Klein. 1989. "Public Opinion Trends." In *The Election of 1988: Reports and Interpretations,* ed. Gerald M. Pomper. Chatham, NJ: Chatham House Publishers, Inc.

Fair, Ray C. 1978. "The Effects of Economic Events on Votes for the President." *The Review of Economics and Statistics* 60:159-73.

_____. 1984. *Specification, Estimation, and Analysis of Macroeconometric Models.* Cambridge, MA: Harvard University Press.

Felderer, B. and S. Homburg. 1987. *Macroeconomics and the New Macroeconomics.* Berlin: Springer-Verlag.

Feldman, Stanley. 1982. "Economic Self-Interest and Political Behavior." *American Journal of Political Science* 26:426-43.

Feldman, Stanley and Patricia Conley. 1991. "Explaining Explanations of Changing Economic Conditions." In *Economics and Politics: The Calculus of Support,* ed. Helmut Norpoth, Michael S. Lewis-Beck, and Jean-Dominique Lafay. Ann Arbor, MI: University of Michigan Press.

Ferejohn, John. 1986. "Incumbent Performance and Electoral Control." *Public Choice* 50:5-25.

Fiorina, Morris P. 1978. "Economic Retrospective Voting in American National Elections: A Micro-Analysis." *American Journal of Political Science* 22:426-43.

_____. 1981. *Retrospective Voting in American National Elections.* New Haven and London: Yale University Press.

Fisher, S. 1987. "Monetary Policy." In *The Performance of the British Economy,* ed. R. Dornbusch and R. Layard. Oxford: Clarendon Press.

Fiske, Susan T. and Susan E. Taylor. 1984. *Social Condition.* New York: Random House.

Frank, H. Jack. 1966. *Crude Oil Prices in the Middle East.* New York: Praeger Publishers.

Freeman, John. 1983. "Granger Causality and Time Series Analysis of Political Relationships." *American Journal of Political Science* 27:327-58.

Frey, Bruno S. 1980. *Modern Political Economy.* New York: John Wiley and Sons.

_____. 1984. "Modelling Politico-Economic Relationships." In *What is Political Economy: Eight Perspectives,* ed. David Whynes. New York: Basil Blackwell.

Frey, Bruno S. and Frederick Schneider. 1975. "On the Modelling of Politico-Economic Interdependence." *European Journal of Political Research* 3:339–60.

———. 1978a. "A Politico-Economic Model of the UK." *Economic Journal* 88:243–53.

———. 1978b. "An Empirical Study of Politico-Economic Interaction in the U.S." *Review of Economics and Statistics* 60:174–83.

———. 1981. "Recent Research on Empirical Politico-Economic Models." In *Contemporary Political Economy,* ed. Douglas A. Hibbs and Heino Fassbender. Amsterdam: North-Holland.

Friedman, Benjamin M. 1988. "Lessons on Monetary Policy from the 1980s." *Journal of Economic Perspectives* 2:51–72.

Friedman, Milton. 1968. "The Role of Monetary Policy." *American Economic Review* 63:1–17.

Frizzell, Alan, Jon H. Pammett, and Anthony Westell. 1989. *The Canadian General Election of 1988.* Ottawa: Carleton University Press.

Garrett, Geoffrey and Peter Lange. 1986. "Performance in a Hostile World: Domestic International Determinants of Economic Growth in the Advanced Capitalist Democracies, 1974–80." *World Politics* 38:517–45.

Gilpin, Robert. 1987. *The Political Economy of International Relations.* Princeton: Princeton University Press.

Golden, David and James Poterba. 1980. "The Price of Popularity: The Political Business Cycle Re-examined." *American Journal of Political Science* 22:426–43.

Goodhart, Charles A. E. 1984. *Monetary Theory and Practice.* London: Macmillan.

Goodhart, Charles A. E., and R. J. Bhansali. 1970. "Political Economy." *Political Studies* 18:43–106.

Gordon, R. J. 1975. "The Demand for and the Supply of Inflation." *Journal of Law and Economics* 18:807–36.

———. 1978. *Macroeconomics.* Boston: Little Brown.

———. 1990. "What is New-Keynesian Economics?" *Journal of Economic Literature* 28:1115–71.

Granger, C.W.J. 1969. "Investigating Causal Relations by Econometric Models and Cross-Spectral Methods." *Econometrica* 37:424–35.

Granger, C.W.J. and P. Newbold. 1974. "Spurious Regressions in Econometrics." *Journal of Econometrics* 2:111–20.

Gratton, Michel. 1988. *So What Are the Boys Saying?: An Inside Look at Brian Mulroney in Power.* Toronto: Paperjacks.

Greenwald, B. C. and J. E. Stiglitz. 1988. "Examining Alternative Macroeconomic Theories." *Brookings Papers on Economic Activity* 1:207–70.

Grier, Kevin B. 1987. "Presidential Elections and Federal Reserve Policy: An Empirical Test." *Southern Economic Journal* 54:475–86.

———. 1989. "On the Existence of a Political Monetary Cycle." *American Journal of Political Science* 33:376–89.

Grodzins, Martin. 1966. *The American Federal System.* Chicago: Rand McNally.

Hamilton, Earl J. 1977. "The Role of War in Modern Inflation." *Journal of Economic History* 37:13–19.

# References

Hartz, Louis. 1955. *The Liberal Tradition in America*. New York: Harcourt, Brace.

Hayduk, Leslie A. 1987. *Structural Equation Modeling with LISREL*. Baltimore: John Hopkins University Press.

Haynes, Stephen E. and Joe Stone. 1988. "Does the Political Business Cycle Dominate U. S. Unemployment and Inflation?: Some New Evidence." In *Political Business Cycles: The Political Economy of Money, Inflation, and Unemployment*, ed. Thomas D. Willett. Durham, NC: Duke University Press.

Heilbroner, Robert L. 1972. *The Worldly Philosophers*. 4th edition. New York: Simon and Schuster.

Hendry, David. 1980. "Econometrics—Alchemy or Science?" *Economica* 47:387–406.

Hibbing, John R. 1987. "On the Issues Surrounding Economic Voting: Looking to the British Case for Answers." *Comparative Political Studies* 20:3–33.

Hibbs, Douglas A. 1977. "Political Parties and Macroeconomic Policy." *American Political Science Review* 71:1467–87.

———. 1979. "Communication." *American Political Science Review* 73:185–90.

———. 1982a. "The Dynamics of Political Support for American Presidents among Occupational and Partisan Groups." *American Journal of Political Science* 26:312–32.

———. 1982b. "Economic Outcomes and Political Support for British Governments Among Occupational Classes: A Dynamic Analysis." *American Political Science Review* 76:259–79.

———. 1983. "Comment on Beck." *American Political Science Review* 77:135–38.

———. 1985. "Inflation, Political Support, and Macroeconomic Policy." In *The Politics of Inflation and Economic Stagnation*, ed. Leon N. Lindberg and Charles S. Maier. Washington, DC: The Brookings Institution.

———. 1987a. *The American Political Economy: Macroeconomics and Electoral Politics*. Cambridge, MA: Harvard University Press.

———. 1987b. *The Political Economy of Industrial Democracies*. Cambridge, MA: Harvard University Press.

Hibbs, Douglas A. and Christopher Dennis. 1988. "Income Distribution in the United States." *American Political Science Review* 82:467–90.

Hibbs, Douglas A. and Nicholas Vasilatos. 1981. "Macroeconomic Performance and Mass Political Support in the United States and Great Britain." In *Contemporary Political Economy*, ed. Douglas A. Hibbs and Heino Fassbender. Amsterdam: North-Holland Publishing Company.

HMSO 1980. *Financial Statement and Budget Report 1980-81*. House of Commons, 500, London: HMSO.

———. 1989. *Economic Trends, Annual Supplement 1989*. London: HMSO.

Horowitz, Gad. 1966. "Conservatism, Liberalism and Socialism in Canada: An Interpretation." *Canadian Journal of Economics and Political Science* 32:144–71.

Hudson, John. 1984. "Prime Ministerial Popularity in the UK: 1960–81." *Political Studies* 32:86–97.

Isaak, Robert A. 1991. *International Political Economy: Managing World Economic Change.* Englewood Cliffs, NJ: Prentice-Hall.
Iyengar, Shanto and Donald R. Kinder. 1987. *News That Matters: Television and American Opinion.* Chicago: University of Chicago Press.
Jackson, Robert J. and Doreen Jackson. 1990. *Politics in Canada: Culture, Institutions, Behaviour and Public Policy.* 2nd edition. Scarborough, Ontario: Prentice-Hall.
Jacobson, Gary. 1991. "The Economy in U.S. House Elections." In *Economics and Politics: The Calculus of Support,* ed. Helmut Norpoth, Michael S. Lewis-Beck, and Jean-Dominique Lafay. Ann Arbor, MI: University of Michigan Press.
Jenkins, Gwilym. 1979. *Practical Experiences With Modeling and Forecasting Time Series.* St. Helier, Jersey: Gwilym Jenkins Publications.
Jenkins, Peter. 1988. *Mrs. Thatcher's Revolution: The Ending of the Socialist Era.* Cambridge, MA: Harvard University Press.
Jervis, Robert. 1986. "Cognition and Political Behavior." In *Political Cognition,* ed. Richard Lau and David O. Sears. Hillsdale, NJ: Lawrence Erlbaum Associates, Inc.
Johnston, Richard. 1990. "Do Campaigns Matter?" Unpublished paper presented at the "Analyzing Democracy" Conference, York University, October 12–14.
Johnston, Ron J., C. J. Pattie, and J. G. Allsopp. 1988. *A Nation Dividing? The Electoral Map of Great Britain 1979–1987.* London: Longman.
Jonung, Lars. 1981. "Perceived and Expected Rates of Inflation in Sweden." *The American Economic Review* 71:961–68.
Jonung, Lars and David Laidler. 1988. "Are Perceptions of Inflation Rational? Some Evidence From Sweden." *The American Economic Review* 78:1080–87.
Joreskog, Karl and Dag Sorbom. 1988. *LISREL 7: A Guide to the Program and Applications.* Chicago: SPSS Inc.
Kaldor, Nicholas. 1982. *The Scourge of Monetarism.* Oxford: Oxford University Press.
Kalecki, M. 1943. "Political Aspects of Full Employment." *Political Quarterly* 14:322–31.
Karnow, Stanley. 1983. *Vietnam: A History.* New York: Viking Press.
Katzenstein, Peter J. 1976. "The Small European States in the International Economy: Economic Dependence and Corporatist Politics." In *The Antinomies of Interdependence,* ed. John Gerard Ruggie. New York: Columbia University Press.
Keech, William R. 1982. "Of Honeymoons and Economic Performance: Comment on Hibbs." *American Political Science Review* 76:280–81.
Keech, William R., Robert H. Bates, and Peter Lange. 1989. "Political Economy Within Nations." Durham, NC: Duke University Program in Political Economy. Papers in International Political Economy. Working Paper Number 83.
Keegan, W. 1984. *Mrs. Thatcher's Economic Experiment.* Harmondsworth, Middlesex: Penguin.
Kegley, Charles W., Jr. and Eugene R. Wittkopf. 1985. *World Politics: Trend or Transformation.* New York: St. Martin's Press.
Keil, Manfred W. 1988. "Is the Political Business Cycle Really Dead?" *Southern Economic Journal* 55:86–99.

Kellner, Peter. 1985. "The Labour Campaign." In *Britain at the Polls 1983*, ed. Austin Ranney. Durham, NC: American Enterprise Institute and Duke University Press.

Kenski, Henry C. 1989. "The Politics of Economic Policymaking: The Shift from Carter to Reagan." In *Economic Decline and Political Change: Canada, Great Britain, the United States*, ed. Harold D. Clarke, Marianne C. Stewart, and Gary Zuk. Pittsburgh: University of Pittsburgh Press.

Keohane, Robert O. 1985. "The International Politics of Inflation." In *The Politics of Inflation and Economic Stagnation*, ed. Leon N. Lindberg and Charles S. Maier. Washington, DC: The Brookings Institution.

Kernell, Samuel. 1978. "Explaining Presidential Popularity: How ad hoc Theorizing, Misplaced Emphasis, and Insufficient Care in Measuring One's Variables Refuted Common Sense and Led Conventional Wisdom Down the Path of Anomalies." *American Political Science Review* 72:506–22.

———. 1986. *Going Public*. Washington, DC: Congressional Quarterly Press.

Kernell, Samuel and Douglas A. Hibbs. 1981. "A Critical Threshold Model of Presidential Popularity." In *Contemporary Political Economy*, ed. Douglas A. Hibbs and Heino Fassbender. Amsterdam: North-Holland Publishing Company.

Kettl Donald F. 1986. *Leadership at the Fed*. New Haven: Yale University Press.

Key, V.O., Jr. 1968. *The Responsible Electorate: Rationality in Presidential Voting, 1936-1960*. New York: Vintage Books.

Keynes, John Maynard. 1936. *The General Theory of Employment, Interest and Money*. London: Macmillan.

Kiewiet, D. Roderick. 1981. "Policy-Oriented Voting in Response to Economic Issues." *American Political Science Review* 75:448–89.

———. 1983. *Macroeconomics & Micropolitics: The Electoral Effects of Economic Issues*. Chicago: University of Chicago Press.

Kiewiet, D. Roderick and Douglas Rivers. 1984. "A Retrospective on Retrospective Voting." *Political Behavior* 6:369–94.

Kinder, Donald R., Gordon S. Adams, and Paul W. Gronke. 1989. "Economics and Politics in the 1984 American Presidential Election." *American Journal of Political Science* 33:491–515.

Kinder, Donald R. and D. Roderick Kiewiet. 1979. "Economic Discontent and Political Behavior: The Role of Personal Grievances and Collective Economic Judgments in Congressional Voting." *American Journal of Political Science* 23:495–527.

———. 1981. "Sociotropic Politics: The American Case." *British Journal of Political Science* 11:129–61.

Kinder, Donald R. and Walter R. Mebane. 1983. "Politics and Economics in Everyday Life." In *The Political Process and Economic Change*, ed. Kristen R. Monroe. New York: Agathon Press.

King, Anthony. 1975. "Overload: Problems of Governing in the 1970s." *Political Studies* 23:284–96.

Kirchgassner, G. 1985. "Economic Conditions and the Popularity of West German Parties: A Survey." Paper presented at the annual meeting of the Midwest Political Science Association, Chicago.

Klorman, Ricardo. 1978. "Trends in Personal Finances and the Vote." *Public Opinion Quarterly* 42:31–48.

Kornberg, Allan. 1970. "Parliament in Canadian Society." In *Legislatures in Developmental Perspective*, ed. Allan Kornberg. Durham, NC: Duke University Press.

Kornberg, Allan and Harold D. Clarke. 1988. "Canada's Tory Tide: Electoral Change and Partisan Instability in the 1980s." In *The Resurgence of Conservatism in Anglo-American Democracies*, ed. Barry Cooper, Allan Kornberg, and William Mishler. Durham, NC: Duke University Press.

———. 1992. *Citizens and Community: Political Support in a Representative Democracy*. New York: Cambridge University Press.

Kornberg, Allan, William Mishler, and Harold D. Clarke. 1982. *Representative Democracy in the Canadian Provinces*. Scarborough, Ontario: Prentice-Hall.

Kramer, Gerald H. 1971. "Short-Term Fluctuations in U.S. Voting Behavior, 1896–1964." *American Political Science Review* 65:131–43.

———. 1983. "The Ecological Fallacy Revisited: Aggregate-versus Individual-Level Findings on Economics and Elections and Sociotropic Voting." *American Political Science Review* 77:92–111.

Krell, Gert. 1981. "Capitalism and Armaments: Business Cycles and Defense Spending in the United States." *Journal of Peace Research* 18:221–40.

Kuklinski, James H. and Darrell M. West. 1981. "Economic Expectations and Voting Behavior in the United States House and Senate Elections." *American Political Science Review* 30:315–46.

Landes, Ronald G. 1983. *The Canadian Polity: A Comparative Introduction*. Scarborough, Ontario: Prentice-Hall.

Laney, L. O. and T. D. Willett. 1983. "Presidential Politics, Budget Deficits, and Monetary Policy in the United States: 1960–1976." *Public Choice* 40:53–69.

Lau, Richard R. and David O. Sears. 1981. "Cognitive Links Between Economic Grievances and Political Responses." *Political Behavior* 3:279–302.

LeDuc, Lawrence. 1989. "The Canadian Federal Election of 1988." *Electoral Studies* 8:163–67.

Leeman, Wayne A. 1962. *The Price of Middle East Oil*. Ithaca, NY: Cornell University Press.

Lewis-Beck, Michael S. 1980. "Economic Conditions and Executive Popularity: The French Experience." *American Journal of Political Science* 24:306–23.

———. 1985. "Pocketbook Voting in U.S. National Election Studies: Fact or Artifact?" *American Journal of Political Science* 29:348–56.

———. 1986. "Comparative Economic Voting: Britain, France, Germany, Italy." *American Journal of Political Science* 30:315–46.

———. 1988a. *Economics and Elections: The Major Western Democracies*. Ann Arbor, MI: University of Michigan Press.

———. 1988b. "Economics and the American Voter: Past, Present, Future." *Political Behavior* 10:5–21.

Lindenfeld, Frank. 1964. "Economic Interest and Political Involvement." *Public Opinion Quarterly* 28:104–11.

Ljung, G. M. and G. E. P. Box. 1978. "On a Measure of Lack of Fit in Time Series Models." *Biometrika* 65:297–304.

# References

Long, J. Scott. 1983a. *Confirmatory Factor Analysis: A Preface to LISREL.* Sage University Paper Series on Quantitative Applications in the Social Sciences, 07-033. Beverly Hills: Sage Publications.
———. 1983b. *Covariance Structure Models: An Introduction to LISREL.* Sage University Paper Series on Quantitative Applications in the Social Sciences, 07-034. Beverly Hills: Sage Publications.
Lovell, M. C. 1986. "Tests of the Rational Expectations Hypothesis." *American Economic Review* 76:110–24.
Lowery, David. 1985. "The Keynesian and Political Determinants of Unbalanced Budgets: U.S. Fiscal Policy from Eisenhower to Reagan." *American Journal of Political Science* 29:428–60.
Lucas, R. E. 1972. "Expectations and the Neutrality of Money." *Journal of Economic Theory* 4:103–24.
———. 1980. "Methods and Problems in Business Cycle Theory." *Journal of Money, Credit and Banking* 12:696–715.
Lucas, R. E. and T. J. Sargent, eds. 1980. *Rational Expectations and Econometric Practice.* Minneapolis: University of Minnesota Press.
MacKuen, Michael. 1983. "Political Drama, Economic Conditions, and the Dynamics of Presidential Popularity." *American Journal of Political Science* 27:165–91.
MacKuen, Michael, Robert Erikson, and James A. Stimson. 1989. "Macropartisanship." *American Political Science Review* 83:1125–42.
MacRae, G. Duncan. 1977. "A Political Model of the Business Cycle." *Journal of Political Economy* 85:239–63.
Maloney, Kevin J. and Michael L. Smirlock. 1981. "Business Cycles and the Political Process." *Southern Economic Journal* 48:377–92.
Mansbridge, Jane J., ed. 1990. *Beyond Self-Interest.* Chicago: University of Chicago Press.
Marcus, George. 1988. "The Structure of Emotional Response: 1984 Presidential Candidates." *American Political Science Review* 82:737–62.
Markus, Gregory B. 1988. "The Impact of Personal and National Economic Conditions on the Presidential Vote: A Pooled Cross-sectional Analysis." *American Journal of Political Science* 32:137–54.
Markus, Gregory B. and Philip E. Converse. 1979. "A Dynamic Simultaneous Equation Model of Electoral Choice." *American Political Science Review* 73:1055–70.
Martinez, Michael. 1990. "Partisan Reinforcement in Context and Cognition: Canadian Federal Partisanships, 1974–79." *American Journal of Political Science* 34:822–45.
McCleary, Richard and Richard A. Hay, Jr. 1980. *Applied Time Series Analysis for the Social Sciences.* Beverly Hills: Sage Publications.
McClosky, Herbert and John Zaller. 1984. *The American Ethos: Public Attitudes toward Capitalism and Democracy.* Cambridge, MA: Harvard University Press.
Mebane, Walter R. 1988. "Popular Evaluations of Economic Conditions and Policy in the United States, 1978–85." Revised version of a paper presented at the 1987 Annual Meeting of the Midwest Political Science Association, Chicago, Illinois, April 1987.

Miller, Arthur H. and Martin P. Wattenberg. 1985. "Throwing the Rascals Out: Policy and Performance Evaluations of Presidential Candidates, 1952-80." *American Political Science Review* 79:359-72.

Miller, Arthur H., Martin P. Wattenberg, and Oksana Malanchuk. 1986. "Schematic Assessments of Presidential Candidates." *American Political Science Review* 80:521-40.

Miller, Warren E. and J. Merrill Shanks. 1982. "Policy Directions and Presidential Leadership: Alternative Interpretations of the 1980 Presidential Election." *British Journal of Political Science* 12:299-356.

Miller, William L. 1989. "Studying How the Economy Affects Attitudes and Behavior: Problems and Prospects." In *Economic Decline and Political Change: Canada, Great Britain, the United States,* ed. Harold D. Clarke, Marianne C. Stewart and Gary Zuk. Pittsburgh: Pittsburgh University Press.

Miller, William L., Harold D. Clarke, Martin Harrop, Lawrence LeDuc, and Paul F. Whiteley. 1990. *How Voters Change: The 1987 British Election Campaign in Perspective.* Oxford: Oxford University Press.

Miller, William L. and William M. Mackie. 1973. "The Electoral Cycle and the Asymmetry of Government and Opposition Popularity." *Political Studies* 21:263-79.

Milne, David. 1990. "Canada's Constitutional Odyssey." In *Canadian Politics in the 1990s,* 3rd edition, ed. Michael S. Whittington and Glen Williams. Scarborough, Ontario: Nelson Canada.

Mishler, William, Marilyn Hoskin, and Roy Fitzgerald. 1988. "'Hunting the Shark': Or Searching for Evidence of that Widely Touted but Highly Elusive Resurgence of Public Support for Conservative Parties in Canada, Great Britain, and the United States." In *The Resurgence of Conservatism in Anglo-American Democracies,* ed. Barry Cooper, Allan Kornberg, and William Mishler. Durham, NC: Duke University Press.

_____. 1989. "British Parties in the Balance: A Time Series Analysis of Long-Term Trends in Public Support for Major Parties." *British Journal of Political Science* 19:211-36.

Mitchell, William C. 1988. "Inflation and Politics: Six Theories in Search of Reality." In *Political Business Cycles: The Political Economy of Money, Inflation, and Unemployment,* ed. Thomas D. Willett. Durham, NC: Duke University Press.

Monroe, Kristen R. 1978. "Economic Influences on Presidential Popularity." *Public Opinion Quarterly* 42:360-69.

_____. 1979a. "God of Vengeance and Reward?: The Economy and Presidential Popularity." *Political Behavior* 1:301-29.

_____. 1979b. "Econometric Analyses of Electoral Behavior: A Critical Review." *Political Behavior* 1:137-74.

_____. 1980. "Presidential Popularity: An Almon Distributed Lag Model." *Political Methodology* 6:211-36.

_____. ed. 1983a. *The Political Process and Economic Change.* New York: Agathon Press, Inc.

_____. 1983b. "Political Manipulation of the Economy: A Closer Look at Political Business Cycles." *Presidential Studies Quarterly* 13:37-49.

———. 1984. *Presidential Popularity and the Economy.* New York: Praeger Publishers.
———, ed. 1991. *The Economic Approach to Politics: A Critical Reassessment of the Theory of Rational Action.* New York: Harper Collins.
Monroe, Kristen R. and Lynda Erickson. 1986. "The Economy and Political Support: The Canadian Case." *Journal of Politics* 48:616–47.
Monroe, Kristen R. and Maurice D. Levi. 1983. "Economic Expectations, Economic Uncertainty, and Presidential Popularity." In *The Political Process and Economic Change,* ed. Kristen R. Monroe. New York: Agathon Press.
Mosley, Paul. 1978. "Images of the 'Floating Voter' or the 'Political Business Cycle' Revisited." *Political Studies* 26:375–94.
———. 1984. "'Popularity Functions' and the Role of the Media: A Pilot Study of the Popular Press." *British Journal of Political Science* 14:117–29.
Mueller, Dennis C. 1979. *Public Choice.* Cambridge: Cambridge University Press.
Mueller, John E. 1970. "Presidential Popularity From Truman to Johnson." *American Political Science Review* 64:18–34.
———. 1973. *War, Presidents and Public Opinion.* New York: John Wiley and Sons.
———. 1986. *Party and Participation in British Elections.* New York: St. Martin's Press.
Nelles, H. V. 1990. "'Red Tied': Fin de Siecle Politics in Ontario." In *Canadian Politics in the 1990s,* 3rd edition, ed. Michael S. Whittington and Glen Williams. Scarborough, Ontario: Nelson Canada.
Nincic, Miroslav and Thomas R. Cusack. 1979. "The Political Economy of U.S. Military Spending." *Journal of Peace Research* 16:101–15.
Niskanen. William A., Jr. 1971. *Bureaucracy and Representative Government.* New York: Aldine, Atherton.
Nordhaus, William D. 1975. "The Political Business Cycle." *Review of Economic Studies* 42:169–90.
———. 1989. "Alternative Approaches to the Political Business Cycle." *Brookings Papers on Economic Activity.* Washington, DC: The Brookings Institution 2:1–68.
Norpoth, Helmut. 1984. "Economics, Politics, and the Cycle of Presidential Popularity." *Political Behavior* 6:253–73.
———. 1986. "Transfer Function Analysis." In *New Tools for Social Scientists: Advances and Applications in Research Methods,* ed. William D. Berry and Michael S. Lewis-Beck. Beverly Hills: Sage Publications.
———. 1987a. "Guns and Butter and Government Popularity in Britain." *American Political Science Review* 81:949–59.
———. 1987b. "The Falklands War and Government Popularity in Britain: Rally without Consequence or Surge without Decline?" *Electoral Studies* 6:3–16.
Norpoth, Helmut, Michael S. Lewis-Beck and Jean-Dominique Lafay, eds. 1991. *Economics and Politics: The Calculus of Support.* Ann Arbor, MI: The University of Michigan Press.
Norpoth, Helmut and Thom Yantek. 1983. "Macro-Economic Conditions and Fluctuations in Presidential Popularity: The Question of Lagged Effects." *American Journal of Political Science* 27:785–807.

O'Connor, James. 1973. *The Fiscal Crisis of the State.* New York: St. Martin's Press.
———. 1986. *Accumulation Crisis.* Oxford: Basil Blackwell.
Odell, John S. 1982. *U.S. International Monetary Policy: Markets, Power, and Ideas as Sources of Change.* Princeton: Princeton University Press.
OECD. 1961-86. *Monthly Trade Indicators.* Paris: OECD.
Offe, Claus. 1972. *Struckturprobleme des Kapitalistischen.* Frankfurt am Main: Suhrkamp.
———. 1984. *Contradictions of the Welfare State.* London: Hutchinson.
Olson, Mancur. 1965. *The Logic of Collective Action.* New York: Schocken Books.
———. 1982. *The Rise and Decline of Nations.* New Haven: Yale University Press.
Ostrom, Charles W., Jr. 1990. *Time Series Analysis: Regression Techniques.* 2nd. edition. Sage University Paper series on Quantitative Applications in the Social Sciences, series no. 07-009. Beverly Hills and London: Sage Publications.
Ostrom, Charles W., Jr. and Dennis M. Simon. 1985. "Promise and Performance: A Dynamic Model of Presidential Popularity." *American Political Science Review* 79:334–58.
Ostrom, Elinor. 1991. "Rational Choice Theory and Institutional Analysis: Toward Complementarity." *American Political Science Review* 85:237–43.
Page, Benjamin I. 1978. *Choices and Echoes in Presidential Elections: Rational Man and Electoral Democracy.* Chicago: University of Chicago Press.
Page, Benjamin I. and Calvin C. Jones. 1979. "Reciprocal Effects of Policy Preferences, Party Loyalties and the Vote." *American Political Science Review* 73:1071–89.
Paldam, Martin. 1981. "A Preliminary Survey of the Theories and Findings on Vote and Popularity Functions." *European Journal of Political Research* 7:1–26.
———. 1991. "How Robust Is the Vote Function? A Study of Seventeen Nations over Four Decades." In *Economics and Politics: The Calculus of Support,* ed. Helmut Norpoth, Michael S. Lewis-Beck, and Jean-Dominique Lafay. Ann Arbor, MI: University of Michigan Press.
Parkin, M. 1984. *Macroeconomics.* Englewood Cliffs, NJ: Prentice-Hall.
Peffley, Mark. 1984. "The Voter as Juror: Attributing Responsibility for Economic Conditions." *Political Behavior* 6:175–94.
Petit, P. 1986. "Full Employment Policies in Stagnation: France in the 1980s." *Cambridge Journal of Economics* 10:393–406.
*Petroleum Economist.* February 1986.
*Petroleum Intelligence Weekly.* Various Issues. New York: PEI, Inc.
Phillips, A. W. 1958. "The Relationship between Unemployment and the Rate of Change of Money Wages in the UK 1861-1957." *Economica* 25:283–99.
Phlips, L. 1988. *The Economics of Imperfect Information.* Cambridge: Cambridge University Press.
Pissarides, Christopher A. 1972. "A Model of British Macroeconomic Policy 1955-69." *Manchester School* 40:245–59.
———. 1980. "British Government Popularity and Economic Performance." *Economic Journal* 90:569–81.

Plott, Charles R. 1990. "Psychology and Economics." In *The New Palgrave: Utility and Probability,* ed. John Eatwell, Murray Milgate and Peter Newman. London: Macmillan Press.
Pollard, S. 1982. *The Wasting of the British Economy.* London: Croom Helm.
Popkin, Samuel L., John W. Gorman, Charles Phillips, and Jeffrey A. Smith. 1976. "Comment: What Have You Done For Me Lately? Toward An Investment Theory of Voting." *American Political Science Review* 70:779–805.
Popkin, Samuel L. 1991. *The Reasoning Voter: Communication and Persuasion in Presidential Campaigns.* Chicago: University of Chicago Press.
Powell, Bingham. 1989. "Constitutional Design and Citizen Electoral Control." *Journal of Theoretical Politics* 1:107–30.
Ranney, Austin. 1954. *The Doctrine of Responsible Party Government.* Urbana, IL: University of Illinois Press.
_____. 1981. "British General Elections: An Introduction." In *Britain at the Polls, 1979,* ed. Howard R. Penniman. Washington, DC: American Enterprise Institute.
_____. ed. 1985. *The American Elections of 1984.* Durham, NC: Duke University Press.
Rasler, Karen and William R. Thompson. 1985. "War and the Economic Growth of Major Powers." *American Journal of Poltical Science* 29:513–38.
Rasmussen, Jorgen. 1981. "David Steel's Liberals: Too Old to Cry, Too Hurt to Laugh." In *Britain at the Polls, 1979,* ed. Howard R. Penniman. Washington, DC: American Enterprise Institute.
_____. 1985. "The Alliance Campaign, Watersheds, and Landslides: Was 1983 a Fault Line in British Politics?" In *Britain at the Polls, 1983,* ed. Austin Ranney. Durham, NC: Duke University Press.
Rees, Albert. 1970. "The Phillips Curve as a Menu for Policy Choice." *Economica* 37:227–38.
Riker, William. 1982. *Liberalism Against Populism.* San Francisco: Freeman.
Rogoff, K. 1987. "Equilibrium Business Cycles." Working Paper 2428. Cambridge, MA: National Bureau of Economic Research.
Rogoff, K. and A. Sibert. 1988. "Elections and Macroeconomic Policy Cycles." *Review of Economic Studies* 55:1–16.
Rose, Richard and Guy Peters. 1978. *Can Government Go Bankrupt?* New York: Basic Books.
Rosenstone, Steven J. 1982. "Economic Adversity and Voter Turnout." *American Journal of Political Science* 26:25–46.
_____. 1983. *Forecasting Presidential Elections.* New Haven: Yale University Press.
_____. 1985. "Explaining the 1984 Presidential Election." *The Brookings Review:* Winter.
Rostow, Walter. 1978. *The World Economy: History and Prospect.* Austin: University of Texas Press.
Russell, R. Robert. 1983. "Can Income Policies Work?" In *The Political Process and Economic Change,* ed. Kristen R. Monroe. New York: Agathon Press.
Russett, Bruce. 1982. "Defense Expenditures and National Well-Being." *American Political Science Review* 76:767–77.

Sanders, David, Hugh Ward, and David Marsh (with Tony Fletcher). 1987. "Governmental Popularity and the Falklands War: A Reassessment." *British Journal of Political Science* 17:281-313.

Sarlvik, Bo and Ivor Crewe. 1983. *Decade of Dealignment*. Cambridge: Cambridge University Press.

Schlozman, Kay Lehman, and Sidney Verba. 1979. *Injury to Insult: Unemployment, Class, and Political Response*. Cambridge, MA: Harvard University Press.

Schmidt, Manfred. 1982. "The Role of Parties in Shaping Macroeconomic Policy." In *The Impact of Parties*, ed. Francis G. Castles. Beverly Hills: Sage Publications.

Schneider, Friedrich. 1984. "Public Attitudes Toward Economic Conditions and Their Impact on Government Behavior." *Political Behavior* 6:211-27.

Schneider, Friedrich and Bruno Frey. 1988. "Politico-Economic Models of Macroeconomic Policy: A Review of the Empirical Evidence." In *The Political Economy of Money, Inflation, and Unemployment*, ed. Thomas D. Willett. Durham, NC: Duke University Press.

Schumpeter, Joseph A. 1962. *Capitalism, Socialism and Democracy*. New York: Harper Torchbooks.

Sears, David O., Richard R. Lau, Tom R. Tyler, and Harris M. Allen, Jr. 1980. "Self-Interest vs. Symbolic Politics in Policy Attitudes and Presidential Voting." *American Political Science Review* 74:670-84.

Seymour, Ian. 1981. *OPEC: Instrument of Change*. New York: St. Martin's Press.

Sheffrin, Steven M. 1983. *Rational Expectations*. Cambridge: Cambridge University Press.

Shiller, R. J. 1990. *Market Volatility*. Cambridge, MA: MIT Press.

Simon, Herbert. 1959. "Theories of Decision-Making in Economics and the Behavioral Sciences." *American Economic Review* 49:253-83.

Small, Melvin and J. David Singer. 1982. *Resort to Arms: International and Civil Wars, 1816-1980*. Beverly Hills: Sage Publications.

Smiley, Donald V. 1980. *Canada in Question: Federalism in the Eighties*. 3rd edition. Toronto: McGraw-Hill Ryerson.

Sniderman, Paul M. and Richard Brody. 1977. "Coping: The Ethic of Self-Reliance." *American Journal of Political Science* 21:501-22.

Spero, Joan Edelman. 1981. *The Politics of International Economic Relations*. New York: St. Martin's Press.

Stein, Herbert. 1988. *Presidential Economics: The Making of Economic Policy from Roosevelt to Reagan and Beyond*. 2nd revised edition. Washington, DC: American Enterprise Institute for Public Policy Research.

Stein, Jerome L. 1984. *Monetarist, Keynesian & New Classical Economics*. New York: New York University Press.

Stevenson, Garth. 1989. *Unfulfilled Union: Canadian Federalism and National Unity*. 3rd edition. Agincourt, Ontario: Gage Publishing.

Stewart, Marianne C. and Gary Zuk. 1989. "Global Forces and American Electoral-Economic Cycles." In *Economic Decline and Political Change: Canada, Great Britain, the United States*, ed. Harold D. Clarke, Marianne C. Stewart and Gary Zuk. Pittsburgh: University of Pittsburgh Press.

Stewart, Michael. 1983. *The Age of Interdependence: Economic Policy in a Shrinking World.* Cambridge, MA: MIT Press.
_____. 1986. *Keynes and After.* 3rd edition. Harmondworth, Middlesex: Penguin.
Stigler, George S. 1973. "General Economic Conditions and National Elections." *American Economic Review* 63:160–67.
Stimson, James A. 1976. "Political Support for American Presidents: A Cyclical Model." *Public Opinion Quarterly* 40:1–21.
_____. 1985. "Regression in Space and Time: A Statistical Essay." *American Journal of Political Science* 29:914–47.
_____. 1989. "Perceptions of Politics and Economic Policy: A Macroanalysis." In *Economic Decline and Political Change: Canada, Great Britain, the United States,* ed. Harold D. Clarke, Marianne C. Stewart and Gary Zuk. Pittsburgh: University of Pittsburgh Press.
Surveys of Consumers Monthly Time Series Data Base: PC Disk Documentation. 1991. Ann Arbor, MI: University of Michigan, Survey Research Center, Monitoring Economic Change Program.
Suzuki, Motoshi. 1989. "Assessing the Rationality of Retrospective Voting." Paper presented at the Annual Meeting of the Midwest Political Science Association. Chicago, Illinois, April 1989.
Thomas, Norman C. 1989. "Adapting Policy-Making Machinery to Fiscal Stress: Canada, Great Britain, and the United States." In *Economic Decline and Political Change: Canada, Great Britain, the United States,* ed. Harold D. Clarke, Marianne C. Stewart and Gary Zuk. Pittsburgh: University of Pittsburgh Press.
Thompson, William R. and Gary Zuk. 1982. "War, Inflation and the Kondratieff Long Wave." *Journal of Conflict Resolution* 27:621–44.
_____. 1983. "American Elections and the International Electoral-Economic Cycle: A Test of the Tufte Hypothesis." *American Journal of Political Science* 27:464–84.
Thornburn, Hugh G. 1985. "Interpretations of the Canadian Party System." In *Party Politics in Canada,* 5th edition, ed. Hugh G. Thorburn. Scarborough, Ontario: Prentice-Hall.
Triffin, Robert. 1978. "The International Role and Fate of the Dollar." *Foreign Affairs* 57:269–86.
Tufte, Edward R. 1975. "Determinants of the Outcomes of Midterm Congressional Elections." *American Political Science Review* 69:812–26.
_____. 1978. *Political Control of the Economy.* Princeton: Princeton University Press.
U.S. Bureau of the Census. 1949-61. *Quarterly Summary of Foreign Commerce of the United States* Washington, DC: GPO.
U.S. Bureau of Labor Statistics. 1975–76, 1979–80. *Monthly Labor Review.*
U.S. Central Intelligence Agency. May/September, 1983. *International Energy Statistical Review.* Washington, DC: GPO.
U.S. Department of Commerce. 1976, 1986. *Business Conditions Digest.* Washington, DC: GPO.
Wagner, R. E. 1977. "Economic Manipulation for Political Profit: Macro-Economic Consequences and Constitutional Implications." *Kyklos* 30:395–410.

Walker, J. 1985. "The UK Economy: Analysis and Prospects." *Oxford Review of Economic Policy* 1:39–62.

Watchel, P. 1977. "Survey Measures of Expected Inflation and Their Usefulness." In *Analysis of Inflation 1965-74*, ed. J. Popkin. Studies in Income and Wealth, Vol. 42. Cambridge: National Bureau of Economic Research.

Weatherford, M. Stephen. 1983a. "Parties and Classes in the Political Response to Economic Conditions." In *The Political Process and Economic Change*, ed. Kristen R. Monroe. New York: Agathon Press.

_____. 1983b. "Evaluating Economic Policy: A Contextual Model of the Opinion Formation Process." *Journal of Politics* 45:866–88.

_____. 1983c. "Economic Voting and the 'Symbolic Politics' Argument: A Reinterpretation and Synthesis." *American Political Science Review* 77:158–74.

_____. 1987. "The Interplay of Ideology and Advice in Economic Policy-Making: The Case of Political Business Cycles." *Journal of Politics* 49:925–52.

Whiteley, Paul. 1979. "Electoral Forecasting From Poll Data: The British Case." *British Journal of Political Science* 9:219–36.

_____. 1980. "Politico-econometric Estimation in Britain: An Alternative Interpretation." In *Models of Political Economy*, ed. Paul Whiteley. Beverly Hills: Sage Publications.

_____. 1984a. "Inflation, Unemployment and Government Popularity—Dynamic Models for the United States, Britain and West Germany." *Electoral Studies* 3:3–24.

_____. 1984b. "Perceptions of Economic Performance and Voting Behavior in the 1983 General Elections in Britain." *Political Behavior* 6:395–410.

_____. 1986a. *Political Control of the Macro-Economy*. London: Sage Publications.

_____. 1986b. "Macroeconomic Performance and Government Popularity—The Short Run Dynamics." *European Journal of Political Research* 14:45–61.

_____. 1988a. "Party Incumbency and Economic Growth in the United States, 1929–1984." *Political Behavior* 10:1–23.

_____. 1988b. "The Causal Relationships between Issues, Candidate Evaluations, Party Identification, and Vote Choice—The View from 'Rolling Thunder.'" *Journal of Politics* 50:961–84.

_____. 1991. "The Objective and Subjective Economies and Party Popularity—The Case of Britain in the 1980s." Unpublished manuscript, Department of Government, College of William and Mary, Williamsburg, VA.

Willett, Thomas D. and King Banaian. 1988. "Explaining the Great Stagflation: Toward a Political Economy Framework." In *Political Business Cycles: The Political Economy of Money, Inflation, and Unemployment*, ed. Thomas D. Willett. Durham, NC: Duke University Press.

Williams, Glen. 1990. "Regions Within Region: Canada in the Continent." In *Canadian Politics in the 1990s*, ed. Michael S. Whittington and Glen Williams. Scarborough, Ontario: Nelson Canada.

Williams, John T. 1990. "The Political Manipulation of Macroeconomic Policy." *American Political Science Review* 84:767–95.

Winer, Stanley L. 1986. "Money and Politics in a Small Open Economy." *Public Choice* 51:221–39.

Woolley, John. 1984. *Monetary Politics: The Federal Reserve and the Politics of Monetary Policy.* New York: Cambridge University Press.
_____. 1988. "Partisan Manipulation of the Economy: Another Look at Monetary Policy with Moving Regression." *Journal of Politics* 50:335-60.
Yantek, Thom. 1985. "Government Popularity in Great Britain under Conditions of Economic Decline." *Political Studies* 33:467-83.
_____. 1988. "Polity and Economy Under Extreme Economic Conditions: A Comparative Study of the Reagan and Thatcher Experiences." *American Journal of Political Science* 32:196-216.
Yeric, Jerry and John R. Todd. 1989. *Public Opinion: The Visible Politics.* 2nd edition. Itasca, IL: F. E. Peacock Publishers.
Young, Walter D. 1969. *Anatomy of a Party: The National CCF.* Toronto: University of Toronto Press.
Zuk, Gary. 1985. "National Growth and International Conflict: A Reevaluation of Choucri and North's Thesis." *Journal of Politics* 47:269-81.
Zuk, Gary and William R. Thompson. 1982. "The Post-Coup Military Spending Question: A Pooled Cross-Sectional Time Series Analysis." *American Political Science Review* 76:60-74.
Zuk, Gary and Nancy R. Woodbury. 1986. "U.S. Defense Spending, Electoral Cycles, and Soviet-American Relations." *Journal of Conflict Resolution* 30:445-68.
Zysman, John. 1985. "Inflation and the Politics of Supply." In *The Politics of Inflation and Economic Stagnation,* ed. Leon N. Lindberg and Charles S. Maier. Washington, DC: The Brookings Institution.

# Index

Alliance, 25, 75, 76, 77, 81, 82, 86, 87, 89–93, 94, 95, 96, 96(n1), 97(n3), 181
  economic effects on support, 26, 79, 82, 85–86, 89–93, 94
  effect of Falklands War on support, 57, 68, 76, 87, 92–93, 94–95, 96
  effects of electoral system on support, 77, 80, 95, 96
  effects of political events on support, 68, 86, 87, 88, 89–93, 94–95
  trends in support, 26, 76–77, 79, 81, 87, 89–93, 94–95, 96, 98(n12)

Bretton Woods. *See* Exchange rates
Broadbent, Ed, 108
Budget, annual
  effects on party support, 12, 57, 66, 107
Bush, George, 23, 123, 131, 132, 133, 134, 137, 140(nn 6, 7)
Butskellism, 14
By-elections
  and effects on party support, 16, 80, 82, 87, 91–92, 94

Canada
  1988 federal election, 101, 102, 103, 108, 110, 114–115, 121(nn 3, 7, 8), 138, 142, 149, 159, 160
  1984 federal election, 101, 102, 108, 112, 115, 118, 121(nn 7, 8), 159
  regions of, Atlantic Provinces, 102, 104, 110, 114, 117, 162(n8)
  regions of, British Columbia, 100, 102, 103, 104, 117
  regions of, Ontario, 13, 101, 102, 103, 109, 110, 111, 121(n6), 153, 162(n8), 164(n18)
  regions of, Prairies, 101, 104, 109, 110, 111, 114, 117, 121(n6), 153, 164(n18)
  regions of, Quebec, 100, 102, 104, 109, 110, 111, 112, 114, 115, 116, 117, 121(n7), 160, 161
Candidate images
  effects of economic evaluations on, 134
  and effects on voting in 1988 presidential election, 134–137
Carter, Jimmy, 192, 194, 195, 197
CDU. *See* Christian Democratic Party
Chretien, Jean, 109
Christian Democratic Party (CDU), 13
Cognitive Miser Theory, 55
Collective action
  problems of, 5–6, 169
Conservatism
  and monetarist economic theory, 2–3, 181
  and neo-classical economic theory, 2, 28
  and political culture, 22
  resurgence in 1970s and 1980s, 22–23
  and supply-side economic theory, 3
Conservative Party (Britain), 24, 28, 63, 67, 68, 69, 70, 78, 79, 86, 93, 94, 96, 181, 182, 186
  economic effects on support, 66–70, 78, 79, 182
  effects of political events on support, 22, 24–25, 57, 66–70
  and 1986–1987 PBC, 28, 184–186
  trends in support, 22, 24–25

Conservative Party (Canada). *See*
  Progressive Conservative Party
Consumer confidence index
  measure of subjective economic
  evaluations, 10, 110
Cooperative Commonwealth Federation
  (CCF). *See* New Democratic Party
Currency
  value of, 178, 180, 187

Decisionmaking
  optimizing strategies, 14–15, 131
  satisficing strategies, 15
Deficits, 132, 152, 167, 168, 176, 182,
  187, 192, 193, 203
Democratic Party
  economic effects on support, 49(n1),
  130, 179
  effects of political events on support,
  49(n1)
Depression of 1930s, 25, 169
Downs, Anthony, 1, 5, 8, 12
Dukakis, Michael, 123, 131, 132, 133,
  140(nn 6, 7)

Economic conditions
  government reports of, 54, 55–56, 57,
  71
Economic evaluations
  effects of economic conditions on, 16,
  27, 31, 32, 45–47, 60–66, 127–129
  effects of economic events on, 60–66,
  71–72
  effects of noneconomic events on, 7,
  8, 31–32, 45, 56, 57, 60–66, 68, 71
  effects on voting, 130–131, 137–139,
  egocentric, 5, 7, 27, 32, 47, 62, 81–82,
  83, 124–125, 125–126, 130–131, 137
  mediated, 6, 131
  and political culture, 6, 22, 78, 100,
  119–120
  sociotropic, 5, 6, 7, 32, 47, 81–82,
  124–125, 125–126, 130–131
  structure of, 125–126, 147–149
Economic policy
  demand-side, 182
  fiscal, 4, 18, 19, 100, 167, 170, 171,
  172, 176, 180, 182, 185, 186, 187
  Medium Term Financial Policy (with
  monetary policy), 181
  monetary, 4, 18, 19, 167, 170, 171,
  172, 176, 177, 181, 182, 184, 185,
  187
  supply-side, 3, 186
Economy
  and beliefs about government
  responsibility, 78, 100, 105, 120,
  159
  emotional reactions to, 56
  government role as manager, 120
  and Keynesian economic theory, 105–
  106, 166, 170, 171
  regional differences in, 100, 103–106,
  117–118
  regional differences in and political
  support, 100–103, 106–110, 112–
  117
EEC. *See* European Economic
  Community
Eisenhower, Dwight, 49, 193, 195, 202
European Community, 15
European Economic Community (EEC),
  55, 187, 203
Exchange rates
  fixed, 189, 191, 193, 193–194, 195–
  196, 202, 203
  floating, 193–194
Expectations, economic
  adaptive model of, 9, 124
  extrapolative model of, 9, 124
  rational expectations model of, 9,
  74(n12), 124, 168, 169, 174, 175,
  176
Exports
  195, 196, 202, 203

Falklands war
  effect on Alliance support, 57, 76, 87,
  94–95
  effect on Conservative Party support,
  10, 57, 68, 87, 94–95
  effect on support for Prime Minister
  Thatcher, 7, 26, 57, 87, 94–95, 183

# Index

Federalism
  Canada, 12, 23, 100, 141
  United States, 23, 187
Federal Republic of Germany, 13
Federal Reserve Board (United States), 187
Fiscal Policy. *See* Economic policy
Foot, Michael, 94
Ford, Gerald, 192, 194, 195, 199, 202
Free Democratic Party (FDP), 13
Free Trade Agreement (FTA), 108, 109, 111, 115, 138, 142, 149–150, 152–156, 159, 160, 162(n8), 163(n13)
  and effects on PC support since 1988, 108, 138, 142, 150, 159
  and evaluations of economic conditions, 138, 150, 156
  as issue in 1988 Canadian federal election, 108, 109, 111, 115, 142, 149–150, 156
  public support, 109, 142, 149–150, 153–156, 159, 160

Gallup Poll
  measure of most urgent problem, 65
  measure of party support, 76, 97(n4)
  measure of presidential approval, 29(n2), 33
  measure of subjective economic evaluations, 58–59, 81–82, 97(n6)
General Goods and Services Tax (GST), 142, 150–152, 152–156, 159, 160, 163(n9)
  and effects on PC support, 142, 153–156, 159
  and evaluations of economic conditions, 142, 152–156, 159
  public support for, 142, 151(table), 150–152, 153–156, 159, 160, 163(n9)
Gorbachev, Mikhail, 87, 95
Great Britain
  1987 general election, 28, 63, 73(n6), 82, 84, 87, 98(n12), 185, 186
  1983 general election, 63, 65, 73(n6), 82, 85, 98(n12), 183

GST. *See* General Goods and Services Tax

Hysteresis hypothesis, 171, 178

Income, real
  effects on economic evaluations, 10, 56, 62
  effects on party support, 10, 56
Inflation
  in Britain, 56, 65, 81–82, 84, 90, 93, 180, 183, 184, 185, 186
  in Canada, 103, 114, 150
  effects of wars on, 74(n12), 82, 192–193, 195–196, 199
  increases after 1973 Arab oil embargo, 178, 194, 199, 202
  and Keynesian economics, 18–19, 170, 171, 172
  party differences in levels of, 13, 79, 197, 202
  and party support, 10, 11, 15, 31, 33, 79, 81–82, 90, 183
  and political business cycles, 17, 172, 174, 183, 184, 185, 186, 189, 191, 192, 202
  and presidential approval, 37, 43, 44, 193
  presidential differences in levels of, 190, 192, 193, 197, 202, 204(n5)
  surprises, 168, 174
  in United States, 13, 33, 36–37, 191, 193, 195, 197, 199, 202
Information
  economic. *See* Economic conditions; Economic evaluations
  and economic evaluations, 7, 9, 53–56, 71, 137, 174
  imperfect information assumption, 7, 9, 56, 71, 174
  perfect information assumption, 9, 53
Interest rates, 4, 56, 60, 61, 62, 65, 142, 184
International economy
  and effects on domestic economies, 15, 178, 191
  and effects on party support, 15

Intra-party disputes
  and effects on Alliance support, 80, 81, 87, 92
Iran-Contra Affair. *See* Reagan, Ronald
Issue-Priority Model, 13, 14, 25–26, 33, 79, 85, 105, 130

Jenkins, Roy, 76, 87, 92
Johnson, Lyndon, 49, 192, 193, 195, 202

Kalecki, Michael, 166, 171, 172
Kennedy, John, 49
Key, V. O.
  and reward-punishment model, 11–12, 130
Keynes, John Maynard, 166
Keynesian economic theory, 166–171, 175, 177, 178, 184
  critiques of, 166
  perceived failure of in 1970s, 2, 166
  and political business cycles, 18–19, 28, 171, 177, 184
  utilization after World War II, 2, 169
Korean War
  economic effects of, 193, 195, 199, 201

Labour Party
  economic effects on support, 63, 66–67, 78, 79, 86, 94
Legitimacy crisis
  of advanced capitalism, 2
Liberal Democratic Party, 96
Liberalism
  and individualism, 22
  and political culture, 22, 24
  and responsibility attributions for economic conditions, 22, 24
Liberal Party (Britain), 24, 25, 75, 77, 78, 79, 81, 94, 98(n12), 181
  economic effects on support, 78, 79, 181
  effects of electoral system on support, 75, 77
  effects of political events on support, 75, 77
Liberal Party (Canada), 24, 100, 102, 104, 106, 107, 108, 109, 110, 114, 115, 116, 117, 119, 121(n6), 122(n8), 142, 149, 159, 160
Lucas, Robert, 168

Media
  effects on economic evaluations, 54, 55, 56, 71, 106
  and issue agenda, 106, 108–109, 119–120
  reports of economic conditions, 55, 62, 70, 71, 82
Medium Term Financial Strategy. *See* Economic policy
Meech Lake Accord, 109, 111, 112, 114, 115, 142, 156, 159, 160
  and effects on party support, 109, 111, 112, 114, 115, 142, 156–159
  and effects on PC support since 1988, 142, 156–159
  public support, 142, 159, 160
Methodology
  Box-Jenkins-Tiao models, 29(n3), 34, 39, 182, 196, 205
  confirmatory factor analysis, 126, 128, 137, 148, 161(n3), 162(n5)
  covariance structure analysis, 134, 138
  model specification, 20, 21, 31, 34, 77
  pooled cross-sectional time series analysis, 6–7, 72(n1), 100, 111, 118–119, 121(n5)
  time series analysis, 3, 10, 21, 86, 121(n5)
Miners strike (Britain), 182, 183
Monetarism
  rebirth of interest in 1970s, 2–3
Monetary policy. *See* economic policy
Mulroney, Brian, 99, 107, 109, 138, 141, 142, 159, 160

National Energy Programme, 112
NDP. *See* New Democratic Party
Neo-classical economic theory, 2, 18, 28, 166, 166–171, 172, 175, 177, 184
  rebirth of interest in 1970s, 2–3, 166
Neo-Keynesianism. *See* Keynesian economic theory

# Index

New Deal, 23, 190
New Democratic Party (NDP), 13, 25, 27, 100, 102, 104, 106, 107, 108, 109, 110, 114, 115, 116, 117, 119, 121(n6), 122(nn 8, 9), 142, 149, 160
Nixon, Richard, 49, 193, 195, 199, 202

O'Connor, Sandra Day, 35, 43
Olson, Mancur, 5
Outcome functions, 4, 165, 166, 180, 185
Owen, David, 77, 87, 92

Parliament
  and attribution of responsibility for economy, 12, 23
  elections and absence of majority party (hung parliament), 95
  Westminster-model, 23, 100
Party identification
  as a long-term affective orientation, 133
  as a running tally of party performance evaluations, 134
  and support for PC party in Canada, 138–139, 152–153
  and voting in 1988 U.S. presidential election, 134–137
  weakness and instability in Canada, 153
Party leader debates
  in 1988 Canadian federal election, 108–109, 149–150
  in 1988 U.S. presidential elections, 131–132, 137–138
Party leader support
  effects of evaluations of national economy, 31–32, 83–84, 134, 138
  effects of evaluations of personal economic situation, 31–32, 83, 134, 138
  effects of prospective economic evaluations, 8, 32, 138
  effects of retrospective economic evaluations, 8, 32, 83, 134, 138
Party popularity. *See* Party support

Party support
  and choice sets provided by party system, 12–13, 16, 120
  economic effects on, 4–5, 10, 16, 17, 51, 66, 78–79, 94, 99, 103–106, 183
  effects of domestic political events, 16, 87, 100, 112
  effects of emotional reactions to economic conditions, 16, 31–32
  effects of evaluations of national economy, 6, 7, 10, 16, 31–32, 82–84, 86, 99, 103–106, 123, 127, 147–149
  effects of evaluations of personal situation, 2, 5–8, 27–28, 31–32, 82–84, 86, 123, 127, 147–149
  effects of inflation, 10, 11, 15, 17, 31–32, 51, 78–79, 81–82, 94, 110, 114, 125
  effects of international political events, 10, 15, 16, 20–21, 33, 68, 79, 87, 106
  effects of prospective evaluations, 8–10, 27–28, 32, 54, 81–82, 83–84, 124–125
  effects of retrospective evaluations, 8–10, 27–28, 32, 54, 81–82, 83–84, 86, 124–125
  effects of unemployment, 10, 11, 15, 17, 20–21, 31–32, 51, 81–82, 94, 105, 110, 117, 125
  emphasis on incumbent governments in studies of, 8, 10, 17, 11, 75, 76–77, 96, 105–106, 179
  importance of context, 12, 22, 106, 120
  for Progressive Conservative Party (Canada) since 1988 federal election, 28, 104–105, 138, 142, 158–160
  trends and volatility in Canada, 100–103, 114–117, 142, 160
Party system, 13
Party system (Canada), 12–13, 24, 25, 100, 101, 119
  and brokerage strategies, 24, 100

and ideological differences among
parties, 24, 25, 101
Party system (Great Britain), 13, 24, 25,
93–96
and brokerage strategies, 24
and ideological differences among
parties, 24, 25
Party system (United States), 12, 13, 24,
25, 190
and brokerage strategies, 24, 190
ideological differences between
parties, 13, 24, 25
Party systems, 8, 12, 13, 24, 25, 94, 101
and coalition governments, 13, 25
multiparty systems, 13, 26, 75, 77, 94
and third parties, 24–25, 26, 75, 78,
94, 108
two-party systems, 8, 24–25, 101
PBC. *See* political business cycle
Phillips Curve, 17, 36, 170, 172, 177,
178, 179, 181, 184, 186, 190
and inflation and unemployment in
U.S., 36, 179
*See also* Political business cycle
Pocketbook voter
and rational choice theory, 6, 124, 130
*See also* Economic evaluations
Policy mandates
and elections, 138–139
Political behavior, theories of
rational choice, 8–9
social psychological, 9
Political Business Cycle, xv, 17, 18, 19,
28, 166, 171, 172, 173, 174, 175,
177, 178, 179, 183, 186, 187, 188,
189, 191, 192, 199, 202, 203
effects of European Community on,
187
effects of free trade agreement on, 189
effects of international economy on
and wars, 29, 189, 191, 199, 202,
203
and Keynesian economic theory, 18–
19, 166, 171, 172, 177
and 1987 British general election, 28,
166, 185–186

and Phillips curve, 17, 172, 177, 179,
187, 190
and rational expectations theory, 18,
28, 173, 174, 175
Political contexts
and economic effects on party
support, 184
and economic effects on presidential
voting, 131–134, 137–139
and party systems, 13–14, 24–25,
131–132, 138
Political economy
history of, 1–3
resurgence of interest in 1970s, xvi,
1–3
Political issues
volatility of, 108–109, 161
Pooled Cross-Sectional Time Series
Analysis. *See* Methodology
Popularity functions, 2, 11. *See also*
Presidential approval
Presidential approval
economic effects on, 26, 31, 34, 39, 52
effects of domestic political events,
31, 33
effects of evaluations of national
economy, 31, 34
effects of evaluations of personal
situation, 26, 31, 34
effects of inflation, 31, 36–37
effects of international political
events, 26, 33, 203
effects of prospective evaluations, 32,
33–34, 47
effects of retrospective evaluations,
32, 33–34, 47
effects of unemployment, 31, 36–37,
132
Progressive Conservative Party
(Canada), 12–13, 24, 27, 28, 100,
101, 102, 106, 107, 108, 109, 112,
117, 119, 121(n6), 138, 142, 149,
153–154, 155, 156–159, 160
economic effects on support, 12–13,
27, 28, 100, 101, 102–103, 112, 117,
119, 159

# Index

effects of free trade agreement on support, 108, 112, 142, 149–150, 156–159
effects of GST on support, 112, 142, 156–159
effects of Meech Lake Accord on support, 109, 112, 142, 156–159, 163(n15)
effects of political events on support, 27, 100, 101, 102–103, 112, 119
Public Sector Borrowing Requirement, 182. *See also* Deficits

Rational Choice Theory
and self-interest, 5–6, 8, 9, 15
theories of political behavior, 1, 2, 8–9, 14–15, 18, 124, 139
*See also* Party identification; Party support
Reaction functions, 4, 17–19, 165, 166, 171–175, 176, 180, 182, 185
Reagan, Ronald, 23, 25, 26, 31, 32, 34, 35–36, 37, 38–39, 41, 43, 46, 47–49, 107, 132, 192, 194, 195, 202
effect on support of Grenada invasion, 35, 39, 43, 47
effect on support of inflation, 25, 36–37, 43–45, 194
effect on support of Iran-Contra affair, 36, 39, 42–43, 47, 50(n3), 132
effect on support of unemployment, 25, 35, 36–37, 43–45, 132, 194
effect on support of 1981 tax cut, 35, 39, 43, 45, 46
effect on support of 1987 stock market crash, 39, 43, 45, 46, 48, 132
and effects of economic evaluations on support, 25, 31–32, 38–39, 45–47
effects on support of Libyan bombing, 36, 39, 43, 47
issue-priority effects on support, 25–26
and teflon image, 25–26, 47–49

trends in public support, 25–26, 35–36
Reform Party (Canada), 164(n18)
Republican Party
economic effects on support, 44, 130, 134, 197
Responsibility attributions, 5, 6, 11–17, 78, 84, 100, 105, 120, 145–147
asymmetric, 14, 27, 106, 120, 145–147, 159
in federal system, 12–13, 23
to government for economic management, 2–3, 6, 11–12, 84
in presidential systems, 12, 23–24, 134
in Westminster-model parliamentary systems, 12, 23–24, 84, 100
Retail prices. *See* Inflation
Reward-punishment model, 11, 12, 14, 25–26, 33, 44, 48, 77, 78, 79, 85, 90, 105, 106, 130, 139

Scandals
and effects on party support in Britain, 79–80
and effects on party support in Canada, 106–107, 110–111, 112, 114, 119
Schumpeter, Joseph, xvi
Social Democratic Party (Britain), 13, 25, 26, 75, 77, 78, 79, 81, 82, 86, 91, 94, 96(n2), 98(n12), 181
demise after 1987 election, 77
economic effects on support, 26, 75, 78, 79
effects of political events on support, 26, 86–87
Socialism
and political culture, 22
Stagflation, 2, 14, 119, 143, 194
Stigler, George, xv
Stock market crash. *See* Reagan, Ronald
Summit meetings
and effects on party leader support, 16, 87, 107, 111

Thatcher, Margaret
  effects of economy on support, 53, 82, 93–94
  effects of Falklands war on support, 7, 26, 57, 87, 183
  effects of political events on support, 87, 94–95
  and monetarist economic policies, 181–183
  neo-conservative ideology, 24, 85
Third parties
  effects of electoral system on, 80, 86, 87
Time Series Analysis. *See* Methodology
Trade deficit
  effects on unemployment, 202
Trudeau, Pierre, 109
Truman, Harry, 192, 193, 195, 197, 199, 202, 203
Turner, John, 107, 108, 109, 112, 114, 115, 138, 149

Unemployment
  in Britain, 56, 79, 81, 84–85, 90, 93, 181, 184, 185, 186
  in Canada, 103, 110, 114, 117, 143
  effects of wars on, 74(n12), 191, 192–193, 195–196, 199, 201
  increases after 1973 Arab oil embargo, 166, 194, 201, 202
  and Keynesian economics, 18–19, 167, 169, 171, 172
  natural rate of, 170, 171, 172, 173, 177, 179
  party differences in levels of, 199, 202
  and party support, 10, 11, 13, 15, 31, 33, 81–82, 90, 110, 114, 117

  and political business cycles, 18–19, 172, 179, 184, 185, 186, 189, 191, 202
  and presidential approval, 33, 36, 43, 192
  presidential differences in levels of, 33, 179, 192, 195–196, 199, 204(n7)
  in United States, 13, 36–37, 179, 190, 191, 192, 194, 195, 199, 201, 202
Unions
  effects of contracts on economy, 172, 175
United States
  1988 presidential election, 123, 127
  *See also* Presidential approval

Vietnam War
  effects on inflation, 193, 199, 202
  effects on unemployment, 193, 195–196, 201
Volcker, Paul, 194
Vote functions, 3, 11
Voting behavior
  effects of evaluations of national economy, 5, 6, 27, 123
  effects of evaluations of personal economic situation, 6, 27, 123
  effects of prospective economic evaluations, 27, 130–131, 138
  effects of retrospective economic evaluations, 6, 27, 130, 138
  and self-interest. *See* Pocketbook voter

Wage-and-price controls
  Nixon policy of, 193–194, 199, 201–202
  Truman policy of, 193, 199
Walrus, Leon, 167
Wilson, Michael, 107, 150